Filicide

DEVELOPMENTS IN CLINICAL PSYCHIATRY

A SERIES OF BOOKS EDITED BY
ANTHONY L. LABRUZZA, M.D.

The books in this series address various facets of the role of psychiatry in the modern world.

Using DSM-IV: A Clinician's Guide to Psychiatric Diagnosis
  Anthony L. LaBruzza
Filicide: The Murder, Humiliation, Mutilation, Denigration,
  and Abandonment of Children by Parents
  Arnaldo Rascovsky
Return from Madness: Psychotherapy for People Suddenly
  and Unexpectedly Recovering from Severe, Lifelong, and
  Disabling Schizophrenia
  Kathleen Degen and Ellen Nasper
Chambers of Memory: Vietnam in the Lives of US Combat
  Veterans with PTSD
  H. William Chalsma

FILICIDE:
The Murder, Humiliation, Mutilation, Denigration, and Abandonment of Children by Parents

by Dr. Arnaldo Rascovsky
Translated by Susan Hale Rogers

JASON ARONSON INC.
Northvale, New Jersey
London

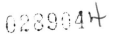

This book was set in 11 point Goudy by TechType of Upper Saddle River, New Jersey, and printed and bound by Haddon Craftsmen of Scranton, Pennsylvania.

Library of Congress Cataloging-in-Publication Data

Rascovsky, Arnaldo.
    [Filicidio. English]
    Filicide : the murder, humiliation, mutilation, denigration, and abandonment of children by parents / by Arnaldo Rascovsky ; translated by Susan Hale Rogers.
        p. cm.
    Includes bibliographical references and index.
    ISBN 1-56821-456-1
    1. Filicide. I. Title.
    [DNLM: 1. Child Abuse. 2. Homicide. 3. Maternal Behavior—psychology. 4. Paternal Behavior. 5. Family—psychology.
    6. Literature. 7. Religion. WA 320 R223f 1995a]
    HV6542.R3713 1995
    364. 1'5554—dc20
    DNLM/DLC
    for Library of Congress   94-46705

Manufactured in the United States of America. Jason Aronson Inc. offers books and cassettes. For information and catalog write to Jason Aronson Inc., 230 Livingston Street, Northvale, New Jersey 07647.

A mis nietos Florencia, Alejandro y Fernando

Florencia responde con su poema:

El abuelo

Una caricia de cuentos e historias para contar
Sus ojos conocen todos los tiempos, todos los mares
todos los hombres, toda la vida.
De su barba brotan flores, de su mano la lealtad.

To my grandchildren Florencia, Alejandro, and Fernando

Florencia answers me with her poem:

My grandfather

A caress of tales and stories to tell
Your eyes know all times, all seas, all men, all life.
From your beard sprout flowers, from your hand loyalty.

Contents

Acknowledgments

In the first place, I would like to thank my patients, whose long periods of treatment enabled me to understand and to elucidate the different aspects of filicide. Their courage and depth allowed them to penetrate with me into the most uncanny strata of the psyche. It was only through their effort and cooperation that I was able to elaborate the criteria that we offer the reader at this time.

I also wish to express my gratitude for the work of my wife Matilde, for the incalculable scientific collaboration she offered at all times and for having organized the atmosphere that was necessary for me to carry out my work.

I must also add my thanks to Drs. Julio Aray and Emanuel K. Schwartz, who provided me with the most excellent stimuli and useful constructive criticism on many occasions. Their solidarity, understanding, and appreciation of the complex problems involved in filicide were of the greatest assistance.

I also wish to thank Mrs. Haydee Fernandez de Breyter for

her understanding cordiality and advice, Miss Eve Ansotegui for her difficult, zealous, and effective work as my secretary, and Mr. Martin Renaud and Mr. Ricardo Zelarayan for their stimulating contributions to the correction and publication of the Spanish text. I am also grateful for the assistance of Anthony L. La-Bruzza, M. D., with the English version.

Finally, my gratitude goes to all the members and assistants of "Filium," who have contributed so much to advancing public awareness of the concepts relating to the harmful treatment of children.

Introduction

The murder, humiliation, mutilation, denigration, and abandonment of children by parents has become such a glaring fact of everyday life that to broach it scientifically, we must begin by exposing the universal denial of this ever recurring, pervasive phenomenon in which each of us plays an active or passive part.

Acts of partial or total aggression and destruction inflicted by parents on their own children are universal, being found in all social groups, both primitive and modern. The facts supporting these statements are recorded throughout the world. In effect, corporal or mental punishment, neglect or abandonment, mutilation or murder of children, infants, or youths—among which war is the foremost example—are practiced in all regions of the globe. In our Western world, a high percentage of boys and young men are circumcised on the grounds of tradition, religion, or hygiene. Thus, in the United States, one of the most highly developed sociocultural systems, eighty percent of the male population is circumcised at birth. This rite of genital mutilation is so widely institutionalized in our cultural process that our yearly cycle begins on the first of January in commemoration of the circumcision of Jesus Christ.

When we study any group in which the relationship between children and their parents or parent substitutes can be observed, we find clear evidence of violence practiced on the young in different ways and for various reasons. In this book, we intend to expose filicide and the cruelty inflicted on children by discussing and interpreting it. We can anticipate that, due to its nature and magnitude, filicide constitutes a specific characteristic of the human species; moreover, the killing of children is closely linked to the development of the sociocultural process.

The most ancient historical documents and primitive myths and legends reveal the universality of filial sacrifice. Throughout this book, we will show how filicide coexists with the origins of most of the mythological or religious processes that formed the beginnings of the sociocultural process. Thus, for example, in the case of agriculture, one of the first cultural advances, we find the widespread rite of child sacrifice to ensure a good harvest. Mars was originally a vegetation god before becoming the god of war.

Sociocultural advances not only begin with filicide but also evidence a flagrant or veiled need to preserve it in order to ensure the process we call civilization. It can be demonstrated that the sacrifice of one's children is the method and price set for the passage from individual, endogamic organization to social, exogamic organization. The ambivalence resulting from the simultaneous existence of strong destructive and strong loving tendencies can be observed quite precisely in the ritual of death and resurrection practiced in many cultures, and is implicit, we think, in all.

Diverse primitive tribes commonly practice initiation rites that consist of subjecting the child (or youth) to a fictitious death and resurrection. Frazer (1944) explains this rite in the following way:

> These rites become intelligible if we suppose that in essence they consist in extracting the youth's soul with the object of transferring it to his totem, since the extraction of his soul naturally involves killing the youth or at least placing him in a deathlike "trance" which the primitive hardly distinguishes from death. His recovery will then be attributed either to the gradual recovery of his system, to the violent experience he has had, or more probably to the infusion of new life which he receives from his totem. Thus, the substance of these initiation rites with their simulation of death and resurrection would be an exchange of lives or souls between the man and his totem. The primitive belief in the possibility of such a change is patent in the story of a Basque hunter who asserted that he was killed by a bear, but that after having killed him, the bear breathed his own soul into the dead body so that the bear's body lay there dead and he was the same bear, since he was animated by the bear's soul. This revival of the dead hunter as a bear is exactly analogous, based on the theory discussed here, to what happens in the ceremony of killing the youth and reviving him afterwards. The boy dies as a human being and revives as an animal; the animal soul is now in him and his soul in the animal. In all right he calls himself a bear, wolf, etc., and in all right he treats bears, wolves, etc., as brothers, since his and their souls are in those animals. [p. 821]

Frazer mentions a number of examples of this remarkable rite of initiation, confirming its universality. Although he specifies that it pertains to totemic systems, we are aware that totemism, in either the superficial or the deeper layers of all cultures, is also universal. Certainly, the death and resurrection of Jesus is the comparable rite in our culture. Further, the Jewish Passover commemorates the killing of the Egyptian first-born sons from which the Jewish babies are saved by means of the modified pact with the Lord, the *pars pro toto* that replaces killing with circumcision.

If we turn to the moment in the child's development when the image (soul) of the father is definitely introjected, we observe its coincidence with the culmination of the castration complex when the boy renounces the direct sexual drive toward his mother.

This integration of death and resurrection may be seen as the expression of the death of the endogamic relationship and its exogamic resurrection. The identification with the totem that unifies the entire tribe results from the resurrection and thus represents precisely an exogamic rebirth. This means that the boy acquires an identity shared with his whole tribe at the cost of losing his former endogamic identity. Consequently, the rite of death and resurrection is an essential requirement for attaining exogamy, the main base of the socialization process.

This method and price have been extended in various ways. The most characteristic of them is the rite of initiation imposed especially on the male members of the community. However, since they are boys, this also involves their mothers, who are still closely connected with their sons, so that the entire community is affected by the sacrificial process applied preferentially to the male children.

Contemporary psychology and sociology now delve into enclaves once esoterically restricted to the initiated minority involved in the concealment of the holocaust of the offspring, that is to say, filicide. Investigations of mental phenomenology, access to the unconscious psyche, and mass information and education have begun to shed light on processes that formerly were rejected, repressed, or denied. And nothing is more sinister and more intensely denied than filicide in both its violent and its attenuated forms. Consequently, the exposition of filicide and the genesis of this most important factor in individual and social pathology undoubtedly offer encouraging perspectives for both therapy and prevention.

Psychological interpretation of the battle between the generations has focused on parricide. Freud laid the foundations of this manifest assertion in accordance with gerontocratic norms that, since time immemorial, have attributed premeditated guilt to the children. Thus, he analyzed Oedipus' character only in part when he held him up as the prototype of parricide.

However, when we examine the destiny of all the heroes who, like Oedipus, have achieved the feat of killing their parents, we find that it was necessary to deny the parents' prior filicidal attitude, an attitude that leads to parricide by way of identification. First of all, Oedipus is condemned to death by his parents. The sentence is not carried out, not because the wish is lacking in his parents (since it is partially executed in his abandonment in any case) but because of positive and erotic factors that permit the baby to survive. These factors are represented by the shepherd who hands the newborn Oedipus over to the messenger from Corinth, by the messenger himself, and finally by Polibus and Merope, the king and queen of Corinth, who wish to accept Oedipus as their son and to raise him with love.

The parents' stronger tender and loving tendencies, which allow the child's survival, coexist alongside their filicidal wishes. This parental ambivalence and the variable proportions of its essential ingredients decide the final lot of the child, which is seriously threatened in our time.

Just as the erotic, tender, and protective attitudes of parents toward their children have been praised and recommended universally, the destructive and denigrating tendencies have been repeatedly denied, thus thwarting their elucidation due to the strong resistance they provoke. We shall attempt to discover the reasons and sources of such a powerful resistance against the awareness of this most sinister feeling: the feeling that our best-loved objects, our parents, hold strong destructive wishes toward us and analogously, the feeling that we also hold strong desires for the destruction of our children.

We propose to contribute specifically to an open investigation of the parent–child relationship as it relates to filicide and to cruelty toward one's children. We cannot foresee now what forms and extent the concept of filicide may adopt in the immediate future, but we are sure that it will be as varied as are human groups and even as varied as are family groups. In addition, we must consider the meaning of the parental function and the responsibility for assuming it in anyone who has a child. We must also consider the child's extreme defenselessness, a specifically human characteristic. In fact, the child's slow development and protracted dependency on its parents demands intense and prolonged protection from them and also determines many aspects of the problems studied and analyzed in this book.

Various contemporary disciplines have collected and provided information on the criminal cruelty of today's parents. Criminology, for example, supplies statistics showing that in the United States in 1966, one in twenty-two crimes was the murder of a child by its parents (Hoover 1966). Similarly, Harder (1967) has shown that in Denmark, in 1967, half of all crimes were committed against children: of these, eighty-five percent were children murdered by their parents. Similar data is provided by pediatrics. Kempe (1962) wrote about the *battered child syndrome*, which was later corroborated throughout the world and whose frequency increases daily in all pediatric emergency rooms. Anthropology and sociology record incredible child sacrifices, while mutilating rites or attitudes toward children are no less frequent today than the systematic murder of the first-born was in ancient societies. The study of the phenomenon of war, polemology, leads to the same conclusions, while psychoanalytic investigation reaches ever deeper into its unconscious dynamics.

The battle against filicide requires the community's unwavering support for the defense of all children and for the promotion of a more positive relationship between the generations through the intensification of the initial love relationship, parental love; in this way, it can contribute to neutralizing the hypertrophied development of hatred in contemporary society. Because of the anxiety that awareness of the sinister nature and magnitude of filicide arouses in our consciousness, we feel the need to propose three avenues of clarification and response to it: (1) the creation of scientific institutions for the study and investigation of the extension, institutionalization, etiology, and motivations of filicide by means of the methods of the different interrelated disciplines dealing with the problems of parents, their children, and the organization of the parent–child relationship; (2) the creation of social institutions for the education of parents and parental substitutes on procedures or behavior that might hinder or impede children's development or inhibit their capacities; also for the elucidation and determination of the basic factors that promote good parenting; and (3) constant alertness and denunciation of everything connected with filicide and filicidal institutions.

En la paz los hijos entierran a sus padres mientras que en la guerra son los padres los que entierran a sus hijos.

—HERODOTO

In peace it is the children who bury their parents while in war it is the parents who bury their children.

—Herodotus

PART I

THE HISTORY OF FILICIDE

1

The Origins of Filicide

Our early semi-human progenitors would not have practiced infanticide . . . for the instincts of the lower animals are never so perverted as to lead them regularly to destroy their own offspring.

—Charles Darwin

ON THE PARENTAL FUNCTION

In mammals, extrauterine development begins with the oral-cannibalistic phase in which the newborn feeds by sucking on parts of the mother's body. Later on, the young one no longer ingests parts of the maternal object. Adult mammals never return to this oral type of relationship with their objects. In the higher vertebrates, cannibalism and the destruction of the offspring by the parents are rare and occur only in situations of extreme stress. By contrast, humans seem to suffer constantly from stressful conditions due to the unrelenting intensity of their regressive states.

At this point, we must discuss some concepts related to the origin and development of the destructive tendencies. The individual develops in accordance with two types of basic instinctive drives that impel him or her to integrate the erotic tendencies or life instincts and the thanatic tendencies or death instinct. Absolute interrelation between the two drives is essential for the preservation of life. The principal function of the thanatic tendencies is the breaking down of the organic molecule, indispensable for the organism to obtain energy for its subsistence. Animals are able to live because the death instincts give them this innate capacity for disintegration, for killing living matter and reducing it to inorganic matter after its energy is released; unlike plants, they lack the chlorophyllic function that would allow them to use solar energy. Thus, animals must obtain this energy directly or indirectly from the plants that have stored it. Here, we can see how the death instincts are just as indispensable for subsistence as the erotic instincts are.

As we have already mentioned, at the beginning of development, during intrauterine life, the umbilical cord provides the fetus with all the elements that neutralize its instinctive needs. At birth, this flow of supplies from the umbilical cord is cut off and instinctive tension accumulates increasingly, along with the death instinct, which up to then had been cushioned or attenuated by the substances provided by the mother. The pressure from this instinct is peremptory because of the organism's constant and unavoidable need for the energy required for subsistence. If the individual lacks organic substances to break down, his internal aggression is turned against his own bodily ego, the only substance available for catabolism and thus subsistence. This phenomenon can be easily observed in the newborn baby[1] who loses an average of nine percent of its weight immediately after birth until the mother's milk, the natural substitute for the flow from the umbilical cord, begins to be secreted in sufficient

---

[1] The same occurs in the person being treated for obesity with food deprivation.

quantities. Thereafter, in the first months of life, the child feeds on parts of its mother's body. This early cannibalistic relationship has specific psychological meanings that form what has been called the *paranoid-schizoid position*[2] that characterizes the beginning of extrauterine life.

With the ingestion of the breast, the oral cannibalistic phase offers the supreme alternative between eating (destroying) and being eaten (destroyed). Actually, the urgency of the disintegrating impulse is irrepressible and constitutes the organism's essential expression: the fight for life. Thus, the first postnatal relationship, the first derivative connection that allows the liberation and expression of the internal pressure that threatens to destroy the individual's own ego, is directed toward the breast or its substitute.

From another point of view, the new mother must at first consider herself as a part of her child's own ego. Since one of the ego's functions is intermediation with the external world, the mother is an "auxiliary ego," taking over the child's yet undeveloped capacities for expressing itself and relating to reality. In this way, she functions in two ways as (1) the child's "auxiliary ego," and (2) the immediate external world.

---

[2]Melanie Klein introduced the concept of the paranoid-schizoid position to describe the anxieties and defenses pertaining to the first phase of the child's postnatal development. First, she discusses the anxiety arising from the threat of annihilation of the ego posed by the death instinct because of birth and shows how a partial relation is formed with the breast. Then, she describes the dissociation between what is frustrating and what is pleasurable. She mentions that the outstanding mechanisms or characteristics of the paranoid-schizoid position are dissociation, idealization, denial, and omnipotence. The concept of the object is essential for understanding cannibalistic regression.

In her second function, the mother acts as a depositary for all the newborn child's drives and this interrelation will later be the pattern for its future relation with society, which is at first represented by the mother. In other words, the mother's reception and elaboration of her child's instinctive tendencies anticipates and structures the bases for the child's orientation, control, sublimation, and socialization of those instincts in his future relationship with society.

We have already said that the child, at birth, encounters his first external world, the breast, and devours it. The divided and partial object enters through the mouth, and the digestive function takes care of annihilating it. But there is a process prior to the oral function: the vision of the internal representations and later the external vision of the objects. Through this process, the individual effects the constant play of projections and introjections that forms the most important mechanism in his relation with his objects. In this process there is a visual introjection of the total object representation and the partial incorporation of the same object by way of the mouth, not only of its representation. This integration of the total representation with partialized reality leads, thanks to the introjective process,[3] to identification which is the basis for all development and growth.

THE FAMILY MEAL AND IDENTIFICATION

We have shown how the individual's initial identificatory processes deal with real external objects, above all through the introjection of the mother's breast; later, through the introjec-

---

[3]Introjection into the ego of both id objects and objects of the external world.

tion of the mother and the father; and finally, of the parental couple. Following the paranoid-schizoid phase, in which the child is in a dyadic situation (there are two: the child and the breast), the infant elaborates a complex system through which he or she displaces the ingestion of parts of the mother's body to the food that represents both parents, following an archaic pattern: the totemic model.

Thus, food acquires an anthropomorphic meaning and is ingested in the family meal according to a configuration and through mechanisms that lead to unconscious identification of this food with the parents. Consequently, in the family meal the child observes and introjects, visually and through other means of perception, his parents and the food that they serve him as well.[4] As we have already said, the process of identification is effected through this double introjection: total through sight and other senses and partial through the mouth.

The child's erotic development leads him to integrate the partial aspects of the external mother and to leave behind the primitive partial object relation. This means that the destruction of the object ceases once the loving feelings predominate over the aggressive ones; the latter are displaced to objects or ends with which no erotic relationship has been established that would impede their destruction. Later, the child will acquire increasing capacity for expressing his aggressiveness in social situations.

Under conditions of excessive stress, the adult individual loses the equilibrium he or she has gained during development and returns to primitive levels. The most generalized form is paranoid-schizoid regression. Total regression is quite rare and is only seen in severe paranoid psychoses; however, partial regres-

---

[4]"This bread is my body and this wine is my blood": Jesus at the Last Supper.

sion is common and universal, its intensity varying quantitatively. In these regressive states, the individual returns to a
partial object relation and has cannibalistic phantasies that he or
she does not act out. However, if tension is too great and if its
sum passes the threshold of containment, those cannibalistic
phantasies may possibly manifest in the form of destruction of
offspring-objects. This type of regression can be observed in
mammals under experimental conditions. When humans are
subjected to objective conditions of extreme stress such as war,
earthquakes, catastrophes, famine, etc., they may return totally
to the paranoid-schizoid phase and, under the effects of this
primitive structure, resort to eating their own children, who are
the objects they preserve when affective equilibrium is normal.

The capacity for caring for one's children is innate in the
woman, who has an essential structure, a complex psychobiological apparatus involving ovarian progesterone, a hormone
lacking in men. The care and protection of the children depends
fundamentally on this psychosomatic apparatus that develops
and is stimulated by the child itself. But its development also
depends on the psychological and social influences acting upon
the girl who will later become the woman; in the course of her
development, these will have formed the internal images she has
of her mother and her father or their substitutes. The experience
the woman receives as a daughter is converted into active
maternal tendencies that lead her to repeat with her own children the patterns imposed on her by her own parents. This
reiteration of imposed patterns is extremely varied and can even
produce contrary results, that is, identification with the opposite. Although it sometimes seems that the woman has drawn
away from her mother's model, deep analysis reveals the same
identificatory pattern in her modified conduct or behavior.

Thus, although the woman possesses an innate apparatus

for caring for her children, the process of identification with her mother, her father, and equivalent figures must be added to it. Her maternal capacity is structured according to the characteristics of these ego ideals. Of course, the first relevant figure in the identification process is the mother and all her behavior. This is fundamentally the basis for the process of acquisition of the maternal function that is exercised when the woman achieves maturity. This narcissistic relation of identification with the mother is followed by several important steps in the process of formation of the maternal capacity:

- The object relation with her father.
- The birth of siblings. Her mother's attitude toward them. Feelings of rivalry and hate triggered by the mother's pregnancy and the arrival of the siblings. Intensity of early envy.
- The time-lapse between her own birth and the birth of her siblings, which could interfere with her early development by limiting her exclusive relationship with her mother when she still needs it.
- The influence of substitute parental figures: grandparents, caregivers, and so on.
- Her parents' and her own traumatic experiences during her infancy, etc.

Summing up, we can enumerate three processes that complement the aptitude for maternity: (1) the innate psychobiological apparatus; (2) the active reproduction of the experiences received passively from parents and parental substitutes with varied forms of identification. The learning this involves is included here; (3) the reinforcement of the active protective function based on the real care given passively by those who protect her present maternity, particularly her spouse.

This complemental series determines the optimal conditions for the development of her offspring; its deficiencies provoke serious disturbances in the behavior of the child's "auxiliary ego," represented by the mother.

THE PATERNAL FUNCTION AND COUVADE

The human being's prolonged infancy, the extreme helplessness, and the lack of integration that characterizes the first years of life demand a long process of protection that the mother cannot exercise alone. Consequently, the father's cooperation is indispensable. Human parenting includes the need to satisfy the demands for adaptation posed by the child's exogamic socialization.

The father's cooperation in the nutritive, protective, identificatory, and adaptive functions has, during the evolution of the species, become an increasingly important factor for the child's eventual structuring. But since the male lacks the female's psychobiological equipment, the process by which he acquires or reinforces the parental function is more complex. If we ponder the meaning of the word "matrimony," we can easily see that it expresses the maternal unity of the conjugal binome: *mater* = mother; *mono* = one. This implies that the primitive maternal function shows two united agencies: mother and father. The child is born in an extremely immature condition and therefore needs a more intense and prolonged parental function.

According to anthropological and psychoanalytic investigation, the primitive father—like the primitive man who survives within every father today together with his amorous and protective tendencies—holds (as he once actually held) intense unconscious destructive and cannibalistic desires toward his children, expressed in the form of feelings of envy, rivalry, hate, and so on. These feelings become more evident in moments of paranoid exasperation when the individual regresses to primitive phases involving sado-cannibalistic relationships with his objects. We have already mentioned that during this regression these objects are once again treated as parts rather than as totalities. Our hypothesis is that gravely stressful circumstances reactivated the latent paranoid conditions that led primitive humans to devour their children.

It is remarkable how the Bible[5] (*Deuteronomy 28:49-57*) describes this regression in no uncertain terms:

> 49 The Lord shall bring a nation against thee from far, from the end of the earth, as swift as the eagle flieth; a nation whose tongue thou shalt not understand;

> 50 A nation of fierce countenance, which shall not regard the person of the old, nor shew favour to the young;

> 51 And he shall eat the fruit of thy cattle, and the fruit of thy land, until thou be destroyed: which also shall not leave thee either corn, wine, or oil, or the increase of thy kine, or flocks of thy sheep, until he have destroyed thee.

> 52 And he shall besiege thee in all thy gates, until thy high and fenced walls come down, wherein thou trustedst, throughout all thy land: and he shall besiege thee in all thy gates throughout all thy land, which the Lord thy God hath given thee.

> 53 And thou shalt eat the fruit of thine own body, the flesh of thy sons and of thy daughters, which the Lord thy God hath given

---

[5]All biblical quotations in this book are taken from *The Holy Bible with Ideal Helps*, published in 1919.

thee, in the siege, and in the straitness, wherewith thine enemies shall distress thee:

54 So that the man that is tender among you, and very delicate, his eye shall be evil toward his brother, and toward the wife of his bosom, and toward the remnant of his children which he shall leave:

55 So that he will not give to any of them of the flesh of his children whom he shall eat: because he hath nothing left in the siege, and in the straitness wherewith thine enemies shall distress thee in all thy gates.

56 The tender and delicate woman among you, which would not adventure to set the sole of her foot upon the ground for delicateness and tenderness, her eye shall be evil toward the husband of her bosom, and toward her son, and toward her daughter.

57 And toward her young one that cometh out from between her feet, and toward her children which she shall bear: for she shall eat them for want of all things secretly in the siege and straitness, wherewith thine enemy shall distress thee in thy gates.

In the process of creation or reinforcement of the parental function, the father not only had to identify with the mother and acquire her tender, tolerant, and protective attitudes, but at the same time had to overcome his destructive and cannibalistic wishes. This does not mean that the male can be defined just by these wishes, since the woman has them in similar situations, not only because of her identifications with the man, but also because of the same regression to the paranoid-schizoid phase.

During the process of gestation, the mother–child relationship intensifies greatly with exclusion of the father, reaching its highest point after delivery. Over the first forty days of extrauterine life, the object relation is strictly limited to the mother, who has an exclusive libidinous relationship with her baby.

At the end of the puerperal period (puerperal: *puer* + *pare* = to give birth to the child), there is a dramatic rift in this exclusive mother–child relationship, expressed in a resulting decrease in milk production, the concrete evidence of this rift. This acute crisis in the mother–child relationship leads to the consequent depressive process in the mother–child unit, which lasts no more than two or three days. At this time, the woman again feels sexual desire for the father, having rechannelled the portion of libido she has withdrawn from her child. As for the child, he initiates his relationship with his father because he has withdrawn an equivalent portion of libido from his mother. Thus, when the parents take up their sexual activity again, the dyadic situation becomes triangular. The father's entry into his child's affective world compensates the child for the loss he has experienced because of the distance his mother has recently placed between them. At this point, the oral level of the Oedipus complex is initiated.

In order to take up his function as father, the husband must undergo a change by identifying with his wife's maternal attitude. Though he has few innate aptitudes, the father's past circumstances may prepare him for this function. The most important of these is the tendency to actively repeat the treatment he passively received from his parents and the compulsion to repair the negative aspects of that treatment. Even so, these hereditary and historical experiences seem to require considerable effort and updating through identification with the mother-wife's behavior.

An important mechanism leading to identification is the possession and loss of the object. In order to understand the process of identification in the father, we must emphasize that during the nine months of gestation the mother experiences a progressive withdrawal of libido from her partner as her relationship with the fetus deepens. In that situation, as we have said, the father is temporarily excluded from the mother–child relationship and the loss of his sexual object produces his identification with it. But now, his wife-object is impregnated with intense maternal feelings so that, through identification, the father also becomes impregnated with tender and protective attitudes toward the child, thus reinforcing his innate and historically acquired parental aptitudes. The process of identification with the mother-wife develops progressively before, during, and after delivery; it acquires maximum intensity in a singular custom called *couvade*, which has been observed and studied in diverse cultures. Theodor Reik made an exhaustive study of it.

Frazer (quoted in Reik 1958a) defines and sums up *couvade* in the following way:

> 1. Under the general name of couvade two quite distinct customs, both connected with childbirth, have been commonly confounded. One of these customs consists of a strict diet and regimen observed by a father for the benefit of his new-born child, because the father is believed to be united to the child by such an intimate bond of physical sympathy that all his acts affect and may hurt or kill the tender infant. The other custom consists of a simulation of childbirth by a man, generally perhaps by the husband, practised for the benefit of the real mother, in order to relieve her of her pains by transferring them to the pretended mother. The difference between these customs in kind is obvious, and in accordance with their different intentions they are commonly observed at different times. The simulation of travail-pangs takes place simultaneously with the real pangs before the child is born. The strict diet and the regimen of the father begin only after the child is born. [p. 45]

Frazer suggests calling the first custom prenatal couvade and the other postnatal couvade because of the differences in procedures. He goes on to say:

> 2. Both customs are founded on the principle of sympathetic magic, though in different branches of it. The post-natal or dietetic couvade is founded on that branch of sympathetic magic which may be called contagious, because in it the effect is supposed to be produced by contact, real or imaginary. In this case the imaginary contact exists between father and child. The prenatal or pseudo-maternal couvade is founded on that branch of sympathetic magic which may be called homeopathic or imitative, because in it the effect is supposed to be produced by imitation. . . .
>
> 3. Neither the one custom nor the other, neither prenatal or dietetic couvade, nor post-natal or pseudo-maternal couvade, appears to have anything to do with an attempt to shift the custom of descent from the maternal to the paternal line, in other words, to initiate the change from the mother-kin to father-kin. [pp. 45–46]

Reik simply offers the following definition:

> Couvade is the custom observed among many races that the father of a new-born child lies in bed for a certain period, eating only prescribed foods, abstaining from severe work and from the chase, etc., while his wife who has just given birth to a child carries on her usual occupation . . . The impression which these phenomena have made on outside observers shows that in applying the name they were trying to convey the idea of a lying-in on the part of the man.

Then, Reik gives a series of examples and adds that our knowledge of couvade is old but not always based on trustworthy report.

Further on, he mentions the description by Diodorus of this custom among the Corsicans and in Straba in the north of Spain, mentioning its development in peoples of South Africa, Sardinia, Spain, Corsica and the Basque Region. He also speaks of Marco Polo's mention of it in China and Lockart's in India, and points out the existence of couvade in the Malaysian Archipelago, in the Caribbean and in South America, especially in Brazil. Also, it is practiced by natives who live in very primitive conditions such as those who live at the source of the Shingu River, the Melanesians and even the Japanese and the Philippines.

Finally, Reik says:

If we survey the present sphere of the father-rites comprised in couvade, we find that they occur only in South America and south-east Asia, although traces of them are still found in many lands and even in south-west Europe. The reports which have been preserved show that it and similar customs were formerly widely spread, and all observers agree that their practice has steadily decreased with the advance of civilisation. Hartland states, "America inhabited by a homogeneous race, displays it everywhere, even among the Eskimos of Greenland, save apparently in Tierra del Fuego. On the eastern continent Mr. Ling Roth puts the matter somewhat strongly when he says that it "is only met with in isolated and widely separated localities." In Australia it is unknown; nor is there any record of it among the extinct Tasmanians. Summing up the facts, the same writer says: "The custom does not appear to exist or to have existed among those people to whom the term most *degraded* is erroneously applied, people which were better described as savages living in the lowest known forms of culture, such as the Australians, Tasmanians, Bushmen, Hottentots, Veddahs, Sakeys, Aetas, and Fuegians. Neither does the custom exist among the so-called civilised portion of mankind. In other words, couvade appears at first sight to be limited to people who hold an intermediate position between those in the highest and those in the lowest states of culture. As such it may be said to represent an intermediate or transition state of mental development." E. B. Taylor ascribed the same importance to the custom in the cultural history of mankind. "The isolated occurrences of a custom among particular races surrounded by other races who ignore it, may be sometimes to the ethnologist like those outlying patches of strata from which the geologist infers that the formation they belong to once spread over intervening districts, from which it has been removed by denudation." The same idea is expressed in the *Encyclopaedia Britannica* (1966, vol. 7): "It is far more likely that so universal a practice has no trivial beginnings, but it is to be considered as a mile-stone marking a great transitional epoch of human progress." [p. 46]

If we accept this interpretation of the value of *couvade*, it would be an important cultural acquisition. Perhaps this custom has enabled the father to identify himself with his wife–mother so as to overcome not only his aggression against his offspring but also his relative inability for taking care of them. This cultural acquisition would be expressed in its most primitive forms in intermediate cultures and would have been internalized and definitively incorporated into the higher cultures. Thus, the primitive oral-cannibalistic regression that leads to the sacrifice and ingestion of one's children would have tended to be overcome through different techniques and procedures. *Couvade* seems to be one of these fundamental procedures. We will later discuss other techniques, especially circumcision.

But *couvade* is interesting to us not only from the anthropological point of view but also because of its unconscious contents today and because of the models of behavior it produces, which can be observed clinically in the psychoanalyses of patients who have pregnant wives or whose children are born while they are in treatment. Further, the phenomenon of *couvade* today or, in other terms, the father's identification with his wife-mother is seen not only in psychoanalytic investigation. If one can break through the intense denial covering this phenomenon, its universality can be observed in manifest rather than just latent form. Thus, the husband's relative obesity during the wife's pregnancy as well as the disappearance of this obesity when the wife regains her pre-pregnancy state is a rather common fact. The husband frequently shares his pregnant, delivering, or puerperal wife's pains and may even undergo a simulated anal delivery. In addition, themes of conception and delivery appear constantly at this time in the husband's dreams. But the acquisition of the identification that reinforces his parental attitude follows a determined course that we will describe as a function of the process that the male experiences when he takes his wife-mother as a model.

We know that the loss of the object produces principally an identification with the lost object. Such is the main mechanism in the male's identification when he feels temporarily excluded from the erotic relations of his wife due to her pregnancy, delivery, and puerperal period. During her pregnancy the wife can be seen to withdraw libido increasingly from her external objects, including her husband, since her libido is directed progressively toward the interior of her body where the fetus is. This erotic withdrawal is felt by her husband to be a loss that grows more intense as the pregnancy progresses. The husband reacts with an increasing identification with his wife, who is also growing as a mother. The situation comes to a head during the delivery and the days immediately following it. The couple's sex life then breaks off completely, and the benefit that derives from this temporary loss is precisely the consolidation of the father's identification with his wife-mother.

During the first six weeks after the baby's birth, the relationship between mother and child is dyadic, meaning between two, since the father has been excluded. But suddenly, thirty-five to forty days after delivery, mother and child experience an acute crisis triggered by a sharp decrease in milk production. This frustrating circumstance—frustrating because of the separation—indicates the child's first great moment of depression after the trauma of birth. The mother complains, reproaching herself for her deficiency and incapacity. At the same time she again feels sexual desire for her husband or partner, which had been dormant until then because of her pregnancy and delivery. The period of hypogalaxia lasts no more than two or three days, and both mother and child emerge from this brief depressive situation with the entry of the father into their emotional constellation. The dyadic relationship between mother and child ends in this way, and the triangular relationship including mother, father, and child begins. At this time, the oral level of the Oedipus complex sets in and the child's depressive attitude begins, only to come to an end in the second trimester of his first year of life.

Our interest here is to show how the father's identification with the mother reinforces his paternal feelings. This identification deepens with the temporary loss of his sexual object, his wife, who has become a mother and even for a brief period of time only a mother. If this crucial moment is taken into account, many aspects of the pathology of the mother–child and of the father–child relationship are more easily understood.

In effect, if the mother fails to turn aside the exclusive charge of libido that she has placed into the child (a charge that after the puerperal period again acquires genital meanings), she will inevitably genitalize the oral relationship with the child, a dangerous situation for both of them.

The father can be seen then to act in two ways. First of all, he acquires maternal functions by identification with the mother, thus contributing to the care of the child. Second, he becomes the depository of the wife–mother's genital desires and thus averts precocious erotization of the child's orality. The principal point of fixation in those materno-filial relationships in which that necessary separation has not taken place during development is precisely the final moment of the puerperal period. That moment effectively marks, just as birth does, the beginning of the separation between mother and child.

Returning to the main subject, that is, the development of the paternal aptitudes, we must emphasize that the child's entry into the father's emotional life depends on the recovery of his sexual object, his wife. When there are difficulties in this recovery, serious obstacles for the tender, loving, and protective relations of the father with his child arise along with the consequent aggressive and destructive impulses that the spectrum of direct or attenuated filicide includes.

We can summarize the man's situation regarding his paternal aptitudes as follows: (1) innate psychobiological equipment that is much poorer than the woman's, (2) active reproduction of the experiences received passively from his parents and substitutes, with diverse identification models, plus learning, and (3) acquisition of loving and protective impulses through identification with the equivalent aptitudes of his wife-mother by means of the unconscious process manifested in *couvade*.

THE BREAKDOWN OF THE PATERNAL FUNCTIONS AND FILICIDE

Lorenz (1966) says:

> I believe that the specifically human tendencies to cannibalism, amply evidenced perhaps by psychoanalysis, have nothing to do with the occasional ingestion of young mammals by their parents. A carnivorous animal eats practically any appetizing and small being. What demands an explanation is not the fact of eating the cub but the inhibition against doing it. In any case, this inhibition disappears in abnormal circumstances or when the parents' health is impaired. [pp. 128–129]

He thus shows that the primitive cannibalistic impulses are inhibited through a process of evolution that implies the later acquisition of parental aptitudes. This acquisition, which guarantees the preservation of the offspring, breaks down in the grave paranoid-schizoid regressions that overpower the human species. Therefore, if the process of acquisition of the parental capacity lacks vigor, the risks of temporary or permanent regression increase. Further, in the temporo-spatial conditionings of infantile development, based on the indispensable identification with the parents, it is also evident that it is important for the child's normal development that his or her demands be satisfied. These intense demands and the parents' difficulties in satisfying them lead to conflicts that take many shapes. The most common of these include all the aspects of flagrant or attenuated filicide.

There is no doubt that the tendencies that drive parents to destroy their children are the former paranoid-schizoid tendencies that have been reactivated by stressful shocks suffered by these parents in their infancy, in their historical development, or in their present life. Manic inductions produced by alcohol or by other drugs weaken the parents' control of their primitive hostility toward their children and encourage them to commit the gravest forms such as murder. But the deepest conclusion emerges from the fact that infanto-juvenile sacrifice has been the basis for the sociocultural process by becoming the essential means by which incest is prohibited, with all the important civilizing consequences this implies: the organization of exogamic displacement and the development of sublimation of the transmission from generation to generation governed by exogamic society.

The consequence has been the systematic organization of the intimidation and the murder of the children. While at the beginning the killing of the children was a result of the paranoid-schizoid regression of their parents, this later became the enslavement or the indiscriminate use of the children, thus increasing the parents' power. Still later, the process was systematized with attenuations and intensifications that resulted from the conflict between the loving, protective tendencies and the aggressive, criminal tendencies toward the children.

Conditions of sufficient maturity and development lead to the fusion of these tendencies and the predominance of the erotic impulses that underlie the positive attitude of good parents; but defusion, with the consequent independent activity of the aggressive tendencies, increases with regression or with the difficulty in acquiring the parental models.

The corollary of this defusion of loving and aggressive

tendencies is filicide. Its intensity depends on many factors. The need to attenuate the violent form of primitive murder has emerged during the cultural process. Responses to this need are *couvade* and also circumcision which, by way of the *pars pro toto*, replaces the murder of the son with the partial sacrifice of his foreskin. Even so, other systems have replaced the primitive pyre where the sons were immolated to the cult of Moloch. The most representative of these systems has been, in all times, war, which we will study in this book.

2

Filicide in Basic Western Myths

Students of the origin of beliefs have been especially interested in certain themes that run through the myths of the most diverse cultures. The myth of the Flood, for example, exists in many cultures that share no cultural communication. Some authors consider this the demonstration of man's psychic unity or of the universality of human experience. Thus, polygenesis would explain the coincidences and affirm that the same myth may be created independently in different places and in different times. On the other hand, those researchers who advocate monogenesis regard the myth as having been created only once and in a certain place, spreading later to other regions.

Through myth, we may explain the phylo- and ontogenetic development of peoples and of individuals. In this sense, the flood myth would be the projection and working-through of the "flood" coming from the breaking of the amniotic sac during birth. In the accounts of Homer and also in the Bible, the Koran, or the Popol-Vuh, essential moments in human life can often be clearly seen. Myths, their symbols and their plots, are projections of experiences and psychological problems similar to those we observe in dreams. For this reason it has been said that they are humanity's universal dreams through which we express our unconscious desires and conflicts. Just as there exist typical dreams in which the individual repeats unconscious psychic experiences of deeply traumatic significance, myths also repeat the great universal events of individuals and of peoples, and, as it were, allow the exposure and drainage of the wounds through their repeated telling and transmission. Myths may be examined from many different angles, but all of these refer to their origin, their function, or their structure. We are presently interested in their origin, since myths can be manifestations of unconscious tendencies or residues of a traumatic historic past that is struggling to be worked through or simply to be expressed.

Malinowski (1948) has said that myths must be considered as carriers of beliefs whose function is to reinforce traditional morals, social structure, and magic by tracing their origins back to superior beings or supernatural events. Further, myths offer socially acceptable ways of violating institutionalized behavior, albeit by proxy. Thus, a myth in which the hero breaks a taboo or a prohibition performs at least two functions. It not only reminds the audience of the defined code of behavior, but also allows them to enjoy the flagrant violation of what is culturally sacred by the hero who also escapes the normally unavoidable consequences. Boas (1938) thinks that mythology is a reflection of the daily life of peoples and that myths clearly express what is considered right and wrong.

In reference to the persistence of filicide in the universal myths, we find the conception of Levi-Strauss (1969) especially interesting; this author supposes that binary oppositions coexist in the myth and are interposed or resolved in it. Examples would be: woman–man, life–death, heaven–earth, man–god, and so on. Levi-Strauss considers the resolution of binary opposition as characteristic of mythical thought, the purpose of the myth being to provide a logical model capable of overcoming a contradiction.

The specific problem of filicide involves one of these binary contradictions that is represented by the ambivalence in feelings toward one's children; this ambivalence is, of course, part of all human affective relationships. But in filicide the aggressive impulse against the offspring becomes more important because of the intense erotic meaning it implies. Thus, the contradiction is extreme because of the intensity of the impulses involved. Another binary opposition is the conflict between parricide and filicide, although the latter is subject to a conditioned continuity, since it is suffered passively and afterwards leads to the active parricidal attitude.

THE HOLOCAUST AS A DEMAND FROM THE DEITY

The demand for the killing of the child is portrayed baldly in various myths that signal the beginning of the beliefs at the origins of the culture. This demand is often essential for the initiation of harmonious relations between the individual or the society and the deity, or is instead the basis for a pact with the godhead.

For example, the Old Testament says:

Exodus 13:1–And the Lord spake unto Moses, saying,
Sanctify unto me all the firstborn, whatsoever openeth the womb among the children of Israel, both of man and of beast: it is mine.

Under other circumstances, the covenant is consecrated through partial mutilation as an attenuated form of sacrifice:

> *Genesis 17:10–14–* This is my covenant, which ye shall keep, between me and you, and thy seed after thee; Every man child among you shall be circumcised. And ye shall circumcise the flesh of your foreskin; and it shall be a token of the covenant betwixt me and you. And he that is eight days old shall be circumcised among you, every man child in your generations; he that is born in the house, or bought with money of any stranger, which is not of thy seed. He that is born in thy house, and he that is bought with thy money, must needs be circumcised: and my covenant shall be in your flesh for an everlasting covenant. And the uncircumcised man child whose flesh of his foreskin is not circumcised, that soul shall be cut off from his people; he hath broken my covenant.

The original killing was only consummated socially on the first-born or on some of the children. The other siblings were threatened without being sacrificed or were partially mutilated as in circumcision. The purpose was to observe the prohibition against incest and its cultural implications or to institutionalize it through the deity or the gerontocratic society. The internalization of the parental images, allowing successful identification and the acquisition of social structures, determines the entry of those structures into the superego. In this way, the punitive and restrictive forms of external parental behavior become attenuated filicidal demands operating from within the personality.

THE GREEK MYTHS

In Greek mythology, filicide marks the first conflicts in the line of generations. The beginnings were established by Chaos, who is followed immediately by Uranus and Gaea, who undertake to people the world (Larousse 1959).

> Uranus could only regard his offspring with horror, and as soon as they were born, he shut them up in the depths of the earth. Gaea at first mourned, but afterwards grew angry and meditated terrible vengeance against her husband. From her breast she drew forth gleaming steel, fashioned a sharp sickle or harpe, and explained to her children the plan she had made. All of them hesitated, struck with horror. Only the astute Cronus, her last-born, volunteered to support his mother. When evening fell, Uranus, accompanied by Night, came as usual to rejoin his wife. While he unsuspectingly slept, Cronus, who with his mother's aid lay in hiding, armed himself with the sickle, mutilated his father atrociously and cast the bleeding genitals into the sea. [p. 88]

Cronus was Uranus' successor, and the destructive relationship with his children became frankly cannibalistic (Grimal 1966):

> But Cronus also wanted descendents. He lay with his sister the Titan Rhea who bore him three daughters: Hestia, Demeter and Hera, and three sons: Hades, Poseidon and finally Zeus, the youngest. But a curse weighed upon Cronus. Astute and violent, he had refused, after dethroning his father, to satisfy Gaea. Instead of freeing his siblings, condemned by Uranus to live in darkness, he had kept them shut up in their underground prison, irritating Gaea. She promised him that he would suffer the same fate that he had inflicted upon his father and would be dethroned by his children. And so, to preserve himself from this threat, he devoured the children Rhea bore him, as soon as they were born. He ate the first five, but when little Zeus was about to be born, Rhea decided to save this child. With Gaea's complicity, she found shelter in a cave in Crete, where she delivered the child.

Then she took a stone and wrapped it in swaddling clothes before taking it to Cronus, telling him that it was his son. Cronus, realizing nothing, took the stone and ate it. Zeus was saved and at the same time, Cronus was condemned. [p. 102]

In later Hellenic accounts, the persecution and killing of offspring comes up quite frequently. It is a reiterated action that reveals the antiquity, intensity, and continuity of this ambivalent conflict. The reasons given for consciously committing this crime take various forms. Thus, Cronus devoured his children to keep them from doing to him what he had done to his father, Medea kills them to take revenge on her husband Jason for having deserted her, and Agamemnon sacrifices Iphigenia to placate Artemis and to ensure his victory in the war. Perseus was persecuted by his mother's father because the oracle had prophesied that he would be his grandfather's assassin, and so on. One of the legends that is most typical because of its cannibalistic meaning and its later inclusion in other myths is that of Tantalus and Pelops, retold by Bunker (1952):

Having been invited by the gods to eat nectar and ambrosia at their table, Tantalus asked them in return to a banquet on the summit of Mount Sipylus. As the "second course," he served them the flesh of his own son Pelops, whom he had cut in pieces and boiled in a cauldron. Demeter, distraught with grief for the loss of Persephone (her daughter, whom Hades had abducted to be his wife), ate part of one shoulder; but Zeus, perceiving the deception that had been practiced, ordered that the flesh be put back into the cauldron, the missing part replaced by a shoulder of ivory, and the child restored to life, whole and sound. It was the mother-goddess Rhea who, according to the poet Bacchylides, revived Pelops by passing him through the cauldron. . . . Finally,

Zeus blasted Mount Sipylus with thunder and earthquake, to punish Tantalus for his impiety. [p. 356]

Bunker (1952), who has made a special study of this fundamental mythic legend, points out the meaning of death and resurrection referring both to all of Pelops and also to a part of him, since, when his body is assembled in order to bring it back to life, the shoulder that Demeter has unknowingly eaten is replaced by an ivory shoulder. Bunker also mentions that:

in a curiously similar story of Magyar origin cited by Mannhardt, . . . the hero is cut in pieces, but the serpent-king lays the bones together in their proper order and washes them with water (that frequent birth symbol; compare the cauldron of the Pelops story), whereupon the hero revives, undergoes a second birth brought to pass by the serpent-king, much as Pelops' second birth took place at the command of Zeus. The Magyar hero's shoulder has been lost, so the serpent-king supplies in its place one of gold and ivory. [p. 358]

In a note, Bunker adds:

The element common to these two tales of being cut in pieces, of dismemberment, is shared also (along, likewise, with being put together again) by such beings as Dionysus, Zagreus, Pentheus, Orpheus, Osiris and, in the attenuated form of the division of his raiment among the centurions, Christ. [p. 358]

Bunker later compares the myth of Pelops with that of Osiris, the main figure in Egyptian mythology, who was cut into pieces and

whose phallus, after his dismemberment, was thrown into the sea and there swallowed by a fish. Set, the brother of Osiris, had cast into the Nile the coffer which he had tricked Osiris into entering (much as Tantalus had put the dismembered Pelops into a cauldron); after various journeyings, the coffer was recovered by Isis, his sister and wife, who with her sister Nephthys lamented for the fate of the fair youth thus cut off in his prime. . . . Coming upon the coffer, in Isis' absence, as he was hunting a boar by the light of the full moon, Set rent the body of Osiris into fourteen pieces and scattered them abroad. However, Isis eventually succeeded in recovering them and—with the help of Nephthys, of the jackal-headed god Anubis, of Thoth and Horus—in piecing them together: all of the *disjecta membra*, that is, except the phallus, which had been thrown into the sea and there swallowed by a fish, the oxyrhynchus. So Isis made an image of it, replacing the phallus with one of wood. The striking parallelism between Pelops and Osiris, and specifically between the shoulder of Pelops and the phallus of Osiris, can be further extended . . . it was a mother-goddess (Demeter) who deprived Pelops of his shoulder by devouring it, thereby (*pars pro toto*) introjecting the child and thus retaining it, so that a part of him remains with the mother for ever, in a kind of magical denial of their separation, an undoing of the dissolution of the mother–child unity; . . . [p. 362]

This *pars pro toto* introjection of the child by the mother, as symbolized in the reception or retention or eating by the mother of the knocked-out tooth it is in connection with the puberty rite (or, among the Nullakun, the foreskin; or, in the Feast of Tantalus, the shoulder blade) whereby is magically effected an undoing of the mother-child separation. . . . [p. 365]

Among the Thonga, for example, the mother, having lost through childbirth part of herself, reintrojects it in the form of a cock if the infant is a boy or a hen if it is a girl. . . . Among the Kayans of Borneo the foetal membranes are dried and preserved by the mother. . . . In Silesia, according to Dreschler, the first milk tooth that falls out must be swallowed by the mother; and the child's first nails should be bitten off by the mother, not cut;

otherwise the child may become a thief . . . Trevelyan has made
the identical observation with regard to Wales. [p. 365]

What interests us most in the myth of Tantalus and Pelops
is that Pelops subsequently pronounces the curse against Laius
that will later extend to Oedipus. We wish to emphasize this here
and to repeat it with special insistence because it is a displacement of Pelop's hatred toward his cannibalistic father, Tantalus.

THE OEDIPUS MYTH

The Oedipus myth raises an endless series of questions whose
answers are frequently found in other related mythological
developments. If we search for the origin of the curse against
Laius, expressed time and again by the oracle, we learn that it is
Pelops, the son assassinated by Tantalus, who proffers it on a
particular occasion. As the story goes, Laius has been banished
from his country by Lycus, who intends to dethrone him. Pelops
shelters Laius in his exile and names him tutor of his son
Chrysippus. But Laius, who was homosexual, not only seduces
young Chrysippus but also kidnaps him, carrying him away
during the sacred Nemean games. At that critical moment,
furious and pained, Pelops curses Laius, wishing that he may
never have a son and, if he were to have one, that he assassinate
his father and marry his mother.

The son who had to die the victim of an undeniably
cannibalistic sentiment is precisely the one who proffers the
classical curse that weighs heavily on all humanity. In effect,
when Laius agrees to be Chrysippus' tutor, he thereby accepts
the substitutive parental functions that Pelops grants him; his
later attitude is similar to that of Pelops' criminal father who is,

on a more primitive plane, the origin of the curse. Thus, Oedipus, the eternal symbol of the son, becomes the last depositary; and the guilt of the original paternal cannibalism, initiated by Tantalus in Greek mythology, falls upon him. Tantalus was condemned by Zeus to suffer unquenchable thirst, submerged in a crystal-clear lake whose waters drew away when he tried to drink from them. Over his head hung branches with appetizing fruits, and every time Tantalus wanted to satisfy his hunger the branches swung out of his reach. Such was Zeus' punishment for Tantalus' filicidal cannibalism: total and eternal oral frustration.

The elements provided by mythology allow us to understand the reasons for Laius' homosexuality and for his inability to exercise his paternity.

Laius is orphaned at a very early age. His father Labdacus dies when he is only one year old. At that time a regent is designated to rule Thebes until Laius reaches the age required to be king. But it is not only the absence of his real father that robs him of developing his masculine and parental conditions. Lycus, the substitute father, is worse than the actual dead father because he fails to function as protector and also attempts to rob Laius of his throne. In the case of Laius, just as with any homosexual, the failed identifications with the male parent are important causal factors; these circumstances are brought up in the mythological narrative. Consequently, Oedipus is destined to be just as bad a father as his own was and he will curse his children, leading them to fratricidal struggle and to their eventual perdition, continuing the chain of parental ruptures.

Roheim's research (1925) into the figures of the primitive Oedipus myth are especially interesting. This author thinks that the Sphinx is a close relative of the Empusa: "It has been said that the Empusa eats human flesh and takes on the appearance of a beautiful woman in order to attract her victims" (p. 529). And he adds:

> In a modern folk tale, a queen seated on a rock in Thebes asks each passerby three riddles. If they fail to answer correctly she devours them, but if they solve the three riddles she spares their lives or marries them. The prince says he knows all the answers. The first riddle is the following: Who eats his own children? Answer: The ocean, because the rivers come from him and return to him. The second riddle: It is black and white and never grows old. Answer: Time which is made of days and nights and is always here. The third is the riddle that Oedipus resolved.

> The answers to the first two riddles cannot be independent of the answer to the last one. Thus, the Sphinx or Jocasta herself is the mother who devours her son. This applies equally to the second answer: the attitude toward the mother is *ambivalent* and in the unconscious is ageless . . .

> The Sphinx is a woman who flies over those she wishes to devour, siezes them in her claws, flies away with them and eats them. Therefore, she is the answer to the second riddle, the mother who devours her children. And if we suppose that the concept of time derives from the nursling's oral frustration, time would then be the Sphinx mother herself again. [p. 530]

Innumerable myths and the associations connected with them offer us a basis for understanding the initial filicidal elements that are constantly denied. This text by Devereux (1953) is interesting:

> It must be supposed that this constant scotomization of the complementary Oedipus complex is due to the adult's profound

need to place all the responsibility for the Oedipus complex on the child and to ignore, whenever possible, certain parental attitudes that actually stimulate the child's Oedipal tendencies. Unfortunately, since then he (Freud) also began to ignore rather obstinately the truly seductive behavior of parents, perhaps because the concept of the Laius and Jocasta complexes was more egodystonic and culturally unacceptable than the theory of the Oedipus complex, which in a way only confirms the poor opinion that 19th-century adults generally had of children. The scotomization of the Laius and Jocasta complexes seems to have induced some modern authors to develop and elaborate a not too convincing theory of a phylogenetically determined infantile phantasy life. This theory maintains that if the child does not notice the amorous and humane virtues of his parent, he will see him as quite a monster because of the child's own instinctively determined and phylogenetically established phantasies. [p. 132]

OEDIPUS' FILICIDAL PROGENITORS[1]

Oedipus, son of Laius, son of Labdacus, son of Polydorus, son of Cadmus, founder of Thebes, descends from a family line in which the murder of the children by their parents or by easily recognizable substitutive displacements is repeated. In the family tree presented here, the most important personages of the house of the Labdacids are included, beginning at its origins with Zeus;

---

[1]The following conclusions and also the family tree presented here summarize the work of a study group that was directed by the author and included Drs. Adela Cositorto, Raul Dolgei, Raquel Augustovsky, Lidia Lisman, Eduardo Mandelbaum Pieczansky, and Liliana Ziamurriz. The results, entitled "Oedipus' filicidal progeny," were read at the Argentine Society of Medical Psychology, Psychoanalysis and Psychosomatic Medicine in the session of April 17, 1969.

a branch of the house of the Pelopids is also shown because of the close relationship between Laius and Lycus, regent of Thebes. Of Cadmus, only the ascendent line is shown, although the fate of his descendents is quite detailed.

Cadmus, the founder of Thebes, has five children from his union with the goddess Harmonia: Semele, Autonoe, Ino, Agave, and Polydorus, the first four being girls and the fourth a boy. Zeus loves Semele zealously and from their union Dionysus is born. But counselled by the malignant Juno, Semele dies when she gazes at Zeus' splendor, a sight that was fatal for mortals. Autonoe, the second daughter, marries Aristaeus with whom she conceives Acteon, murdered by Diana for having viewed her naked. In this case, Diana is a displacement of Autonoe. Ino, the third daughter, marries Atamas and begets Learchus and Melicertes. Learchus is killed by an arrow shot by his father who has mistaken him for a deer. Melicertes dies in a cauldron of boiling water at the hands of his mother Ino, who commits suicide immediately afterwards. Agave, the fourth sister, marries Echion and gives birth to Pentheus, but this time it is she herself who kills her son when she confuses him with a lion. Such is the first generation following Cadmus. And we go on with Oedipus' progenitors. Labdacus, son of Polydorus, dies when his son Laius is only one year old, torn to pieces by the bacchantes for having fought against the cult of Dionysus. Laius marries Jocasta, daughter of Menoeceus and sister of Creon. Creon marries Eurydice who bears Athenon. Eurydice and Athenon commit suicide when they see the cadaver of Antigone, beloved of Athenon and faithful daughter of Oedipus, who hangs herself, wearied by Creon's persecution and hardness. Laius dies at the crossroads by the hand of his son Oedipus whom he has previously tried to kill, and Jocasta hangs herself. The house of the Pelopids touches on the life of the Labdacids since, because of the

THE FILICIDAL PROGENY OF OEDIPUS

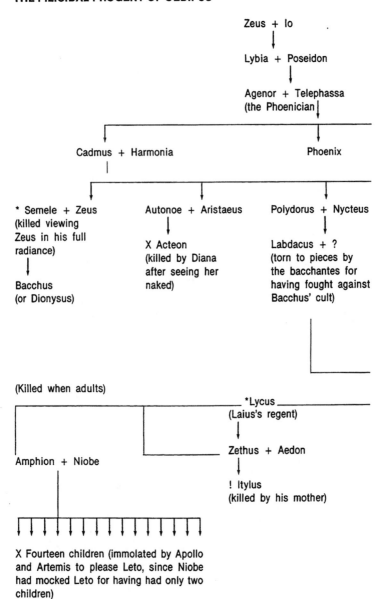

Zeus + Io

Lybia + Poseidon

Agenor + Telephassa
(the Phoenician)

Cadmus + Harmonia   Phoenix

* Semele + Zeus   Autonoe + Aristaeus   Polydorus + Nycteus
(killed viewing
Zeus in his full   X Acteon   Labdacus + ?
radiance)   (killed by Diana   (torn to pieces by
                         after seeing her   the bacchantes for
Bacchus   naked)   having fought against
(or Dionysus)   Bacchus' cult)

(Killed when adults)

                                            *Lycus
                                            (Laius's regent)

Amphion + Niobe   Zethus + Aedon

                                            ! Itylus
                                            (killed by his mother)

X Fourteen children (immolated by Apollo
and Artemis to please Leto, since Niobe
had mocked Leto for having had only two
children)

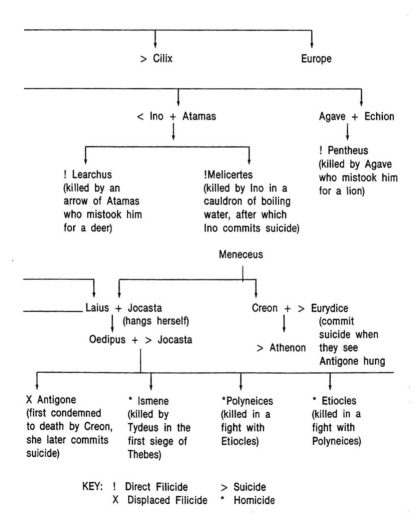

KEY: ! Direct Filicide   > Suicide
      X Displaced Filicide   * Homicide

death of Labdacus, whose son Laius is only a nursling and cannot take the throne, Lycus is named regent of Thebes. Lycus exposes his sons, Amphion and Zethus, on the mountain. They later murder him. Amphion marries Niobe and has fourteen children who are killed by Apollo and Artemis, who Niobe has mocked for having only two children. Zethus marries Aedon, who becomes the murderer of their son Itylus.

Thus we see that few of Oedipus' forebears were saved from dying at the hands of their parents or substitute parents. And not only the progenitors suffer this fate that eventually extinguishes the house of the Labdacids: Oedipus' own descendents will suffer from this thanatic curse. In effect, they will finally destroy each other, and this is doubtless connected with the fact that Oedipus has cursed his sons. Just as Antigone commits suicide because of the persecution by her uncle Creon, father of her beloved Athenon, Ismene is put to death by Tydeus in the first siege of Troy, and Eteocles and Polyneices die while fighting against each other.

Such is the summary of the intensely filicidal background of Oedipus, an expression of human nature and of the grave conflicts involved in the struggle between the generations. Students of psychology cannot ignore knowledge of the Oedipus myth, perhaps the deepest and most far-reaching mythological concept. The Oedipus complex is the main pillar of the theories about the unconscious and, therefore, anything contributing to its clarification is indispensable.

OTHER BASIC OCCIDENTAL MYTHS

All hero myths begin with the hero's condemnation by his parents or their substitutes to a fateful death. We have discussed this theme previously. The interested reader may refer to Rank's classical work, *The Myth of the Birth of the Hero* (1957).

There are some myths that are particularly interesting in which the death of the father is replaced by the holocaust of the son. Frazer (1942) mentions one of the most typical of these from Scandinavian mythology:

> According to tradition, the king of Sweden, Aun or On, sacrificed nine of his sons to Odin in order to preserve his own life. After sacrificing his second son, god told him that he would live as long as he sacrificed a son every nine years. When he sacrificed the seventh son, he still lived but he was already so weak that he was unable to walk and had to be carried in a chair. Afterward, he sacrificed his eighth son and lived nine years prostrated in bed. After sacrificing his ninth son he lived another nine years, but he had to be fed from a horn like a newly weaned baby. He wanted to sacrifice the tenth and only son he had left, but the Swedes did not allow him to do so. Therefore, he died and was buried in Upsala. [p. 290]

Here we find clear reference to the envy that the father feels at the birth of each child. We must accordingly consider the nine years between each sacrifice as a symbolic expression of the nine months of pregnancy preceding each birth that sharpen the father's envy and the accompanying cannibalistic and filicidal desires. Another significant detail is the progressive transformation of king Aun into a babylike man, until at the end he is fed with a kind of baby bottle.   .

Frazer (1942) also mentions similar myths in the cults of the primitive Semites, who worshiped Baal or Moloch:

> Among the Semites of Western Asia (Minor), in times of national danger, the king sometimes sacrificed his son for the good of his

people. Thus, Philon of Byblos says in his work on the Jews: "It was an ancient custom, in times of danger, for the ruler of a city or nation to sacrifice his son for his people, as a ransom offered to the vengeful demons. The immolated children were offered with mystical rites. Thus, Cronus, whom the Phoenicians called Israel, who was king of the country and had an only son called Jeoud (Jeoud in Phoenician means only child), dressed him in kingly robes and sacrificed him on an altar, in times of war when the country was in grave danger threatened by the enemy." [p. 293]

Frazer goes on:

> When king Moab was besieged by the Israelites and saw that he was greatly persecuted, he took his eldest son, who would have been his successor to the throne, and offered him as a burnt offering on the walls. [p. 293]

The forms of sacrifice related to war (and even war itself) have always been fed with the lives of children and youths. For this reason we have affirmed (Rascovsky 1970) that, since remotest antiquity, war represents the sacrificial pyre on which the killing of the offspring is consummated. In this sense, we will also quote an account by Herodotus (1968), written 2,500 years before Christ:

> Then Cresus, according to the Lydians, seeing that the mind of Cyrus had turned in his favor, and that all those present unsuccessfully attempted to extinguish the fire, invoked the god Apollo aloud, asking him that if any of his offerings had met with his favor, he should help him in his distress and free him from the wretched fate that was menacing him. He had scarcely sobbed out this supplication when, in spite of the serene and clear skies, clouds suddenly gathered and showered copious rain that left the blaze quenched. Cyrus was persuaded by this prodigy of what a

friend of the gods Cresus was and what a good character he had, having him taken down from the pyre and then asking him: "Tell me, Cresus, who induced you to undertake an expedition against my States, changing you from my friend to my foe?" "This I did, sir," answered Cresus, "compelled by the fortune that shows favor unto you and adversity unto me. For all this the guilt lies with the god of the Greeks, who deluded me with flattering hopes; because who is so base that he unreasonably prefers war to the sweetness of peace? In the latter children bury their parents and in the former it is the parents who bury their children. But all this must have happened because some deity wished it so." [p. 40]

3

The Prohibition against Incest, Filicide, and the Sociocultural Process

Psychoanalysis has confirmed that incest constitutes the deepest, most intense, and most universal instinctive aim. Endogamic ties form the main emotional obstacle the individual must overcome in the process of development and socialization; this is evidenced by the difficulty involved in working through the Oedipus complex. However, at the beginning of life, the incestuous urge is the fundamental sexual factor both in the child's development and in the future adult's genital behavior.

In view of the absolute generalization of the prohibition against incest in all sociocultural groups, we cannot avoid asking: By what irrevocable and persistent procedures was the most essential instinctive aim distorted?

Together with the universal prohibition against incest, we find another generalized cultural institution: primitive myths

(Devereux 1953, 1966, Rascovsky 1967, 1968, 1970), rites of
initiation, studies of human sacrifice (Devereux 1953, 1966), and
diverse expressions of the social systems show us that the real or
symbolic killing, mutilation, and humiliation of the offspring, in
their most varied expressions, constitute practices that have also
been universal since the dawn of man (Devereux 1953, 1966,
Rascovsky 1970, Rheingold 1964).

In psychoanalytic clinical practice, we can observe the
endopsychic expression of this phenomenology in the relationship between the superego and the ego (Berliner 1966), manifested in disturbances such as obsessional neurosis, melancholia,
or suicide; it also comes to light when we analyze the type of
punitive sanctions imposed on the ego for incestuous phantasies.
This threat from the superego, a result of archaic parental
attitudes that have been introjected, is the basis of the concept of
taboo. For this reason, the concept of filicide acquires special
importance for psychoanalytic theory by adding a new dimen-
sion to the Oedipus complex, to the structure of guilt, and to the
understanding of repressive forces and internalized persecutors.

The hypothesis that parricide is the original crime and the
origin of guilt requires thorough revision. Parricide is the consequence rather than the cause of filicidal behavior and its roots
can be found in the child's identification with the previous
aggressive attitude of its parents. This approach emphasizes the
importance of the parental attitude in the regulation of innate
infantile aggression and explains how the parricidal phantasy
established in later periods of development is created by the
environment.

The "great event" described by Freud (1913) as the "killing
and eating of the father—guilt feelings" (p. 145) must be modified
considering that the original victim was the child; the "great
event" is actually the sequence: killing and eating of the offspring

or of a group of offspring—guilt-provoking intimidation of all the offspring—denial of the true process. The *pars pro toto* substitution for the killing of the son is renewed in the circumcision of newborn males among the Jews and at a later age among the Moslems, and also in the identification experienced by Christians through communion with Jesus who has been circumcised and murdered. We will make only brief mention of the most well-founded anthropological criticism of the conception of parricide. According to Kroeber (1920a,b), in history, typical events are always recurrent. But this is not the case for the killing and eating of the father and the sentiment of guilt. Kroeber considers that certain unconscious processes always tend to be operative and to find expression in human institutions.

Filicide is actually a typical happening demonstrated by those human institutions that re-enact its consummation, generation after generation, perpetuating it in a variety of primitive and contemporary social forms, the most constant of them being war (Rascovsky 1970).

When Freud (1928) stated: "Parricide . . . is the principal and primal crime of humanity as well as of the individual . . . It is in any case the main source of the sense of guilt, although we do not know if it is the only one" (p. 184), he was basing his idea on the fear of the father, as he went on to point out: "What makes hatred of the father unacceptable is *fear* of the father; castration is terrible, whether as a punishment or as the price of love. Of the two factors which repress hatred of the father, the first, the direct fear of punishment and castration, may be called the normal one. . ." (p. 184). Freud also said:

> . . . when a child reacts to his first great instinctual frustrations with excessively strong aggressiveness and with a correspondingly severe superego, he is following a phylogenetic model and is going

beyond the response that would be currently justified, for the father of prehistoric times was undoubtedly terrible, and an extreme amount of aggressiveness may be attributed to him. [p. 184]

In analyzing the fear of the father we must look for that aggressiveness in archaic relationships with the parents, bringing to light the internalized factors that result from the parents' capacity for absorbing, being depositories for, and working through the child's innate primitive aggression. The parents' destructive behavior is then visible in many forms, on a spectrum that varies from rejection or lack of consideration, all the way to direct attitudes that include murdering the child (Berliner 1966, Devereux 1966, Rascovsky 1970). More recently, studies of the effects of the relationship between parents and their offspring (Ainsworth et al. 1963, Bowlby et al. 1956, Bowlby 1958, Burlingham and Freud 1943) have been modified to take into account that parents function initially as their child's "auxiliary ego." The child is able to survive thanks to this "auxiliary ego," which is indispensable for the child's adaptation to the external world. The initial lack of a parental function—exercised by parents or by substitutes—produces the child's "death," which later causes damage that is proportional to the magnitude of the defect. Parental deficiency is expressed through active and/or passive attitudes, most commonly seen in practices such as circumcision, early and/or repeated abandonment, mental or physical punishment, prohibition of instinctual needs, threats, castration, sufferings and abuse, cruelty, physical or verbal attacks, despotic denials, insensitivity to suffering, denigrating judgments, and the various parental attitudes, occasional or constant, that leave immediate or eventual wounds on the child's Self.

Filicide is a corollary of the relation between the prohibition against incest and parricide; in fact, it can be considered as the basic procedure that established both the prohibition and its sociocultural consequences. This explains how the sacrifice of the offspring, the basis of all human sacrifice, became the quintessence of cultural demand on its members and was later extended to include attenuated forms labeled as education. It also enriches the interpretation of guilt feelings, since the increment of paranoia provoked by the direct threat posed by the parents intensifies persecutory guilt (Ginsberg 1963). Facing filicide squarely helps us to unravel its aggressive microforms that act on the ego so as to shape a paranoid organization, including the structuring of internal persecutory objects, on the basis not only of phantasies but also on the basis of parental reality.

THE PROHIBITION AGAINST INCEST AND THE SOCIOCULTURAL PROCESS

Man's most specifically human trait is formed by violently blocking his deepest gratification: incest. This basic event marking the beginning of culture was described by Levi-Strauss (1983) in this way:

> The sexual instinct, because it is natural itself, does not constitute the passage from nature to culture, since this would be inconceivable, but explains one of the reasons for which sexual life more than any other matter is where the transit between the two orders must and can operate . . . the prohibition of incest is simultaneously on the threshold of culture, within culture and, in a certain sense, as we will try to demonstrate, is culture itself. [pp. 41–42]

The prohibition against incest produced: (1) the institution of exogamy and the extension of the social group, including displacement of initial early dependence on the parents to the community; (2) the overdevelopment and organization of sublimation involving the channelling of forbidden instinctive tendencies toward activities that multiplied man's creative and occupational expressions; and (3) the transmission of experiences and knowledge acquired by former generations and the participation of the whole group in the education of infants and children.

This process, which represents the individual's death in incestuous society and rebirth in exogamic society, is the latent content beneath Frazer's (1944) description of the ritual of "death and resurrection" (p. 820) that is found in all cultures.

This evolution is re-experienced by each individual in the vicissitudes of the Oedipus complex. When the child reaches the zenith of genital incest, the onset of the castration complex produces endogamic death, renouncement of orientation toward the mother, and rebirth into society outside the family. Consequently, the child enters the period of latency until puberty when instinctive pressure is reactivated. During this period sublimation increases and the society of school is the first expression of exogamy. Instruction, begun by the parents, is now displaced to teachers and other substitutes.

The prohibition against incest required a force intense enough to oppose the energy of the instinctive desire that it had to block. This traumatic submission at first included the immolation of a group of children: the murder of the firstborn. This demand, institutionalized later by religious systems as a sacred demand from the divinity, is explicit in diverse historical-religious documents (Rascovsky 1967) and must be considered a very ancient norm whose origins date back to the dawn of culture.

THE ORIGINS OF FILICIDE

Although the murder of the offspring eventually became the principal means of establishing the prohibition against incest, it was originally an instinctive urge that was only subsequently converted to an institutionalized norm as "human sacrifice." We have shown (Rascovsky 1967, 1968) that the initial myths of diverse cultures begin with the murder or, what is the same, the abandonment of the offspring.

In the higher vertebrates, Lorenz (1966) says:

> I do not believe that the specifically human tendencies to cannibalism, for which there appears to be ample psychoanalytic evidence, have anything to do with the occasional eating of young mammals by their progenitors. . . . In general, cannibalism is quite rare in the higher vertebrates. [pp. 128–129]

Blin and Favreau (1968), referring to infanticide and puerperal cannibalism, state: "In mammals . . . this fact does not fail to constitute a real behavioral disturbance and must be considered pathological" (p. 282).

Occasional cannibalism in mammals is a response to excessive *stress*. This response became permanent in human beings exposed to constant *stressful* circumstances and created an adaptation based on regression to the oral-cannibalistic stage. In this regressive state, previously acquired erotic capacities that would have served to preserve and care for the offspring were lost.

Cannibalism by ingestion of parts of the mother constitutes a normal process in mammals until the offspring is able to assimilate foods that are more differentiated than the mother's milk. In the human being, it coexists with the partial object relation and is abandoned when the child is able to perceive the totality of the object of its love. Therefore, cannibalism is part of the paranoid-schizoid position. The passage to the total object relation means there has been considerable erotic progress enabling the individual to unite the parts of the totality. This erotic development inhibits cannibalism and, once the child has entered the depressive position, the possibility of destroying the object of its love. Repeated human filicide and its institutionalized perpetuation is understandable considering that in the remote past conditions of extreme *stress* induced oral-cannibalistic regression, which leads to a considerable increase in paranoia. When the inhibitions that have been acquired to avoid killing the offspring are lost, the children are transformed into partial objects at the mercy of intensified oral sadism.

In clinical practice, this regression generally takes place with the arrival of the firstborn. We can illustrate this mechanism with the following sequence of clinical material drawn from the psychoanalysis of a man who was expecting his first child.

When the delivery seemed imminent, the patient said in the following session that his wife had been to the obstetrician, who had told her that the cervix was very dilated. He described two dreams from the previous night:

We were in a hospital corridor. My wife and I saw G. coming toward us, with the front and collar of his shirt spotted. It looked like he'd been drinking. I think that he's been to a banquet at J.'s house. It makes me furious because J. has problems about inviting me and not about inviting G. The corridor turns into the clinic where my wife is going to have the baby.

His associations led him to G., a friend with whom he has an obviously ambivalent relationship. G. represented the patient's future child nursing, with the shirt spotted in the place where babies wear their bibs, and sharing the food with J. (the wife-mother), excluding him from the feast (breast). His oral envy can be seen in his fury at not having been invited. Another dream:

> I go to the movies. It's a holiday. The movie theater is closed but they're going to show the movie. Another couple is with us. It seems odd to me that they're going to show the movie with the theater closed. They give me balcony tickets. I think they're too far away, because I'd rather be downstairs.

When he associated, he said that he couldn't have sexual relations because his wife was too swollen and too full of the fetus. It was a reference to the movie theater that was closed on the holiday (holiday as coitus), which forced him to keep his distance. The couple with them was associated with the genitals. Here, he expresses the feeling of being excluded genitally from the relationship with his wife because of the pregnancy, which he could only watch from far away.

Two days later the child was born and the patient spent time in the clinic with the mother. The next morning he brought in two dreams:

> I was with P. (a friend having attributes referring to the baby), G. (who appeared before as the baby) and V. (the

dreamer). V. says that we must celebrate the birth with a barbecue that could be held in the Luna Park [similar to Madison Square Garden]. G. says it couldn't be done in the Rotary Club. P. scolds me because I haven't received my medical degree and because I'm incapable of studying.

He associated Luna Park with the arena where boxing matches are held, in contrast with the Rotary Club, an expression of love between men. The barbecue represented the killing and eating of the baby. The child protests against this through the superego agency that accuses him of immaturity and incapacity as a father because of the cannibalism he has not overcome.

I see that the mother of my brother-in-law is ill, about to die.

The patient had this dream after having taken care of the baby during the night. It represented his envy and his wish that his wife die, displaced to the mother of his brother-in-law. He was trying to replace his wife in the relationship with the baby. Baby and mother had been at home for two days. The following dream occurred after he had again taken care of the baby during the night:

I go to the kitchen to prepare a bottle. The door of the apartment is open. I want to close it but someone is pushing from outside. I think it's a thief and I try to keep him from entering. But he manages to open it and the door falls over on me. The presumed thief was my brother."

That afternoon he had said goodbye to his brother, giving him a hug. He felt bothered because his brother had leaned on him too much. He also associated that in children's stories babies are brought from Paris; his brother had just come back from Paris. The thief represented the intruding new baby who threatened to displace him; he was expressing his useless opposition to this situation.

This fragmentary account of the patient's experience of the birth of his firstborn child is a sample of the universal unconscious response to the arrival of offspring.

PROCEDURES FOR IMPOSING THE PROHIBITION AGAINST INCEST

We return to our initial question: What procedures were capable of effectively imposing the prohibition against incest? Instinctive demand exerts constant pressure that has been structured through filogenetic evolution. Coercion of it, historically much later, requires incessant antagonistic action, which loses effectiveness as soon as it has been exerted. Repeated opposition to this instinctive demand, imposed from outside and introjected as the superego agency, was necessary in order to maintain the interdiction against incest. The archaic prohibition could be imposed as long as the parents dominated their children physically, mentally, and morally. This supremacy weakened with the children's growing vigor and the parents' corresponding decrepitude, until it was no longer possible to maintain the prohibition. The primitive gerontocracy, after repeated individual and collective experiences and backed by their sadistic and cannibalistic tendencies, permanently instituted parental despotism during childhood when the offspring's weakness and dependency made this possible.

This principle consolidated primitive society; it established a body of procedures that stands in full force even today: the killing of one group of the children and the mutilation and/or intimidation of the rest. The procedure was completed by covering up all knowledge of it, a denial that also persists at full intensity. For this reason, in spite of the obvious, ostensible, and ceaseless evidence of filicide, its recognition is consistently denied, while the importance of parricide is exaggerated. This antagonistic distortion intensifies the persecutory guilt that falls upon the offspring, with an added melancholic connotation intensifying the desired induced submission. Further, the mechanism of denial inverts the observation of parental sadism, twisting it so that it is seen as the justified wrath of the parents or of their institutions (society and its gods). The accusation of parricide is another type of filicidal action that converts the parents' guilt for envying their children and for the mortifying and murderous actions that stem from that envy into a guilt-inducing accusation of the children.

We have already pointed out that the whole process can be traced through the anthropological observation of primitive cultures, through analyzing ancient myths, rites of initiation, and many other archaic social institutions, or by psychoanalytic investigation, since transference brings primitive thinking into the present, reviving its effects. We will thus, time and again, discover a sequence consisting of the real or phantasied murder and consequent satisfaction of oral aggression against the child who is sacrificed with the secondary aim of terrorizing the rest of the offspring. Once the need for calming the parents' oral rivalry has been satisfied, there follows the child's resurrection from this voracious act. Then, genital rivalry comes forward with the intimidating castration, through diverse procedures that vary from real castration, still practiced in some cultures, to introjected genital inhibition organized by different endopsychic mechanisms. Circumcision, widely practiced in our most outstanding cultures, is an intermediate procedure.

We do not believe that the consequences of the prohibition against incest that originated the sociocultural process were the original motivations for killing and humiliating children. It is more credible to assume that the motivation stemmed from parental envy of the offspring, irrespective of an eventual sociocultural intention. Conditions of extreme *stress* provoked the parents' regression and the exacerbation of oral envy that led to the killing and eating of the offspring. Later, it was genital rivalry that impelled them to murder or, *pars pro toto*, to real or attenuated castration. The prohibition against incest can even be seen as a resulting compromise signaling progress, since it avoided killing the offspring and allowed the establishment of a sufficiently erotic bond. This entire process became permanently established in the superego of the species as an internal inhibitory regulator of genital activity.

Summing up: the prohibition against incest and its sociocultural consequences are based on the following triad: (1) the murder of a portion of the offspring, perpetuated through several techniques; the most representative of these is the "eternal sacrificial pyre of war" (Rascovsky 1970); (2) the induction of paranoia in the offspring through repeated intimidation, even to the extreme of terrorizing them; and (3) concealment of the entire process and reversal of its causality, thus effectively denying filicide with the concept of parricide so as to increase the persecutory guilt and anxiety of children and young people.

Filicide arose from the parents' paranoid-schizoid regression and instituted continual paranoid exacerbation of the sociocultural development that organized the prohibition against incest. The process became integrated through the creation of manic defenses that culminated in the idealization of the persecutors and the omnipotent denial of the entire procedure.

4

Filicide in the Origins of Monotheism

Present knowledge of the psychic structures and their dynamics provides us with a basis for understanding the archaic mental constructions underlying the myths and beliefs we are now able to examine. Some of these are universal manifestations or at least are common to entire peoples or to widespread masses of human beings. Freud analyzed the universal myths and established the importance that their meaning has for our knowledge of the unconscious and vice versa. In this way, the oedipal conflict was elucidated and came to be considered an essential feature of the human condition.[1]

---

[1]Freud (1960) analyzed the projective contents of myths in this way (italics are the author's):

"In point of fact I believe that a large part of the mythological view of the world, which extends a long way into the most modern religions, is nothing but psychology projected into the external world. The obscure recognition (the endopsychic perception, as it were) of psychical factors and relations in the unconscious is mirrored—it is difficult to express it

There exists a universal belief that forms the foundation of three of the most widespread religions, namely, Christianity, Islam, and Judaism. The reader has doubtless guessed that I am referring to the biblical account of Abraham and his pact with the Lord, as well as the circumstances signaling the passage from the polytheism of Terah to the beginning of monotheism as taken up by his son Abraham. Now, we will try to shed light on the psychodynamic aspects of this belief, which is consciously or unconsciously rooted in the individual and collective mind, and attempt to discover its relation to the human filicidal tendency, a tendency that is revealingly expressed in the biblical account.

FREUD AND MONOTHEISM

In *Moses and Monotheism*, a work published in the last year of his life (1939), Freud discussed his ideas on the origins of monotheism. Freud's thesis is based on historical roots and begins with the fact that a conception with the grandiosity of monotheism

---

in other terms, and here the analogy with paranoia must come to our aid—in the construction of a *supernatural reality*, which is destined to be changed back once more by science into the *psychology of the unconscious*. One could venture to explain in this way the myths of paradise and the fall of man, of God, of good and evil, of immortality, and so on, and to transform *metaphysics* into *metapsychology*. The gap between the paranoic's displacement and that of the superstitious person is less wide than it appears at first sight. When human beings began to think, they were, as is well known, forced to explain the external world anthropomorphically by means of a multitude of personalities in their own image; chance events, which they interpreted superstitiously, were thus actions and manifestations of persons" (*Standard Edition* 11: 258–259).

could not have sprung from a people as primitive as were the Hebrews at that time and that, just as the undisputably Egyptian name Moses shows,[2] only a superior culture, such as that achieved by the land of the Nile, could reach this degree of evolution. To explain why such a superior Egyptian, raised in a princely palace, joined the enslaved Hebrew people, Freud points out that Moses adopted them as his own people, imposing the knowledge of a unique and true god by circumcision and leading them out of Egypt to free them, thus ensuring the survival of the new religion introduced by the revolutionary pharaoh, Amenhotep IV, who later became Ikhnaton.

Once Ikhnaton had been overthrown, after seventeen years of imposing the monotheistic cult of Aton, his religious conception was violently repudiated by the Egyptian clergy whose rebellion reinstated the polytheistic reign of Osiris. When he fell, it was Moses who saved Ikhnaton's conception by taking it out of Egypt with the Hebrews whom he took to the desert in the Exodus. There, over different difficult periods, several rebellions challenged his authority, culminating in Moses' murder. Freud believes this was the great traumatic event of the Jewish people, that is, the assassination of their father-leader, repressed at the beginning only to return much later after having been forgotten.

Freud (1939) considered there was an analogy that "approaches identity" between the process he discovered in the history of the Jewish religion and the genesis of human neuroses. The latter pertains to individual psychology while the former pertains to the masses, this analogy supposedly being axiomatic.

---

[2]The Egyptian name Mose means male child. The "s" was added later by the Greeks. This formation can be seen in Ramose = Ramses or in Ptahmose.

He also insisted on the sequential formula for the development of the neuroses, that is: early trauma–defense–latency–outbreak of the neurosis–partial return of the repressed, this individual process then being associated with the experience of the species.[3]

---

[3]According to Freud (1939): ". . . that is, that here too events occurred of a sexually aggressive nature, which left behind them permanent consequences but were for the most part fended off and forgotten, and which after a long latency came into effect and created phenomena similar to symptoms in their structure and purpose.

"We believe that we can guess these events and we propose to show that their symptom-like consequences are the phenomena of religion. Since the emergence of the idea of evolution no longer leaves room for doubt that the human race has a prehistory, and since this is unknown—that is, forgotten—a conclusion of this kind almost carries the weight of a postulate. When we learn that in both cases the operative and forgotten traumas relate to life in the human family, we can greet this as a highly welcome, unforeseen bonus which has not been called for by our discussions up to this point."

Freud (1939) also notes, when he refers to the repercussion of the first experiences in life on events of adulthood: "It has long since become common knowledge that the experiences of a person's first five years exercise a determining effect on his life, which nothing later can withstand. Much that deserves knowing might be said about the way in which these early impressions maintain themselves against any influences in more mature periods of life but it would not be relevant here. It may, however, be less well known that the strongest compulsive influence arises from impressions which impinge upon a child at a time when we would have to regard his psychical apparatus as not yet completely receptive. The fact itself cannot be doubted; but it is so puzzling that we may make it more comprehensible by comparing it with a photographic exposure which can be developed after any interval of time and transformed into a picture. I am nevertheless glad to point out that this uncomfortable discovery of ours has been anticipated by an imaginative writer, with the boldness that is permitted to poets. E.T.A. Hoffmann used to trace back the wealth of

Freud was unable to escape the denial of filicide and thus he based his interpretation of original guilt on parricide, taking the assassination of the father-leader as the essential traumatic-genetic event in the configuration of the Jewish religious process. However, in a deeper study of the Mosaic myth, we can find the denied filicide and trace the genesis of the sacrifice of Moses back to his beginnings as an infant, that is, to the desertion that the baby Moses suffered in the waters of the Nile. Is this not equivalent to the myth of the child condemned by his parents to die on Mount Citheron, the same child who later became the prototypical parricidal son, that is, Oedipus?

As Freud (1939) quotes, basing his ideas on those of Rank and of Galton, the myth of the birth of the hero has a recurring sequence:

> The hero is the child of the *most aristocratic* parents; usually the son of a king. His conception is preceded by difficulties, such as abstinence or prolonged barrenness or his parents having to have intercourse in secret owing to external prohibitions or obstacles. During the pregnancy, or even earlier, there is a prophecy (in the form of a dream or oracle) cautioning against his birth, usually threatening danger to his father.

> As a result of this the new-born child is condemned to death or to *exposure*, usually by the orders of *his father or of someone representing him*; as a rule he is given over to the *water* in a *casket*. He is afterwards rescued by animals or by *humble people* (such as

---

figures that put themselves at his disposal for his creative writings to the changing images and impressions which he had experienced during a journey of some weeks in a post-chaise while he was still an infant at his mother's breast. What children have experienced at the age of two and have not understood, need never be remembered by them except in dreams. . ."

shepherds) and is suckled by a *female animal* or by a *humble woman*. After he has grown up, he rediscovers his aristocratic parents after highly variegated experiences, *takes his revenge on his father*, on the one hand, and is *acknowledged* on the other and achieves greatness and fame. (The italics are Freud's.) [*Standard Edition* 23:10–11]

It is easy to see that in this sequence the initial sacrifice is constituted by the desertion or the threat of murdering the child who becomes a hero when he is saved by fortuitous or unusual circumstances. Such a threatening beginning establishes a climax in the child's paranoic anxieties, which constitute the inner driving mechanism that will transform him into a hero. He is a hero through identification with the aggressor (the father or his substitute who ordered him killed) and so he will accomplish the feat of killing his father. Thus, the entire configuration of the myth of the birth of the hero can begin to be broken down into its most primitive psychodynamic elements and come to acquire a genetic meaning that is not only prior and valid but also more quantitative than qualitative, considering the weight of the persecutory threat to the child.

In the case of heroes, over and above the universal paranoid position that originates with birth and is felt by each of us, there is a marked persecutory intensification because of the mentioned desertion and the parents' equivalent attempts at murder. For this reason, Moses, left in the waters of the Nile, like Sargon in the Euphrates or Oedipus on Mount Citheron, together with the series mentioned by Rank (1981) and Freud (1939): Cyrus, Romulus, Karna, Paris, Telephos, Perseus, Heracles, Gilgamesh, Amphion, and Zethos, follows, as they do, the same initial filicidal pattern from which the later sequence will grow, culminating in parricide according to the basic model of child development: identification with the object, in this case identification with the aggressor.

However, these bad parents are described not only in this filicidal attitude as persecutors or deserters of their newborn baby, but are simultaneously idealized as rulers or personages of the highest social rank, according to the plot of the family romance as Freud analyzed it. On the other hand, the good or substitute parents, that is, the good aspects of the parents, are denigrated to the point of making them animals or, if they are human beings, very lowly people whom the son will eventually desert, actively repeating the equivalent pattern to which his parents subjected him previously. Thus, the hero abandons the good parents and sets out to find the idealized bad parents on whom he has remained fixated.[4]

Rather than attempting a historical interpretation of the events that gave rise to monotheism, we prefer to restrict our study to the individual psychological process leading to the universal acceptance of the monotheistic conception. In this way we will be able to understand the developmental stages that each individual experiences in his or her psychodynamics, repeating the pattern established by the species.

We will begin by centering the entire process on the above-mentioned model, that is: the filicidal threat and the resulting institution of manic defenses that lead to the projection and external acceptance of processes that are exclusively endopsychic and that acquire "real" meaning only from the sum of collective projective identifications. For this reason, denial, idealization, omnipotence, denigration of the good object, and

---

[4]Oedipus leaves Corinth and his good parents, Polybus and Merope, to return to Thebes where he will rejoin his persecutory parents, Laius and Jocasta.

overvaluation of the bad object are all essential mechanisms in the religious process. These mechanisms are heightened in monotheism where the predominance of the intensified persecutory character of the introjected filicidal parents reaches full expression. Finally, as in all religious institutions, the process of massive projective identification is organized collectively and is effectively established as a dominant "reality."

Psychologically, both the myth of the birth of the hero and the structuring of the chosen heroic people can be seen to have two salient conditions: (1) serious paranoid intensification at the expense of the intimidatory desertion or murder of a group of children from the firstborn on, and the mutilation (circumcision) and induction of all the rest, and (2) equally intense manic defenses with heightened mechanisms of denial, idealization, omnipotence, overvaluation of the bad object, and denigration of the good object, acted out through collective massive projective identification that converts the internal phantasies into "external pseudorealities."

The mythical stories boldly display the desertion, mutilation, and intimidation of the child-hero, who is thus paranoically induced. The most threatening factor for the life of a child is desertion. In the universal institution of this paranoid induction, the conspicuous act is the mutilation of each individual through circumcision,[5] thus establishing the reality of persecutory castration from the child's birth or infancy.

The denial, idealization, and omnipotence of the perse-

---

[5]Circumcision is practiced when the child is one week old by the Jews, in prepuberty by the Muslims, and through the process of identification (the Communion) with circumcised Jesus by the Christians, who have made this date, the first of January, not only one of their main holidays but also the beginning of their annual cycle.

cutor are transparent in the biblical conception, where Jehovah himself, demanding universal circumcision and later the murder of Isaac's son, constitutes the image of someone on whom all hope of life and of a prolific future depends. In the various individual hero myths, the parents who desert their child or order their child killed are also idealized as kings or wished-for objects of love. As we have already pointed out, the best example is offered by Oedipus, Laius, and Jocasta.

ABRAHAM

Freud examined the myth of Abraham only secondarily. It is interesting to note that in *Moses and Monotheism*, Abraham is mentioned only a few times. The existence of a biblical account attributing the origins of monotheism to the events centering on Abraham and his relationship with Jehovah (the expression Adonai is not used in the biblical text that refers to Abraham) was an obstacle for the thesis Freud held on the Egyptian origins of monotheism. Freud brilliantly swept aside this obstacle by creating a synthesis from the conception of the god Aten-Adonai introduced by the first Egyptian Moses and the cruel and totemic conception of Yahweh-Jehovah imposed by a later Midianite Moses, son-in-law of the priest Jethro, who actually organized the new religion of the Jews in Kadesh.

According to Freud (1939), the two conceptions of Adonai and Jehovah were thus fused into one unique god:

> We cannot dispute the impression that this Moses of Kadesh and Midian, to whom tradition could actually attribute the erection of a brazen serpent as a god of healing, is someone quite other than the aristocratic Egyptian inferred by us, who presented the

people with a religion in which all magic and spells were pro-
scribed in the strictest terms. Our Egyptian Moses is no less
different, perhaps, from the Midianite Moses than is the universal god Aten from the demon Yahweh in his home on the
Mount of God. [p. 36]

Freud (1939) also adds:

We are, I think, justified in separating the two figures and in
assuming that the Egyptian Moses was never at Kadesh and had
never heard the name of Yahweh, and that the Midianite Moses
had never been in Egypt and knew nothing of Aten. In order to
solder the two figures together, tradition or legend had the task of
bringing the Egyptian Moses to Midian, and we have seen that
more than one explanation of this was current. [p. 41]

Freud's explanation of the myth of Abraham is excessively
concise and therefore lacking with respect to its importance. He
only says (1939):

The fact that we find signs of efforts being made to deny explicitly
that Yahweh was a new god, alien to the Jews, can scarcely be
described as the appearance of a fresh tendentious purpose: it is
rather a continuation of the former one. With this end in view
the legends of the patriarchs of the people—Abraham, Isaac and
Jacob—were introduced. Yahweh asserted that he was already
the god of these forefathers; though it is true that he himself had
to admit that they had not worshipped him under that name. He
does not add, however, what the other name was.

And here was the opportunity for a decisive blow against the
Egyptian origin of the custom of circumcision: Yahweh, it was
said, had already insisted on it with Abraham and had introduced it as the token of the covenant between him and Abra-

ham. But this was a particularly clumsy invention. As a mark that is to distinguish one person from others and prefer him to them, one would choose something that is not to be found in other people; one would *not* choose something that can be exhibited in the same way by millions of other people. An Israelite who was transplanted to Egypt would have had to acknowledge every Egyptian as a brother in the covenant, a brother in Yahweh. It is impossible that the Israelites who created the text of the Bible can have been ignorant of the fact that circumcision was indigenous in Egypt. The passage in Joshua [v,9] quoted by Eduard Meyer admits this without question; but for that very reason it had to be disavowed at any price. [p. 44]

An unacceptable point in light of present anthropological knowledge concerns Freud's statement that circumcision was "indigenous in Egypt," since it is a universal practice disseminated throughout the most diverse human groups, primitive and contemporary, whose cultural patterns, both elemental and developed, are extremely varied.

The *Encyclopaedia Britannica* states:

The origin of the practice is unknown. The widespread ethnic distribution of circumcision as a ritual, and the quite widely preferred use of a stone knife rather than a metal one, suggest a great antiquity for the operation. Only the Indo-Germanic, the Mongol and the Finno-Ugrian-speaking peoples were unacquainted with the practice. Wherever the operation is performed as a traditional rite it is done either before or at puberty, and sometimes, as among some Arabian peoples, immediately before marriage. [5:799]

There are numerous theories concerning the origin of circumcision. The following constitute a representative sample: it represents a blood-offering to the gods, in order to maintain the latters' immortality and also to extend the life of the individual; it is a substitute for sacrifice; it is a dedication; the sacrifice of a part to ensure the welfare of the whole; the cutting off and preservation of part of oneself ensures preservation after death, and reincarnation; it represents the atonement made for incestuous desires entertained in childhood, unconsciously expiated by the fathers through their sons; since the foreskin often exerts a constricting effect it was considered magically to inhibit fertility, hence the necessity of its removal; finally, it has been suggested that it was practiced for purely hygienic reasons.

There is probably some truth in some of these conjectures, perhaps in all, but precisely how much or how little it is impossible to say. The origins of the practice are as dark as an Egyptian night. A lucky series of archaeological finds may some day provide a more exact understanding of the origin of the custom. [5:800]

Circumcision seems to be a measure of the way in which most cultures impose the genital submission on their sons and the universal prohibition against incest, which holds equally in the most primitive and in the most advanced among them. For this reason, we cannot consider at present that the primitive Jews needed the Egyptian contribution in order to institute circumcision, which we know was practiced as it is nowadays by culturally inferior tribes including those of Africa, Australia, and America, before there was any possible contact with men who could have brought it from Egypt. On the other hand, circumcision, as it is organized in the myth of Abraham, can lead us to elucidate the universal reasons for this imposition, which is connected, as we shall see, with the prohibition against incest, in the service of the intensification of submission to parents and a consequent increment of paranoid anxieties.

In addition, the convincing argument contributed by Freud is unidirectional in the dual conception that he establishes for the origin of monotheism, since he searches for its origins in the Egyptian source of the Mosaic roots, while failing to scrutinize the predecessors of the Midianite Moses who contributed the conception of the volcanic Jehovah: those who can be traced back to Abraham. It is Abraham who, in the biblical account, initiates the dialogue with Jehovah, whose cruel and bloodthirsty nature can be seen from the beginning when his first demand is for total obedience, shown by his acceptance of the sacrifice of Abraham's son. It is also Jehovah who demands the circumcision of all the males who are to belong to his chosen people, a choice that is later extended to include Jews, Christians, and Moslems, that is, to all the extended descendents of Abraham.

In this way, in the biblical narrative, Abram, son of Terah, seller of idols, initiates the belief in one god and it seems that "there is no doubt that Abram existed" and "at the same time we cannot now specify when he lived or details of his life" (*Encyclopaedia Britannica* 1966, 1:44–45).[6]

In any case, what interests us here is the mythical meaning

---

[6]According to the *Encyclopaedia Britannica* (1:45):

In rabbinic tradition Abraham occupies a position of eminence. His faith atones for the sins of Israel, and he was even the rock upon which God built and established the world. In the *New Testament*, allusions are made to this role of Abraham; *e.g.*, in Matthew 8:11 and Luke 13:28–29, where Abraham is an eschatological figure, represented as the host at the heavenly banquet (*cf.* Luke 16:22). The promises to Abraham are recognized as giving the Jews a special prerogative (Romans 9:8; 11:1 ff.). Yet, being children of Abraham has a spiritual, rather than a national, meaning (Romans 9:7 ff.; *cf.*Galatians 3:9). The true children of Abraham are "children of the promise" (Romans 9:8), and that promise is fulfilled in Christ that describes the institution of monotheism including all the dramatic events that the narrative ascribes to his actions and that culminate in his unconditional submission to the Lord when he attempts to kill his son Isaac. We shall see that after an initial period of rebellious action against the gerontocratic prescriptions limiting incestuous instinctual actions, an equally intense submission is imposed through a covenant that will permanently and more severly establish the same limitations that were initially violated.

Which of the data and references structuring the biblical belief, correlated with coherent psychic dynamics, will allow us to question and discover the total configuration of this narrative? Can we find its place with respect to our knowledge of the causality of mental processes? Finally, does the narrative have coherence and does it offer possibilities for a causal understanding of it?

We shall attempt to demonstrate that the mythical elements at our disposal authorize us to integrate our knowledge with this text accepted by Western humanity as corresponding to the beginnings of monotheism. The reader will also notice that, just as the title of this section indicates, the filicidal episodes

---

(Galatians 3:14). Abraham becomes a precursor of Christ. In Him the promises to Abraham are fulfilled (Galatians 3:25-29; cf. Hebrews 7), and Christians, even the gentile ones, partake in the blessing in Abraham (Galatians 3:8 ff.; cf. Genesis 12:3). Paul seizes upon Abraham's righteousness by faith (Genesis 15:6) in order to expound his central thesis that righteousness is granted through faith rather than through works (Romans 4:1 ff.; Galatians 3:6 ff.). In the epistle to the Hebrews, Abraham is an example of the faith that receives God's promise and responds to it in obedience (Hebrews 11:8 ff.).

established without the least concealment in the development of the monotheistic covenant have led us to study this crucial moment in recorded history, or at least in human mythology, with particular interest.

Before continuing, we must adopt a perspective that will be appropriate for differentiating situations of the collective ego from those of the individual ego in the two conceptions: the polytheistic and the monotheistic. If we delve into the mind's deepest strata, it is not difficult to observe that polytheism deifies all the tendencies of the id whose satisfaction the id demands of the ego; that is, all the instinctive tendencies in their exuberant variety. For this reason, there are as many gods as there are desires, and the meanings of the gods embrace all the human wishes that seek expression. Through the religious technique, these impulses manage to be projected into a social milieu that has been conditioned to accept them as if they were an exterior "conventional reality."

This is perhaps the hedonistic essence of paganism, that is, the deified valuation of the instinctive wish in conflict with the subsequent submission to which it had to yield in monotheism when this wish had to bow before the superego's despotic will. Thus, in monotheism, instinctive expression is only allowed pending examination, censorship, and permissiveness from the absolute power wielded by the superego,[7] which in turn receives nourishment from the same sources it subjugates. The superego

---

[7]We are referring here to the concept of the superego in which the addition of the internalized parental figures results in a later structure that must be distinguished from the primitive one, intertwined with the id whose origin is entirely endogenous and which influences the development of polytheism.

then becomes the regulator of all the anxieties and imposes the ethical norms governing satisfaction.[8]

It is impossible to demarcate strict limits between the two systems since regulations by the superego obviously exist, though to a lesser extent, prior to the institution of monotheism. The nature of their evolution is gradual; and before the superego with exogenous roots achieves absolute dominion, it has already been increasingly active, though still at the service of instinctual predominance, during the entire process of pagan deification. With monotheism the situation of predominance changes, and this change is possible because of the imposition of the prolonged and extremely despotic action of the most important exogenous factor in the organization of the superego: the parents.

We have learned that in the variation of the predominant endopsychic influences that act upon the ego, we observe manifestations that are typical of one state of preponderance or the other. Thus, the melancholic processes show us the overwhelming pressure of the superego, punishing the ego mercilessly and limiting any expression of pleasure that is not at the service of the submission it imposes. In these circumstances, hedonism becomes the type that can be experienced in subservience to the despotic and insatiable superego. We have also learned that there is a state, mania, in which the overwhelming pressure from the superego is denied or suppressed temporarily as a factor inhibiting instinctual expression. We have said "temporarily," since its previous existence can later be seen as more terribly cruel.

---

[8]The Ten Commandments established by Moses are the codification of the instinctual restrictions imposed by the superego, restrictions that place the "thou shalt not" upon the agencies glorified until then in the form of "thou shalt" satisfy the instinctual wish that characterizes heroic idealization.

The early existence of polytheism and the later development of monotheism indicates a developmental process whose
psychological parallel is the passage from early predominance of
the instincts, the superego not yet having been differentiated
antagonistically for the regulation of actions and ethics,[9] to the
predominance of the superego of exogenous origin. We shall try
to show how this development can be seen in the biblical
narrative, personified by Abraham, who is a collective projection of the universal development that each individual repeats
during his unconscious mental metamorphosis.

The central and latent point to be considered in this
biblical tale hinges on the incestuous character of the relationship between Abram (later Abraham) and his sister-wife Sarai
(later Sarah) and the consequent initial sterility of the couple,
overcome later through the covenant with God. Several passages
in the Scriptures support this idea.

In the first reference in *Genesis* to the subject, Sarai (also
called Iscah) is said to be the daughter of Haran, the dead brother
of Abram. *Genesis* describes it thus (*Genesis 11:27–29*):

27 Now these are the generations of Terah: Terah begat Abram,
Nahor, and Haran; and Haran begat Lot.

28 And Haran died before his father Terah, in the land of his
nativity, in Ur of the Chaldees.

29 And Abram and Nahor took them wives: the name of
Abram's wife was Sarai; and the name of Nahor's wife, Milcah,

---

[9]This regressive ethic is the one that prevails again in war, in
which organized crime, rape, and permissiveness for actions resulting
from the most primitive and least worked-through of the instinctual
demands are again rampant, together with idealization and the search
for the heroic condition.

the daughter of Haran the father of Milcah, and the father of Iscah.

This first biblical reference makes no mention of Sarai's kinship but does show Milcah's relation to Nahor, her blood uncle. Sarai is also Abram's blood niece here, contradicting later passages in which she appears as his sister. In other verses, Sarai's name is also Iscah.

In Chapter 12, Abram tells Sarai to introduce herself as his sister[10] to the Egyptians (*Genesis 12: 11–13*):

> *11* And it came to pass, when he was come near to enter into Egypt, that he said to Sarai his wife, Behold now, I know that thou art a woman beautiful to look upon;
>
> *12* Therefore it shall come to pass, when the Egyptians shall see ye, that they will say, This is his wife; and they will kill me, but they will save thee alive.
>
> *13* Say, I pray thee, thou art my sister; that it may be well with me for thy sake; and my soul shall live because of thee.

This is the introduction of Sarai as his sister. It is interesting to point out that afterwards the pharaoh is punished for his relationship with Sarai, suffering the Lord's wrath (*Genesis 12: 17–19*):

> *17* And the Lord plagued Pharaoh and his house with great plagues, because of Sarai, Abram's wife.

---

[10]Here, as in the later episode with King Abimelech, Abraham asks Sarah to go back to her relationship as his sister because he feels intimidated by the kings (parental substitutes) to whom he returns her.

18 And Pharaoh called Abram, and said, What is this that thou hast done unto me? Why didst thou not tell me that she was thy wife?

19 Why saidst thou, She is my sister, so I might have taken her to me to wife; now, therefore, behold thy wife, take her, and go thy way.

The punishment falls upon the pharaoh as a displacement of the one pertaining to Abram for his incest, while at the same time, through denial, he becomes very rich as *Genesis (13:1–2)* describes immediately after:

1 And Abram went up out of Egypt, he and his wife, and all that he had, and Lot with him, into the south.

2 And Abram was very rich, in cattle, in silver, and in gold.

The next mention of Sarah (no longer Sarai) as the sister of Abraham (also no longer Abram) is in *Genesis* when they are living as foreigners in Gerar (*Genesis 20:2–5*):

2 And Abraham said of Sarah his wife, She is my sister: and Abimelech king of Gerar sent, and took Sarah.

3 But God came to Abimelech in a dream by night, and said to him, "Behold, thou art but a dead man, for the woman which thou hast taken; for she is a man's wife."

4 But Abimelech had not come near her; so he said, Lord, wilt thou slay also a righteous nation?

5 Said he not unto me, She is my sister? and she, even she herself, said, He is my brother: in the integrity of my heart, and innocence of my hands, have I done this

Shortly afterwards, Abraham himself admits that Sarah is his half-sister (Genesis 20:11–13):

11 And Abraham said, Because I thought, Surely the fear of God is not in this place: and they will slay me for my wife's sake.

12 And yet indeed she is my sister; she is the daughter of my father, but not the daughter of my mother; and she became my wife.

13 And it came to pass, when God caused me to wander from my father's house, that I said unto her, This is thy kindness which thou shalt shew unto me: at every place whither we shall come, say of me, He is my brother.

This passage also suggests that the two of them were driven from their father's house because of their incestuous relationship. Although these narrations insinuate or indicate the fraternal relationship of Abraham and Sarah, another factor is added to make this seem quite real. This is the couple's sterility, which continues until they establish the relationship with the Lord. Sarah's sterility, or rather of the union between the two siblings, corresponds to the denial or the lack of identification with the father or to the primitive punishment for incest, and although Genesis is not explicit about it in this sense, we cannot reject its meaning.

On the other hand, the essential theme of the initial relationship with the Lord revolves around Abram's desire to have children with Sarai though she seems to be resigned to her sterility. Both Abram's complaints to the Lord and the compensations that the Lord promises him refer to the desire for a child and to Jehovah's promise of many descendents.

Abram, who has remained sterile until the age of 86, tells the Lord of his condition (Genesis 15:1–4):

1 After these things the word of the Lord came unto Abram in a vision, saying, Fear not, Abram, I am thy shield, and thy exceeding great reward.

2 And Abram said, Lord God, what wilt thou give me, seeing I go childless, and the steward of my house is this Eliezer of Damascus?

3 And Abram said, Behold, to me thou hast given no seed: and lo, one born in my house is mine heir.

4 And, behold, the word of the Lord came unto him, saying, This man shall not be thine heir; but he that shall come forth out of thine own bowels, shall be thine heir."

Thus, Abram's first son is born from the failure of his fertility with Sarai, who for this reason gives him permission to impregnate Hagar, the Egyptian slave who later gives birth to Ishmael. According to the biblical account, when Abram reached 99 years of age, Jehovah appeared to him and established the covenant between them (Genesis 17:1–5):

1 And when Abram was ninety years old and nine, the Lord appeared to Abram, and said unto him, I am the Almighty God: walk before me, and be thou perfect.

2 And I will make my covenant between me and thee, and will multiply thee exceedingly.

3 And Abram fell on his face: and God talked to him, saying,

4 As for me, behold, my covenant is with thee, and thou shalt be a father of many nations.

5 Neither shall thy name any more be Abram, but thy name shall be Abraham; for a father of many nations have I made thee.

When Jehovah announces the covenant, he promises to overcome the couple's sterility with the paternity of "a multitude of nations." It is noteworthy that this promise goes together with the modification of the name: an addition to Abram's original name. That is, the modification imposed by the Lord refers to the inclusion of another element in his name, since the components of his original name are retained and something new added. We believe that this addition symbolizes the part that is taken from the father in order to acquire identification and support, in this case from the Lord, who is considered "the father of the multitudes" by religion. Thus, the conversion of Abram to Abraham may psychologically signify the acquisition of the identification with his father, which reinforces Abram's innate structures and leads him to be able to be a father in his own right; he overcomes the former denial of his father, a denial that made his incestuous marriage possible. In another sense, would this not be a primitive expression of our contemporary family name, which adds the name of our father and the equivalent of the paternal lineage to our specific name? This is an interpretation based on the need for support from our identification with our father in order to achieve our own paternity by reinforcing our innate genitality.

But Sarai must also transform her name and, unlike Abram who extended his name, she must shorten it by removing the last letter. Does leaving aside this part of herself indicate the need to leave aside infantile dependency on her parents in order to achieve maternity, in the same sense that contemporary women leave aside their father's name to take possession of that of their legal companion, thus indicating they have overcome incest through their child whose name is different? These conjectures may vary in many directions, but we cannot refrain from showing that the archaic language of many parts of *Genesis* refer not only to the passage from endogamy to exogamy, but also to the changes in personality and the acquisition of identifications leading to the genital maturity indicated by both paternity and maternity.

The conditions of the covenant with the Lord, which began by offering paternity, go on to indicate the demand for genital submission in *Genesis (17:10–16)*.

> *10* This is my covenant, which ye shall keep, between me, and you, and thy seed after thee: Every man child among you shall be circumcised.

> *11* And ye shall circumcise the flesh of your foreskin; and it shall be a token of the covenant betwixt me and you.

> *12* And he that is eight days old shall be circumcised among you, every man child in your generations; he that is born in the house, or bought with money of any stranger, which is not of thy seed.

> *13* He that is born in thy house, and he that is bought with thy money, must needs be circumcised: and my covenant shall be in your flesh for an everlasting covenant.

> *14* And the uncircumcised man child, whose flesh of his foreskin is not circumcised, that soul shall be cut off from his people; he hath broken my covenant.

> *15* And God said unto Abraham, As for Sarai thy wife, thou shalt not call her name Sarai, but Sarah shall her name be.

> *16* And I will bless her, and give thee a son also of her; yea, I will bless her, and she shall be a mother of nations; kings of people shall be of her.

The fulfillment of the covenant, promising fertility and the removal of the couple's sterility on the one hand and the demand for circumcision on the other, occurs after the circumcision of all of Abraham's dependents after which Sarah conceives. The first to be circumcised are Abraham who is ninety-nine years old and Ishmael who is thirteen. Then Isaac is born and circumcised when he is eight days old, according to the covenant.

Total submission to the parents, expressed through obedience and absolute unquestioned faith in the Lord, is shown more crudely in the two filicidal episodes presented from the outset. First it is Sarah who demands that Abraham banish Hagar and her child Ishmael to the wilderness, leaving them there to die (Genesis 21:9–10):

> 9 And Sarah saw the son of Hagar the Egyptian, which she had borne unto Abraham, mocking.
>
> 10 Wherefore she said unto Abraham, Cast out this bondwoman and her son: for the son of this bondwoman shall not be heir with my son, even with Isaac.

Thus, Abraham abandons his son Ishmael in the wilderness and soon thereafter (Genesis 22:1–2):

> 1 And it came to pass after these things, that God did tempt Abraham, and said, unto him, Abraham: and he said, Behold, here I am.
>
> 2 And he said, Take now thy son, thine only son Isaac, whom thou lovest, and get thee into the land of Moriah; and offer him there for a burnt offering upon one of the mountains which I shall tell thee of.

The following verses describe the way Abraham prepares to consummate the slaughter of his son and begins to do so (Genesis 22:9–13):

9 And they came to the place which God had told him of; and Abraham built an altar there, and laid the wood in order; and bound Isaac his son, and laid him on the altar upon the wood.

10 And Abraham stretched forth his hand, and took the knife to slay his son.

11 And the angel of the Lord called unto him out of heaven, and said, Abraham, Abraham: and he said, Here am I.

12 And he said, Lay not thine hand upon the lad neither do thou anything unto him; for now I know that thou fearest God, seeing thou hast not withheld thy son, thine only son, from me.

13 And Abraham lifted up his eyes, and looked, and, behold, behind him a ram caught in a thicket by his horns; and Abraham went and took the ram, and offered him up for a burnt offering in the stead of his son.

These unquestionably filicidal expressions are commonly found at the roots of the most diverse mythologies (Rascovsky 1967). Is there any characteristic differentiating the monotheistic conception from the polytheistic version? Preliminary observation shows us that in the case of Abraham–Ishmael–Isaac, they are their mothers' only sons: Ishmael is Hagar's and Isaac is Sarah's. The next observation is that in both cases, conception has followed a long period of sterility in Abraham, indicating that his paternity is prohibited. This means that the origin of monotheism reveals the father's intense dependency dating from the pre-monotheistic period of its creator. Finally, we observe that the death threat hanging over the sons, nearly consummated, is finally overcome in both cases, particularly through displacement to expiatory animal sacrifice and circumcision.

Another filicidal characteristic of the monotheistic conception is the consciousness instilled by the parent and the precocity of their threat and its consummation, since it is directed against the newborn baby in the covenant with Jehovah. In these conditions, paranoid induction (the fear of God) is correspondingly aggrandized and acts more severely because it is instituted so early in life. But the essential characteristic is probably acquired with the final passage to patriarchy and the denial of the previous matriarchal process. Thus, the Bible refers only to the existence of Terah, Abraham's father, while his mother is not even mentioned. Thus, the son owes unconditional obedience exclusively to the deification of the father, not to the mother.

It is worth noting that the first filicidal demand, that is, the one that is directed against Ishmael in the form of abandonment, is requested by Sarah (*Genesis 21:9–10*), a figure that must be interpreted as a splitting of the maternal imago. The second filicidal demand, the one directed against Isaac, is imposed by the Lord, a splitting of the paternal rather than of the maternal figure. In this way, the filicidal wishes of the parental couple can be seen. Further, the demand for Isaac's death is attributed to the test of unconditional obedience to the figure of Jehovah. The reiterated peremptory nature of the demand for the two sacrifices is confirmed by similar characteristics of their displacement to sacrificial animals. The immolation of Ishmael and Isaac through substitute animal sacrifice, in which they are represented by "the two he-goats," is most clearly seen in a passage from *Leviticus* (16:8–10, 20–22):

> 8 And Aaron shall cast lots upon the two goats; one lot for the Lord, and the other lot for the scapegoat.
>
> 9 And Aaron shall bring the goat upon which the Lord's lot fell, and offer him for a sin offering;
>
> 10 But the goat, on which the lot fell to be the scapegoat, shall be presented alive before the Lord, to make an atonement with him, and to let him go for a scapegoat into the wilderness.

20 And when he hath made an end of reconciling the holy place, and the tabernacle of the congregation, and the altar, he shall bring the live goat;

21 and Aaron shall lay both his hands upon the head of the live goat, and confess over him all the iniquities of the children of Israel, and all their transgressions in all their sins, putting them upon the head of the goat, and shall send him away by the hand of a fit man into the wilderness.

22 And the goat shall bear upon him all their iniquities unto a land not inhabited: and he shall let go the goat in the wilderness.

But we must pause at this point in the biblical account and thereby limit ourselves to the main subject in order to go on to examine the congruence and coherence of the episodes referring to Abraham.

ANALYSIS OF THE MYTH

We must remind the reader that we propose to analyze the mythical narrative, excluding any discussion of its truth or religious meaning. For our purposes, we are interested in the myth itself and the concatenation of circumstances it describes that may offer us interpretative congruence and later coherent understanding of the entire process.

Most if not all the versions about Abraham coincide on several points:

1. Abraham is the son of Terah, seller of idols.
2. He takes as his wife his paternal half-sister, who is also mentioned as being Abraham's blood niece.

3. He leaves his father's house and begins a nomadic life with her.

4. The couple is sterile for many years, a sterility that is removed by the covenant with the Lord years after Terah's death.

5. In the attempt to overcome this sterility, attributed to Sarah or to his union with her, Abraham begets a son with the Egyptian slave, Hagar. This son, called Ishmael, will later be repudiated.

6. God appears to Abraham demanding perfection of him and offering him protection, and when Abraham complains of his sterility, He promises to make him the father of "a multitude of nations."

7. God establishes a covenant with Abraham, demanding that he circumcise all his progeny beginning with himself and his son Ishmael; for His part, He again promises to make him the father of "a multitude of nations."

8. God changes Abram's name to Abraham and Sarai's to Sarah.

9. Immediately after, God announces that Sarah has conceived, an announcement that she ridicules.

10. After Isaac's birth, Sarah demands that Abraham banish and abandon Hagar and her son Ishmael in the desert. God demands that Abraham slaughter his only son as a test of his unconditional submission.

11. The angel stops Abraham when he is about to kill his son; Abraham then offers a ram as a substitute burnt offering.

We must examine two phases in this narrative: first, Abram's actions are prior to and independent of his recognition of Jehovah, and second, his relationship with Jehovah begins and culminates with the establishment of the covenant between them.

What special characteristics do we find in the first period? In the first place, the specific fact that differentiates it from the second is the incestuous meaning of Abram and Sarai's marital relationship. We cannot ignore the fact that the incestuous relationship is the most severely punished violation of the ethical norms of any cultural process and that in the narration we also find it rationalized in aspects that might justify it. Thus, when Abram confesses to Abimelech that his wife is his sister, he softens it by saying that they are siblings on their father's side but not on their mother's. According to Chaldean law at that time, his marriage to Sarai was legal because "they were not children of the same womb" (of different mothers), but under the empirical patriarchal law they were "children of the same father" and therefore reciprocal sexual objects and traditionally taboo.

It is also important to note that Terah, his father, is only mentioned prior to Abram's relationship with Jehovah, really only a later substitute. The marriage of Abram and Sarai is therefore a flagrant violation of the most powerful taboo and for that reason, this incest can be consummated only without the father's approval or support. The absence of this indispensable identificatory reinforcement of paternity determines the couple's sterility. Thus, Abram and Sarai live many long years without having children and in the meantime Terah has lived and died.

During the second period, occurring after the death of Terah, the real deceased father is replaced by the deified father who appears as a hallucination. The sequence of events indicates:

(1) the overcoming of Abram's sterility, twice expressed: first, by the birth of Ishmael from his relationship with Hagar and second, by the birth of Isaac, which implies that the sterility of the incestuous couple has been overcome; (2) together with the affirmation of paternity as the expression of the father's

support and reconciliation, God announces the price for that support (*Genesis 17:9–14*):

> 9 And God said unto Abraham, Thou shalt shall keep my covenant, therefore, thou and thy seed after thee, in their generations.
>
> 10 This is my covenant, which ye shall keep, between me, and you and thy seed after thee: Every man child among you shall be circumcised.
>
> 11 And ye shall circumcise the flesh of your foreskin; and it shall be a token of the covenant betwixt me and you.
>
> 12 And he that is eight days old shall be circumcised among you, every man child in your generations; he that is born in the house, or bought with money of any stranger, which is not of thy seed.
>
> 13 He that is born in thy house, and he that is bought with thy money, must needs be circumcised: And my covenant shall be in your flesh an everlasting covenant.
>
> 14 And the uncircumcised man child, whose flesh of his foreskin is not circumcised, that soul shall be cut off from his people; he hath broken my covenant.

Thus, paternity is granted at the price of the genital subjection expressed in submission to attenuated castration: circumcision. (3) Subsequently, the parental demand intensifies to the extreme of demanding the supreme test of obedience, the slaughter of his own son. This is not only genital submission but also the offering of life itself, represented by the burnt offering of the son's life. Thus, in the second period the two tests of total and unconditional surrender to the image of the father, represented by Jehovah, are passed.

If the endopsychic characteristics of the second period,

which we have just described, are obvious in the straightforward expression of the ego's submission to the superego (i.e., the son's to the father), the characteristics of the pressures predominating in the first period (i.e., the incestuous instinctual tendencies) are no less obvious if we accept the fraternal character of the sterile couple's relationship.

Because Abram and Sarai are siblings, their union is only possible because they ignore or deny the prohibition instituted by the father. This denial of the prohibitions imposed by the superego defines the initial period as antagonistic in relation to the one that is to follow. While the second period is characterized, as we have said, by unconditional submission to parental demands, the first expresses the rebellion against the prohibition of incest, that is rebellion against the father. In that way, endogamic satisfaction or the predominance of the instinctive wishes over their subjection belongs to Abram's initial, polytheistic period. But this type of repudiation of the inhibitory regulations of the superego is what characterizes the manic phenomenon. Before the establishment of dependency of the ego on the parental superego, the ego is dependent on instinctual demand. Although the social organization dictates its norms, they act at first as external intimidations and only later become internalized, after which they exert pressure from within the psychic apparatus. Abram escapes social submission and marries his sister, while the father figure remains externalized. They then take up the nomadic life, lacking the paternal support that is essential for achieving fertility.

But after Terah's death, following a period of insufficient working through of the mourning process, the externally denied father reappears introjected and reprojected hallucinatorily and produces a totally opposite attitude in Abram. This introjection of the father transforms Abram into Abraham and also transforms his rebellion into unconditional submission. If the marriage with Sarai was the denial of paternal authority, universal circumcision and the later attempt to murder Ishmael and Isaac indicate, along with the covenant of total obedience, his submission to the despotic demands of the father and of the superego. The covenant has to be renewed with the birth of each new generation and circumcision practiced on the son when he is eight days old, definitively avoiding any future repetition of the previous incestuous experience. Thus, the prohibition against incest and the submission and intimidation of the offspring are consolidated in this way.

The passage to monotheism and the distortion of direct instinctual satisfaction produced an extraordinary increment of sublimation, which led to the triumph of the ideology of the unique god. But in order that this triumph could become really universal, it was necessary to make a compromise by means of transitory instinctual tolerance which was institutionalized. In creating such an unconditional demand for submission, Judaism also had to create a weekly outlet, the Sabbath. This uses the same type of model as the outlet that dreams provide. In the same way that, during the nightly dream period, we return to the triumph of our desires and to omnipotence, we are also obliged to refrain from working one day a week and we can free ourselves to some extent from the brutal demands the superego imposes the other six days. Thus, because of greater pressure exerted by the superego on the other six days, the ego was allowed to relax on Saturday, the sabbath that Christianity moved to Sunday. This was a temporary denial that made the demands bearable.

The biblical text condenses the process of socialization which structured the human condition based on the prohibition of incest and the demand for sublimation. It establishes the function and mission of the generations, since it is exercised coercively on the child as soon as its earliest and most basic instinctual tendencies emerge. In this way, it intensifies the renunciation of the initial hedonism that paganism exalts and the passage to the structured monotheistic melancholia that finally led to the deification of suffering and pain, glorifying aggression and death at the price of renouncing many aspects of love and of joy, of erotism and of life itself.

In psychopathological terms, the universally submissive human condition, whose social structure was based from the beginning on the prohibition against incest, on the slaughter of one sector of offspring starting with the firstborn and on the constant intimidation and exploitation of the rest, was thus able to sustain a typical paranoid organization alternating with passing manic fits.

It was a deeper and more intense melancholic organization that founded monotheism, institutionalizing the sacrifice of the offspring to a greater degree, compensated perhaps by greater reparatory attitudes that fought for better depressive working through. It was not a new procedure but rather an institutionalized intensification with new developmental characteristics that induced such a greater reparatory factor, either through circumcision (when the child was one week old) or through the veiled techniques for sacrificing the child that did, however, avoid his murder (rigorous education; systematization of child and youth sacrifice in rites of initiation, displaced to a sector of them in military services and in wars; projection to the children of the parents' own guilt for real filicide through the creation of an imaginary parricide; consequent idealization of the persecutory parents, etc.). This configuration acquired dramatic expression in the episode we are studying and in this way signaled the beginning of monotheistic conceptions in the Occident.

There is a conjecture that we must examine, which is the

possibility that the procedure described by the Bible avoided the constant slaughter previously inflicted on the children as was the case in many polytheistic cults and, in the Semitic tradition, in the cult of Moloch. The development of monotheism may have replaced this with the child's subsistence at the price of a paranoid-melancholic intensification. The human sacrifice of the offspring is a ritual that antedates the advent of monotheism. It is probable that the biblical prescription offered an alternative that, by establishing unconditional submission and the *pars pro toto* type displacement to circumcision, allowed the elimination of the sacrifice of the firstborn or allowed surmounting the sacrifice of his life with the advantage that the surviving son could later be utilized. Monotheism seems to have prohibited the cult of Moloch.

Thus, the demand at first placed on the son was displaced and acquired other characteristics for both generations. The sons saved their lives partially, but only their lives, and the gerontocracy derived enormous benefit from constant utilization of the offspring, improving the institutionalization of the exploitation of children by their parents or their substitutes.

Just as the guilt of the parents for the crime against their children is transformed into the contrary accusation of parricide, the child's "auxiliary ego," which the parents should be, was distorted to transform the child into the parents' "auxiliary ego." Paradoxically, the child was forced to become the parents' parent and to do for them what they should have done for the child. The Tables of the Law prescribe the child's obligations to the parents but omit the parents' obligations to their children, except perhaps in "Thou shalt not kill," as it refers to filicide.

The existence of a unique authority as an external phenomenon is rooted much further back in time than the monotheistic institution. Could we say that the establishment of monotheism signals the definitive introjection of that agency and possibly its deified projection? The fact that this development postdates polytheism seems to substantiate our hypothesis. That is, monotheism as a projection of a deified internal agency demanded the previous external creation, later introjected, of this agency. We will examine the individual history of this development, but first we will say that the introjection and the reinforcement of the superego to the point of being capable of controlling instinctual demands was an achievement reached only after a long developmental process which is expressed religiously by the deified projection of that despotic agency.

Although this individual developmental process can easily be followed throughout infantile development, culminating in the organization of the superego now integrated with the father image just before the beginning of the latency period, it is possible to trace its roots back to the first moments of the organization of the Oedipal conflict at the oral level. Before the incorporation of the father figure[11] interferes in the mother–child relationship, the nursling is connected exclusively with its mother and with its desires for her which, according to whether they are gratified or not, configure the diverse internal phantasies that are projected to create the polytheistic world with its innumerable quantity of deities. Thus, as a function of the early paranoid position, the multiple demands on the ego are organized projectively.

In the sixth week of life, with the introduction of the father figure into the child's mental organization, the triangular situation commences. The paternal image added to the maternal one acquires increasing importance until its climax at around six

---

[11]We have demonstrated that this process takes place in the sixth week of the child's life.

years of age. Step by step, it will exert growing influence on the child's instinctual wishes. First it is an external control easy to elude temporarily, but through constant introjection it becomes a permanently established internal agent that exercises permanent control over all the drives. Then, as the Scriptures say, it will be everywhere (in all sectors of the mental apparatus) and it will be represented as a projection of insight, like the eye of God that sees everything.

CONCLUSIONS

The ego is a system for intermediation among the id (the instinctual demands), the superego, and external reality, and it experiences the developmental mutations of those demands. There is no doubt about the concept that the first demands to produce any impact on the ego are the demands from the id. If we begin our observation with the newborn child, we can follow the vicissitudes of its actions and wishes as a function of its instinctual needs with their cyclical rhythm. Thus, we see the baby calm and sleeping in order to replenish energies immediately after its satisfaction at the breast; as the effects of the gratifying experience wear off, anxiety arises and grows. As an expression of instinctual need, ego activities, such as crying and the different associated manifestations that temporarily express and quiet the anxiety, also increase. At this point and during the periods to come, no other agency so intensely pressures the ego to find an outlet. Although the role of internalized external reality gradually comes into play, its predominance in the regulation of demands on the ego is only established much later. This struggle for predominance between demands from the id (the instincts) and the regulation imposed by internalized external reality (the superego) will end, in the socioculturally adapted individual, with the triumph of internalized society. But this triumph is conditioned by the degree of benevolence in the conflict between the two agencies. The compromise triumph is positive and satisfactory to the extent that it takes the defeated agency into account and finally manages to arrange for the combined expression of both agencies. This result leads to the best psychic equilibrium and in most cases is achieved only partially.

The evolution of the projective systems constituted by the monotheistic religions passes similarly from the predominance of the deified instinctual tendencies that appear as polytheism to the conquest of these tendencies through recognition of a total and unique regulator for them, which is the superego. This regulator is represented by the figure of the unique God in the religious conception.

This process must have undergone a more or less parallel development in diverse cultural conditions. Two of those cultures seem to have been Chaldea and Egypt. The exalted degree of socialization, civilization, and aggression imposed by the cultural process forced intensification of coercion of the instincts which, when it was internalized and later reprojected, led to the origin of the monotheistic conception. The essential instinctual coercion was directed against the first orientation of the sexual drives, that is, against the incestuous tendencies. The instrument for the imposition of these restrictions was filicide with its displacements in *totum* to the sacrificial animal and by means of the *pars pro toto* to circumcision, provoking the consequent paranoid induction in all the offspring. The marital relationship between Abram and Sarai and the subsequent covenant with Jehovah is one step in this sequence.

5

Filicide in History and Anthropology

History and anthropology show us numerous forms and frequent episodes of filicide that range widely from the actual murder of the offspring to attenuated forms such as mild neglect. This spectrum of parents' aggressive attitudes exists in all societies, be they primitive or contemporary. Therefore, this constitutes a specific characteristic of the human condition.

William Graham Sumner (1906), pioneer of modern sociology, acknowledged the weight of filicide in the history of humanity in the following terms:

> The sacrifice of the child expresses the deepest horror and suffering produced by the experience of human destiny. Men must do it. Their interests demand it though it much pains them. It may be said that human sacrifice has been universal . . . it has lasted into the semi-civilized period of all nations and has barely ceased in contemporary semi-civilized peoples. [p. 553]

Darwin (1936) associated the rise of man, in the evolution of the species, with filicide: "Our primitive, semi-human ancestors probably did not practice infanticide . . . since the instinct of the animals inferior to us never reached such perversion as to regularly destroy their own young" (p. 430).

Darwin's affirmation can be confirmed if we study any human group in depth. Since the information at our disposal is quite abundant, we shall only indicate some of the universal sources, which are unquestionable and easily accessible for the reader who wishes to verify the facts. We have consulted the *Encyclopaedia Britannica* and different authors. But these indirect sources have been fully confirmed by our psychoanalytic observation of the archaic contents of our patients' unconscious.

We shall begin with the *Bible*, where we can find records that are quantitatively significant. Thus, mass murder of children is described when the pharaoh condemned all the Jewish children to death by drowning in the Nile at the time of Moses' birth. The same process is repeated on the Egyptian firstborn before the Exodus and again when Herod orders the slaughter of all the children born in Bethlehem when he is persecuting Jesus. In all these cases, a figure representing the father—the pharaoh, the king, or the Lord—is the one who demands the universal murder of the children.

We wish to mention a myth in folklore (Rappoport 1966) that describes the birth of Abraham and the persecutions of all the male children, decreed at that time by Nimrod, the cruel Babylonian emperor:

> Nimrod, the great king of Babylonia, was also a great astrologer and in the stars, which he constantly consulted, he had read that a child would be born in Mesopotamia who would one day declare war on him and on his religion and would finally win. His

mind much disturbed, Nimrod consulted his ministers demanding counsel and, following their warnings, he constructed a large house eighty yards long and sixty yards wide where all the women who were about to give birth to a child were kept and closely watched. They ordered all the midwives and nurses to kill any new-born boy without hesitation and on the other hand to give valuable gifts to the mothers who gave birth to a girl. Thus, seventy thousand boys were massacred by order of King Nimrod. . . . Soon after, the time arrived for Emtelai, wife of Terah, to give birth and she was taken into custody by order of the king. But Oh! a miracle took place and all the external signs of her pregnancy disappeared, so that she was freed. When the day of her delivery drew near, she secretly left the city and hid alone in a cavern. There she had a son, Abraham, the radiance of whose face shone brightly in the dark cave. Wrapping the child in her clothes, she left him there, trusting in the pity of Almighty God. And when the Lord of the Universe heard the child's laments, he sent His angel Gabriel to the cave to feed the baby. The angel Gabriel offered a finger of his right hand to the afflicted child to suck on and Oh! from the angelical finger flowed milk abundantly. [pp. 228–229]

Bakan (1971) remarks that the many references in the Bible to the slaughter of children show how much they worried the authors of the biblical narrative. He adds that the prophets often preached against the murder of children and that they doubtless had reason to do so.

On other occasions, we can find cases in the Bible that attribute the filicide directly to the father's doing. In the example of Abraham and Isaac, whose consummation has inspired theological controversies (Spiegel 1969), although the demand came from the Lord, the executor of the sacrifice had to be the father himself, Abraham. Later, we find passages like those referring to King Ahaz:

2 Chronicles 28:1–4:

1 Ahaz was twenty years old when he began to reign; and he reigned sixteen years in Jerusalem: But he did not that which was right in the sight of the Lord, like David his father:

2 For he walked in the ways of the kings of Israel, and made also molten images for Baalim.

3 Moreover, he burnt incense in the valley of the son of Hinnom, and burnt the children in the fire, after the abominations of the heathen, whom the Lord had cast out before the children of Israel.

4 He sacrificed also, and burnt incense in the high places, and on the hills, and under every green tree.

and also to King Manasseh:

2 Chronicles 33:5–6:

5 And he built altars for all the host of heaven in the two courts of the house of the Lord.

6 And he caused his children to pass through the fire in the valley of the son of Hinnom; also he observed times, and used enchantments, and used witchcraft, also dealt with a familiar spirit, and with wizards; he wrought much evil in the sight of the Lord . . .

and even to Solomon:

1 Kings 11:6–8:

6 And Solomon did evil in the sight of the Lord, and went not fully to follow after the Lord, as did David his father.

7 Then did Solomon build an high place for Chemosh,[1] the abomination of Moab, in the hill that is before Jerusalem; and for Molech, the abomination of the children of Ammon.

8 And likewise did he for all his strange wives, which burnt incense, and sacrificed unto their gods.

Bakan (1971) notes that the concept of hell originates in the place where the children were burnt alive according to the ancient cult of Moloch. The word used in the *New Testament* for hell is Gehenna, which derives from Ge-Hinnom. Hinnom is a valley near Jerusalem, which the prophets derided as the site where the children were killed. Jeremiah called it "the valley of slaughter":

Jeremiah 7:32: Therefore, behold, the days come, saith the Lord, that it shall no more be called Tophet, nor the valley of the son of Hinnom, but the valley of slaughter: for they shall bury in Tophet, till there be no place.

This valley where the children were sacrificed, at least in the days of Solomon, Ahaz, and Manasseh, thus acquired a sinister meaning, which later became part of the myths about hell. Finally, it became a refuse heap whose unending fires provided the image of the perpetual fires of hell.

We must remember that the cult of Moloch refers to the divinity to whom children were sacrificed in the last period of the Hebrew kingdom. A biblical passage expresses the following:

---

[1]Chemosh is another name for Moloch, a divinity that demanded the immolation of children.

2 Kings 23:10: And he defiled Tophet, which is in the valley of the children of Hinnom, that no one might make his son or his daughter to pass through fire to Molech.

Although Moloch is considered a foreign deity occupying an illegitimate place in the Hebrew cult as a result of the syncretic policies of some apostate kings, he was probably a former deity, common to different Semitic peoples, especially the Phoenicians. Other biblical texts identify Moloch with Milcom, god of the Ammonites, and there are different gods with the common root of Melek, a distortion of the father-king, including Muluk who was adored on the Euphrates up to the nineteenth century. According to the *Encyclopedia Britannica* (15:676):

> Despite this evidence that gods with names similar to Molech were known in neighbouring countries, and the knowledge that the worship of imported deities was at certain periods encouraged in Israel, it seems unlikely that Molech in the Old Testament is the name of a foreign god. The deity to whom child sacrifice was offered was Yahweh, the chief—and, for normative Hebrew religion, the only—god of the nation, honoured in this connection as "the King." So repulsive was this abnormal practice, largely confined to the apostatizing reigns of Ahaz (II Kings 16:3) and Manasseh (II Kings 21:6), that the later Hebrews transformed the divine title associated with it into the artificial name Molech, as though the sacrifices had indeed been offered to a foreign god.
>
> An attempt by O. Eissfeldt to show that "Molech" was originally the technical name for a legitimate sacrificial offering (*molk*), later distorted into a proper name, has not met with general acceptance, although his evidence is deserving of further study. It is unlikely that child sacrifice was ever regarded, in historical times, as a normal part of Israelite religion . . .; its occasional appear-

ance was due either to a recrudescence of ancient superstition in times of special peril or to foreign influence.

Another common name for an equivalent of Moloch is Baal, the name of a god known especially among the Canaanites, which in Semitic languages means lord or owner. His cult is associated with corrupt licentiousness and gross sensuality and was commonly celebrated on hilltops and under trees. For this reason, the mention of rituals on the hills and under the trees is associated with child sacrifice. The *Old Testament* associates it with human sacrifice, the burning of incense, violent and ecstatic practices, ceremonial acts of prostration, and the preparation of sacred mystic cakes, all of these being the offenses that the prophets repeatedly denounced, suggesting that the cult of Baal appears time and again in different parts of the Semitic scene. What remains uncertain is whether this is actually a distortion of the proper name of Yahweh.

In Carthage, his adoration was considered by the Greeks and Romans as

> abominable because of its brutality and human sacrifices. The burials in the precinct of Tanith are certainly those of children sacrificed to the goddess Tanith and the god Baal Amon, although there is only one figural representation of such a sacrifice taking place, a gravestone which depicts a priest offering a human child. The god Moloch, who was supposed to have images of metal containing furnaces in which human victims were burned alive, is perhaps a Greek invention. . . . [*Encyclopaedia Britannica* 4:977]

We believe that it is more likely that the constant sacrifice of children was depicted in that representation.

We cannot ignore the fact that the slaughter of children was involved in the concept of human sacrifice and therefore, we must listen to the interpretations that some anthropologists make of this ritual. The theory of the offering proposed by Tylor in 1899 (quoted in Robertson Smith 1956) fails to explain the fact that very frequently the sacrificed victims were eaten partly or completely by the adorers. The theory of the meal shared with the gods discussed by Robertson Smith (1956) does not satisfactorily explain the holocaust, although it does seem an important step in the right direction. Both Tylor and Robertson Smith suggest that some concept of divinity precedes the adoration and sacrifice, but they leave the origin of the concept of deity unexplained. Frazer in *The Golden Bough* (1913) leaves no room for doubt that the sacrificial rites must be traced back to a period antedating any concept of deity.

In this sense, Reik (1958a) says:

> We know that among primitive people their god, who desires the sacrifice of the child, is regarded as their father. Psychoanalysis has proved that the idea of God in the life of the individual and of the people has its origin in the veneration and exaltation of the father. The command to sacrifice the first-born child to God as an atonement is therefore really a command to give the grandfather his grandchild. Moreover, the idea is always present that the father is being appeased and satisfied by the sacrifice as though his dignity had before been infringed by a misdeed on the part of his son. The religious sacrifice of the son is always in the nature of an atonement. What offence of primitive man is to be made good thereby, and why by means of such a horrible and inhuman custom as this one? Perhaps we shall gain light on this point if we turn to the second motive given by Frazer in regard to child-sacrifice, i.e., that the death of the son will lengthen the life of the father. In Peru, for example, "the son dies that the father might

live. But in some cases it would seem that the child has been killed, not so much as a substitute for the father, as because it is supposed to endanger his life by absorbing his spiritual essence or vital energy." Frazer assumes that this belief originates in ideas of the migration of souls. The belief in the migration of souls is actually given as the determining factor in this fear. For example, a Bantu negro of the Lower Congo would be much offended if it were remarked that his son resembled him. He would then firmly believe that he would soon die himself. The Galelareese fancy that if a child resembles his father, they will not both live long; for the child has taken away his father's likeness or shadow and consequently the father must soon die. [pp. 73–74]

The introduction of concepts about filicide can elucidate this very primitive impulse to kill and devour one's children as a function of the oral-cannibalistic regression that is acted on by the parents. The latter appear afterward in idealized form, acquiring the nature of gods. The subsequent imposition of norms that prohibit sexuality and other instinctual tendencies, ensuring the development of the sociocultural process, has been based on the slaughter of one sector of the population and the absolute intimidation of the developing generation, that is, the children. Since the civilizing process itself was idealized and overvalued, its sacrificial foundations were established as an indispensable norm or universal obligation with which all adult individuals had to comply in order to preserve their culture. In effect, there is no sociocultural process in the world that does not impose restrictive sanctions and rites of initiation on its children, culminating with the overt or covert murder of a group of them.

It must be emphasized that the organization of the cultural process is based essentially on the family, which is the nucleus for ethical and behavioral norms in the physical habitat of the home. With reference to the home, there is concrete evidence that the walling-up of newborn babies and children within the structure of buildings was required. Thus, Joshua threatens to curse anyone who might attempt to reconstruct Jericho:

> *Joshua 6:26–27:* . . . Cursed be the man before the Lord that riseth up and buildeth this city, Jericho: he shall lay the foundation thereof in his firstborn, and in his youngest son shall he set up the gates of it.
>
> 27 So the Lord was with Joshua; and his fame was noised throughout all the country.

This threat is later carried out in the biblical narrative:

> *1 Kings 16:34:* In his days did Hiel the Bethelite build Jericho; he laid the foundation thereof in Abiram his firstborn, and set up the gates thereof in his youngest son Segub, according to the word of the Lord, which he spake by Joshua the son of Nun.

Thus, the two sons serve as victims for the foundation sacrifice. But this is not an exceptional event limited to Jericho; it is found in the most diverse peoples in primitive conditions. Archeologists have found confirmation in bones of newborn infants alongside pottery, vessels, utensils, and other primitive objects buried under corners, thresholds, and floors. Skeletons of children have also been found inside ancient walls.

Further, in many societies, certain ceremonies must be held before the newborn baby is accepted into life. Thus, among the Greeks in Athens, the ceremony was called *amphidroma* and was held on the fifth day after birth. The newborn was taken by a nurse to the "ancestral heart" to be consecrated and to receive a name. If the father did not want the child, he had to dispose of it in the *amphidroma.* In Egypt, the midwife prayed for union of the child's soul with hers. In Babylonia, the father ensured his child's life by blowing on its face, thus passing his spirit to the baby. Then he gave the child his own name or the name of an ancestor. In Phrygia, the father could only kill or dispose of the child before the baby had been fed, since once the child had been given sustenance its right to life was recognized.

Among the primitive Scandinavians, the ancient Vikings showed the newborn boy a lance. If the child grasped it, they allowed it to live. The child's life also depended on a ceremony similar to modern baptism, called *wasserweihe*. Immediately after birth, the baby was placed in the father's lap or on the floor in front of him. If he decided the child should live, he took it in his arms. Then, water was poured over the newborn baby and it was given a name and a gift. Only then was it fed. If the child was not lifted by its father it was killed immediately, without baptism or food. But if the two conditions had been fulfilled it was illegal to kill the child, since once it was baptized it had certain rights of its own. These customs remained in force in Sweden until 1734, in Norway until 1854, and in Denmark until 1857 (Werner 1917).

The slaughter of newborn babies may be considered a common event in many cultures. Bakan (1971) includes the Eskimos, the Polynesians, the Egyptians, the Chinese, the Scandinavians, the Africans, the American Indians, and the Australian aboriginals. He says that in the Hawaiian Islands it was common practice to kill all progeny after the third or fourth. Among the Australian aboriginals, if a woman was forced to move because of lack of food or water and could not take both her children with her, she generally killed the younger one (Bakan 1971). According to Frazer (1913), the Polynesians killed two-thirds of their children. Reverend Orsmond (Bakan 1971) in Tahiti recorded the killing of more than two-thirds of the children: " . . generally before they saw the light of day. Sometimes when they drew their first breath, they were drowned to death, calling this 'tamari hia' (child drowning)" (p. 30).

Bakan (1971), when he refers to Orsmond's manuscripts, points out a dramatic relationship between the slaughter of offspring and social class, since the obligation to commit filicide depended on the category to which the parents belonged. The inferior members of the community were obliged to kill their children. "If any family saved its children, it fell into disgrace in society" (p. 30). On the contrary, the members of the upper classes were obliged to check their impulse to exterminate their children. It has been estimated that in India, before this century, six-sevenths of the population systematically practiced female filicide. At the beginning of the nineteenth century the British government obliged the people to substitute a sheep for the child who was sacrificed every Friday night on the altar of Kali in the Saiva Temple in Tangore.

The *Encyclopaedia Britannica* (1966, 12:217) confirms many of these data and adds others in its article on infanticide:

> Among the Eskimo conditions of life were so severe that it was sometimes the practice to kill female children shortly after birth, since there might not be husbands able to support them. In Polynesia, where population often reached high density, similar practices prevailed. In the Hawaiian Islands all children, after the third or fourth, were once strangled or buried alive, and in Tahiti chiefs were obliged to kill their daughters. The famous Areoi secret society that originated in Tahiti imposed infanticide on its women members, but apparently this was mainly to allow freedom in their cult activities. In China female infanticide for economic reasons was once common and girls were also sold as servants.
>
> Children also may be allowed to die or are killed with cultural sanction because of irregular marriages, abnormal births or sim-

ilar reasons. Plato recommended destruction of unfit children in *The Republic*. Violation of incest restrictions frequently leads to infanticide, as well as punishment of the parents. Abnormal behaviour of the fetus and irregular birth presentations (*e.g.*, breech delivery) sometimes have been considered reasons for infanticide (as among the Nandi peoples of Africa). Where pre-marital relations are not sanctioned, resulting children are often abandoned or killed in a great number of societies, including modern western cultures.

Multiple births frequently are held to signify future prosperity or impending misfortune. Some groups (as the Pima Indians in Arizona) welcome twins and treat them with special consider-ation. Others (as aborigines in Queensland, Australia, and the Ibo in West Africa) put one or both to death, in the belief that they were evidence of kinship with animals, or because they could not be nursed adequately. In medieval Scotland mothers of twins were believed to have committed adultery . . .

In more advanced societies children were sometimes killed in the belief it would ensure health, good fortune and general fertility, or cure such misfortunes as barrenness. Religious offerings, espe-cially of the first-born, are known from the Bible (Genesis 22) as well as from the histories of Egypt, Greece and Rome. Up to the 19th century first-born sacrifice was almost universal in India. Here the motive was the offering of one's most precious posses-sion to the deities.

Practices of infanticide have been linked to such marriage prac-tices as polyandry, but the correlation is not direct. In Africa where the legitimatization of offspring through proper marriage is of great concern and where reincarnation of ancestors is an important belief, irregular offspring are a danger to the mainte-nance of proper ritual relations. Where age is important, there are often beliefs that elders should cease bearing children after their own children begin to do so, as among certain Chinese groups.

Infanticide has often been interpreted as a primitive method of birth control and as a means of ridding the group of weak and deformed children. But most societies actively desire children, and put them to death (or allow them to die) only under exceptional circumstances. In modern societies regulation of population with contraceptives or through abortion tends to reduce the frequency of infanticide. [vol. 12, p. 217]

We must also refer here to the rites of initiation extant in every culture as an expression of their development.

Reik (1931) says:

Originally the punishment of death was actually carried out by the infuriated fathers. A long path is traversed in the development of peoples from the actual killing of the youths and the consequent strong remorse of the fathers up to the two-period rite-sequences which say in effect, "We love you, but we must rid you of your childishness." [pp. 102–103]

Among the rites of initiation demanded by all cultural processes, the most constant and universally extended one is perhaps war in all its aspects, including, of course, military service. But we are especially interested in showing how the primitive ritual common to so many peoples is performed.

Frazer (quoted in Reik 1958b) refers to the initiation ceremony in the Jabim tribe in German New Guinea:

The initiation of young men takes place at intervals of several years, when there are a number of youths ready to be initiated, and enough pigs can be procured to furnish forth the feasts which form an indispensable part of the ceremony. The principal initiatory rite consists of circumcision, which is performed on all youths before they are admitted to the rank of full-grown men.

The age of the candidates varies considerably, from four years up to twenty. Many are married before they are initiated. The operation is performed in the forest, and the procession of the youths to the place is attended by a number of men swinging bull-roarers. As the procession sets out, the women look on from a distance, weeping and howling, for they are taught to believe that the lads, their sons and brothers, are about to be swallowed up by a monster called a balum, or ghost, who will only release them from his belly on condition of receiving a sufficient number of roast pigs. How, then, can the poor women be sure that they will ever see their dear ones again? . . . The place where the operation is performed on the lads is a long hut, about a hundred feet in length, which dimishes in height towards the rear. This represents the belly of the monster who is to swallow up the candidates. To keep up the delusion a pair of great eyes are painted over the entrance, and above them the projecting roots of a betel-palm represent the monster's hair, while the trunk of the tree passes for his backbone. As the awe-struck lads approach this imposing creature, he is heard from time to time to utter a growl. This growl is, in fact, no other than the humming note of bull-roarers swung by men, who are concealed within the edifice. When the procession has come to a halt . . . they raise a shrill song like a scream and sacrifice pigs to the monster in order to induce him to spare the lives of the candidates. When the operation has been performed on the lads, they must remain in strict seclusion for three or four months, avoiding all contact with women and even the sight of them. They live in the long hut, which represents the monster's belly and their food is brought to them by elder men. . . . Sometimes, though perhaps rarely, one of the lads dies under the operation; in that case the men explain his disappearance to the women saying that the monster has a pig's stomach as well as a human stomach, and that, unfortunately, the deceased young man slipped by mistake into the wrong stomach and so perished miserably. But as a rule the candidates pass into the right stomach, and, after a sufficient period has been allowed for digestion, they come forth safe and sound, the monster having kindly consented to let them go free in consideration of the roast pigs which have been offered to him by the men. Indeed, he is not very exacting, for he contents himself with devouring the souls of the pigs, while he leaves their bodies to be consumed by his worshippers. . . . When the time of seclusion is up . . . the young men are brought back to the village with much solemnity. An eye-witness has described the ceremony . . . In marching back to the village, they had to keep their eyes tightly shut, and each of them was led by a man who acted as a king or god-father. . . . The women were much moved at the return of the lads; they sobbed and tears of joy ran down their cheeks. Arrived in the village, the newly initiated lads . . . stood with closed eyes, motionless as statues. Then a man passed behind them . . . saying, "O circumcised one, sit down." But still the lads remained standing, stiff and motionless. Not till another man had knocked repeatedly on the ground with the stalk of a palm-leaf, crying, "O circumcised ones, open your eyes!" did the youths, one after another, open their eyes as if awaking from a profound stupor. [pp. 93–95]

Frazer adds that:

the candidate is supposed to die or to be killed and to come to life again or be born again; and the pretence of a new birth is not uncommonly kept up by the novices feigning to have forgotten all the most common actions of life, and having accordingly to learn them all over again like new-born babes. We may conjecture that this is why the young circumcised Papuans march back to their village with closed eyes; this is why, when bidden to sit down, they remain standing stiffly, as if they understood neither the command nor the action. The rites among the Bukaua and the Tami are of a similar kind. In these rites it is given out that the lads are swallowed by a ferocious monster called a *balum*, who, however, is induced by the sacrifice of many pigs to vomit them up again. In spewing them out of his maw he bites or scratches them, and the wound so inflicted is circumcision. . . . [p. 95]

Although there is always an allusion in these rituals to fictitious death and resurrection while the boys are frightened, it is interesting to examine another, analogous ceremony:

In the west of Ceram boys at puberty are admitted to the Kakian association . . . in a long wooden shed, situated under the darkest trees in the depth of the forest, and it is built to admit so little light that it is impossible to see what goes on in it. . . . Thither the boys who are to be initiated are conducted blindfold, followed by their parents and relations. Each one is led by the hand by two men who act as his sponsors or guardians during the period of initiation. When all are assembled before the shed, the high priest calls aloud upon the devils. Immediately a hideous uproar is heard to proceed from the shed. It is made by men with bamboo trumpets. . . . Then the priests enter the shed, followed by the boys one at a time. As soon as each boy has disappeared within the precincts, a dull chopping sound is heard, a frightful cry rings out, and a sword or spear, dripping with blood, is thrust through the roof of the shed. This is a token that the boy's head has been cut off, and that the devil has carried him away to the other world, there to regenerate and transform him. So at the sight of the bloody sword the mothers weep and wail, crying that the devil has murdered their children. In some places, it would seem, the boys are pushed through an opening made in the shape of a crocodile's jaws or a cassowary's beak, and it is then said that the devil has swallowed them. The boys remain in the shed for five or nine days. Sitting in the dark, they hear the blast of the bamboo trumpets, and from time to time, the sound of musket shots and the crash of swords. . . . When they are not sleeping, the lads must sit in a crouching posture without moving a muscle. As they sit in a row cross-legged, with their hands stretched out, the chief takes his trumpet, and placing the mouth of it on the hands of each lad, speaks through its strange tones, imitating the voice of the spirits. He warns the lads, under the pain of death, to observe the rules of the Kakian society, and never to reveal what has passed in the Kakian house. . . . Meantime, the mothers and sisters of the lads have gone home to weep and mourn. But in a day or two the men who acted as guardians or sponsors to the novices return to the village with the glad tidings that the devil, at the intercession of the priests, has restored the lads to life. The men who bring this news come in a fainting state and daubed with mud, like messengers freshly arrived from the nether world. . . . When they [the lads] return to their homes they totter in their walk, and enter the house backward, as if they had forgotten how to walk properly; or they enter the house by the back door. If a plate of food is given to them they hold it upside down. They remain dumb, indicating their wants by signs only. . . . Their sponsors have to teach them all the common acts of life, as if they were new-born children. [Frazer quoted in Reik 1958b, pp. 96–97]

The men's behavior toward the youths has led many authors to think that the main objective of initiation is to intimidate and frighten the novices. Thus, Reik (1958b) says:

> . . . Schellong, in his report of the *balum* festival in Kaiser Wilhelms Land says that the men make the preparations for the circumcision with refined deliberation, while the novices await the operation in the stomach of *balum*. The men make the most hideous noise, striking their shields, shrieking, whooping, whistling through their hands, and appear as noisy and unrestrained as possible, "with the unmistakable intention of thoroughly intimidating the trembling youths." [pp. 101–102]

Evidence of filicidal impulses is seen even more clearly in the elaborate tortures to which youths are submitted. [p. 103]

Among the Kai, for example, after the circumcision the men stand in two rows facing one another, and the youths have to pass down between the men who rain violent blows upon them. The boys are beaten with birches, thorny branches, nettles, etc., ostensibly to awaken their warlike spirit. Also among the Tami the youths have to run the gauntlet twice; and it is said that formerly some were left dead on the ground. Among the Karesau islanders the novices are led into the forest to a tree, kakar, on which black ants run up and down, and the boy is placed against it with his head bent forward. A man strikes the tree and an ant falls down and bites into the boy's neck. At each blow the men give the candidates for circumcision they say, "If anyone does you any harm, then spear him." [p. 103]

After referring to other, equally cruel rituals, Reik questions:

What do these cruel rites signify? The explanation given by comparative ethnology, that they represent tests of courage and endurance, does not satisfy us. This certainly may be a secondary motive, but we prefer to take these refined acts of cruelty at their face value, i.e., as cruel and hostile acts of the men against the youths. We have seen that the men among the Australian natives drag the youths to the monster, circumcise and torture them, but at the same time hypocritically assist the novices in the fight against the monster. The role of these fathers now becomes clearer to us. The fathers identify themselves with the *balum* monster. It is they who harbour those wicked impulses against the neophytes which are ascribed to the monster." [p. 104]

Further on, Reik adds:

We know that circumcision represents a castration-equivalent and supports in the most effective way the prohibition against

incest. The fear of castration would be stimulated by the unconscious fear of retaliation which is felt by the man who has now
become a father himself. The unconscious memory of incestuous
and hostile impulses of childhood which were turned upon his
parents still lives in him. He fears the realisation of these wishes,
in which he might be the object injured at the hands of his own
child. [p. 105]

Finally, he interprets:

Perhaps we can now comprehend the peculiar conduct of the
primitive fathers: they project their own hostile feelings towards
their sons on to the monster which devours the youths, and in so
doing make it evident that an essential part of those feelings is
derived from an unconscious fear of retaliation. Their apparently
affectionate and protective actions merely serve to conceal their
hostility towards their sons. [pp. 109–110]

Jewitt (cited in Reik 1958b) offers another illustrative example in
his report on the initiation myths of the Indians of Sondka
Sound:

The chief discharges his pistol close to his son's ear, and the son
immediately falls down as though he were dead. The women utter
terrible cries, tear out their hair and wail, thinking the youth is
dead. Two men covered in a wolf's skin, and having a wolf's mask
on their heads, approach on their hands and feet and carry the
youth away. [p. 121]

Later Jewitt sees the child wearing a wolf mask and adds:

This tribe of Indians belong to the totem clan of the wolf. Frazer
suspects there is some connection between the totem animal and

the youth's transformation, though he does not know how to explain it; but it seems like a confirmation of our view as to the latent meaning of the death and resurrection rite. . . . A parallel may be drawn between the death and resurrection rites and the story of the Basque hunter, "who affirmed that he had been killed by a bear, but that the bear had, after killing him, breathed its own soul into him, so that the bear's body was now dead, but he himself was a bear, being animated by the bear's soul." The identification of the man with the totem plays the chief part in the toemistic system of belief; but we must not forget that the totem animal affords protection and assistance to its worshippers and believers by means of this identification. [p. 121]

Reik (1958b) refers to the ideas of Schurtz and considers that:

The important and widespread institution of age-classes is conditioned by the ambivalent attitude of feelings of the older generation towards the younger generation, i.e., of the fathers towards their sons, and *vice versa*. Clans, age-classes, and men's societies have not developed concurrently, as Schurtz believes, but successively as a result of a development of primitive society which has yet to be investigated. The original purpose of these institutions can be determined from the fact that they are recognizable as attempts to bridge over the gulf between fathers and sons produced by the Oedipus complex. The latent meaning of the men's societies is to prevent incest, to afford protection against the hostile impulses of the sons that arise from incestuous desires, and to establish a reconciliation between fathers and sons, deriving its support from unconscious homosexual tendencies. . . . [pp. 150–151]

We have tried to include a brief discussion of initiation rites as an expression of parental aggression before examining other aspects of filicide. We shall now take up parents' cannibalistic impulses against their children. First and foremost, it is important to describe some anthropological characteristics that are defenses against cannibalism and also to analyze rituals related to what Frazer (1910) calls dietary or nutritional *couvade*. As we know, *couvade* is an institution in many primitive peoples that tends to protect the mother and child from the excluded father's fury during and after pregnancy. Dietary *couvade* prohibits him from carrying out any activity that could be associated with his criminal and cannibalistic desires. Thus, during pregnancy and in the first months of the child's life, the father is prohibited from hunting, eating small animals, using weapons or destructive instruments, and so on. The idea that the death of a small animal could harm the child derives from a direct association between them. Contact with large animals must also be avoided, perhaps to avoid any association with the aggressive relation between the father and his child, which could cause the latter's death. According to Reik, *couvade* represents a stage in cultural development that begins when social groups reach a certain degree of evolution.

Parents' cannibalistic impulses have been the subject of a special study by Devereux (1966). This author points out that the tendency of mammals to eat the placenta immediately after delivery is also observed in some primitive tribes and that it is a partial aspect of the tendency to eat the child. Just as dietary *couvade* is a defense against the father's cannibalism, there are similar prohibitions to counteract the mother's cannibalistic tendency. For example, the Mohave mother (Devereux 1966) cannot eat any kind of meat during the post-partum period. In other cases, maternal or paternal cannibalism takes place only substitutively. Devereux reports the dramatic case of a certain tribe in New Guinea: the mother must take her firstborn to the ravine where the sows are with their piglets and throw the child to these pigs for them to eat it. The woman then takes one of the suckling pigs from the sow that has been the first to attack the baby and nurses it at her own breast. The same author adds that, in a wider sense, the eating and selling of the meat of the offspring was frequent both in periods of famine in the Middle Ages and in Russia after the Revolution. According to Multatuli (cited in Devereux 1966), this was also observed in the past in Java as a consequence of disastrous famines. In at least two Australian tribes, the Ngali and the Yumu, the women aborted (or were made to abort) to feed the family. In another Australian tribe, when the family suffered hunger the youngest was killed by striking his head against the eldest child's back. His meat was eaten by his elder brothers and the rest of the family. Devereux also says that among primitive Australians cannibalism was quite common in times of famine and many of them preferred to kill a useless child rather than a useful hunting dog. He then adds that it would be incorrect to consider that these Australians did not love their children and quotes a case, reported by Roheim, of a small child with whom the parents had played very affectionately during the day and who was later killed and cooked for dinner. Devereux associates this case with the common expression: "I love you so much that I could eat you up."

Cannibalism of the offspring appears in the Bible and in literary works which express, in manifest or latent terms, the characteristics of the societies in which they were written. Thus, in *Deuteronomy* it is prophesied that the Lord's violent reaction to disobedience will lead people to eat their own children:

> *Deuteronomy 28:49–57:* The Lord shall bring a nation against thee from far, from the end of the earth, as swift as the eagle flieth, a nation whose tongue you shall not understand,
>
> 50 A nation of fierce countenance, which shall not regard the person of the old nor shew favor to the young;

51 And he shall eat the fruit of thy cattle and the fruit of thy land, until thou be destroyed; which also shall not leave thee either corn, wine, or oil, the increase of thy kine or the flocks of thy sheep, until he have destroyed thee.

52 And he shall besiege thee in all thy gates, until thy high and fenced walls come down wherein thou trustest, throughout all thy land; and he shall besiege thee in all thy gates throughout all thy land, which the Lord thy God hath given thee.

53 And thou shalt eat the fruit of thine own body, the flesh of thy sons and of thy daughters, which the Lord thy God hath given thee, in the siege, and in the straitness, wherewith thine enemies shall distress thee.

54 So that the man that is tender among you and very delicate, his eye shall be evil toward his brother, and toward the wife of his bosom, and toward the remnant of his children which he shall leave;

55 So that he will not give to any of them of the flesh of his children whom he shall eat, because he hath nothing left in the siege and in the straitness wherewith thine enemies shall distress thee in all thy gates.

56 The tender and delicate woman among you, which would not adventure to set the sole of her foot upon the ground for delicateness and tenderness, her eye shall be evil toward the husband of her bosom, and toward her son and toward her daughter,

57 And toward her young one that cometh out from between her feet, and toward her children which she shall bear, for she shall eat them for want of all things secretly in the siege and the straitness wherewith thine enemy shall distress thee in thy gates.

Coincidentally, Flavio Josefo in *The War of the Jews* (1948) describes a scene recorded during the siege of Jerusalem that corroborates the biblical prophecy:

VIII A woman . . . noble in lineage and rich, fleeing with all the other people, took refuge inside Jerusalem, and there she was surrounded no less than all the others. All the property that she had brought from her land had already been stolen by the tyrants of Jerusalem; whatever she had hidden and all the provisions that they found was taken away by the mutineers who entered her house daily. The woman was extremely angry at this because since she cursed the thieves who entered her house every day, they treated her more roughly: seeing also that none of them as angry as he might be or even out of pity wanted to put her out of her misery; first searching for food for herself, she searched for it for others. Her freedom was also taken away and she could take nothing and was already dying of hunger no less than the others; and the anger she felt incensed her even more, though not against her hunger. With the greatness of her soul's suffering, and moved by need, she rose up to do something against all humanity and nature: because tearing her child from her breast, she said: "Oh, thou unfortunate child! For whom will I keep you amidst so much war, revolt, sedition and such great hunger? Although you live you will be placed in service under the Romans, and your own are even more cruel than they. Serve me then with your meat for sustenance and the evil rebels for fury; and serve as a story in the human life of men, which is only lacking in such great destructions and adversities of the Jews." Saying this, she killed her child and cooked half of it and she herself ate it, keeping the other half very well covered. It happened that the mutineers entered her house and having smelled the awful, rotten odor of the meat, they threatened to kill her if she did not show them what she had gotten to eat. Answering that she had still kept most of it, she gave them what was left over of the child that she had killed. They, seeing such a thing, were seized by such a fearful horror and perturbation that they lost their nerve when they saw such a perverse and execrable thing. However, the woman said: this, then, is my child and this is my doing; you eat, because I have already eaten my part. I do not want you to be more tender than a woman, or to be more merciful to the child than his own mother has been. If you have pity, and honor religion, and reject my sacrifices, I have already eaten; let what is left also be for me. Fearful only for having seen such a wild thing, they went out trembling, although they could barely let the mother have her fill of this food. Later the city was all full of this evil and spread among them all; and putting that slaughter before him, each one was fearful, no less than if he himself had committed such a great evil. All those who were famished ran to seek someone to kill them and those who died rather than suffer were called blessed . . . but the evil of this illicit and execrable food had to be covered with the ruin and destruction of their own country, neither should the sun rise nor shine upon the city in which the mothers eat their own children. The fathers should serve first as these foods before the mothers, since they did not lay down their arms after these deaths. [pp. 388–390]

The third reference that we quote is no less pathetic. It is the story in the 32nd and 33rd cantos, the description of the tragedy of Count Ugolino in "Hell" of Dante's *The Divine Comedy* (1969):

> Leaving him then, I saw two souls together
> in a single hole, and so pinched in by the ice
> that one head made a helmet for the other.
>
> As a famished man chews crusts—so the sinner
> sank his teeth into the other's nape
> at the base of the skull, gnawing his loathsome dinner. . . .
>
> "You there," I said, "who show so odiously
> your hatred for that other, tell me why
> on this condition: that if in what you tell me
>
> you seem to have a reasonable complaint
> against him you devour with such foul relish,
> I, knowing who you are, and his soul's taint,
>
> may speak your cause to living memory,
> God willing the power of speech be left to me."

Canto 33:

The sinner raised his mouth from his grim repast
and wiped it on the hair of the bloody head
whose nape he had all but eaten away. At last
   he began to speak: "You ask me to renew
a grief so desperate that the very thought
of speaking of it tears my heart in two.
   But if my words may be a seed that bears
the fruit of infamy for him I gnaw,
I shall weep, but tell my story through my tears.
   Who you may be, and by what powers you reach
into this underworld, I cannot guess,
but you seem to me a Florentine by your speech.
   I was Count Ugolino, I must explain;
this reverend grace is the Archbishop Ruggieri:
now I will tell you why I gnaw his brain.
   That I, who trusted him, had to undergo
imprisonment and death through his treachery,
you will know already. What you cannot know—
   that is, the lingering inhumanity
of the death I suffered—you shall hear in full:
then judge for yourself if he has injured me.
   A narrow window in that coop of stone
now called the Tower of Hunger for my sake
(within which others yet must pace alone)
   had shown me several waning moons already
between its bars, when I slept the evil sleep
in which the veil of the future parted for me.
   This beast appeared as master of a hunt
chasing the wolf and his whelps across the mountain
that hides Lucca from Pisa. Out in front
   of the starved and shrewd and avid pack he had placed
Gualandi and Sismondi and Lanfranchi
to point his prey. The father and sons had raced
   a brief course only when they failed of breath

and seemed to weaken; then I thought I saw
their flanks ripped open by the hounds' fierce teeth.

    Before the dawn, the dream still in my head,   ·
I woke and heard my sons, who were there with me,
cry from their troubled sleep, asking for bread.

    You are cruelty itself if you can keep
your tears back at the thought of what foreboding
stirred in my heart; and if you do not weep,

    at what are you used to weeping? – The hour when food
used to be brought, drew near. They were now awake,
and each was anxious from his dream's dark mood.

    And from the base of that horrible tower I heard
the sound of hammers nailing up the gates:
I stared at my sons' faces without a word.

    I did not weep: I had turned to stone inside.
They wept. "What ails you, Father, you look so strange,"
my little Anselm, youngest of them, cried.

    But I did not speak a word nor shed a tear:
not all that day nor all that endless night, until I saw another sun
appear.

    When a tiny ray leaked into that dark prison
and I saw staring back from their four faces
the terror and wasting of my own,

    I bit my hands in helpless grief. And they,
thinking I chewed myself for hunger, rose
suddenly together. I heard them say:

    "Father, it would give us much less pain
if you ate us: it was you who put upon us
this sorry flesh; now strip it off again."

    I calmed myself to spare them. Ah! hard earth,
why did you not yawn open? All that day
and the next we sat in silence. On the fourth,

    Gaddo, the eldest, fell before me and cried,
stretched at my feet upon that prison floor:

"Father, why don't you help me?" There he died.
   And just as you see me, I saw them fall
one by one on the fifth day and the sixth.
Then, already blind, I began to crawl
   from body to body shaking them frantically.
Two days I called their names, and they were dead.
Then fasting overcame my grief and me.
   His eyes narrowed to slits when he was done,
and he seized the skull again between his teeth
grinding it as a mastiff grinds a bone. [pp. 96–98]

Devereux (1966) refers to castration, one of the most serious forms of partial filicide, practiced universally to different extents. Total genital mutilation is now an exception but this does not imply that it has disappeared entirely. Its millennial constancy has led to its internalization in the form of an innate psychological structure in all people, evidenced in the castration complex. But we shall see a nearly recent case of objective practice of castration (Encyclopaedia Britannica 5:43). The castrato was

a male soprano or contralto voice of great range, flexibility and power, produced as a result of castration before puberty. . . . The castrato voice was first introduced while women were banned from church choirs and the stage. In 18th-century Italian opera the majority of male singers were castrati and over 200 of them sang in churches in Rome alone. The most famous of them all was Farinelli. The roles created for them, e.g., by Gluck and Mozart, are now sung by women.

Devereux (1966) also mentions the children who were castrated to be sold as eunuchs in China and the Middle East and reminds us that in Byzantium the upper-class families had their sons castrated to ensure that they would become high officials of the court. In other cases, they had themselves castrated to avoid the danger that the emperor, always fearful of being dethroned by a descendant of the aristocratic families, might execute their children. This list would be endless if we included the castration of children by substitute parents practiced by states, kingdoms, and even religious communities.

A pathetic account by Herodotus (1947) tells of Hermothymus who was captured as a boy and sold to a preparer of eunuchs called Paunionios who castrated him. Time passed and Hermothymus became the favorite eunuch of the emperor Xerxes; pretending to be grateful, Hermothymus invited Paunionios to visit him with his family, then forced him to castrate his own sons and forced the sons to castrate their father.

Castration appeared in Assyria as a form of punishment two millennia before Christ. In general, eunuchs appear in history as having been castrated for diverse misdemeanors, but they have most commonly been castrated by their parents or substitute parents for sale as slaves. Since earliest antiquity eunuchs have worked in harems. Their condition of absolute submission has made them faithful servants and reliable counselors to their masters, especially in Islam where they were not only preceptor counselors but often generals and admirals. The markets where castrated boys are sold as slaves exist even today in North Central Africa (Baguirmi, etc.). The Italian custom of castrating boys to make them into sopranos, especially for the Sistine Chapel, ended with the papacy of Leon XII, only in 1878.

Voluntary castration for mystical reasons or as a result of grave psychopathological disturbance is quite common. The classical example is that of Origenes in the third century and sects like the Valessi and the Skoptsi have existed and still exist who castrate themselves as faithful servants of the Lord, thus preserving themselves from sexual sins or temptations. According to modern psychology, these rationalized aberrations are due to the precocious internalization, individual or collective, of extremely cruel and prohibiting parental images that are expressed in acts such as castration imposed on the person's weakened ego. These considerations are equally valid for suicide, which can ultimately be regarded as an expression of endopsychic filicidal organization. In other words, it is the internal representation of the parents that pushes the suicide victim to destroy his own ego. There are other motivations in the genesis and dynamics of suicide, but none of these is as meaningful as the one that begins with the destruction of children by their parents. This experience, at the beginning passive from outside, later becomes an active tendency that develops from within.

Although the complete castration of the genitals is observed in a limited minority, this is not true in the case of partial and attenuated forms of castration. The most widespread and representative of these is circumcision, which can be considered a universal practice in sociocultural development, both primitive and contemporary. Thus, it can be observed in the least developed tribes of Africa, Australia, and South America, in the Jews and the Moslems, and indirectly in the Christians through communion with circumcised Jesus. We must not forget that the first of January, the day of the circumcision of Jesus, marks the beginning of the year.

The origin of circumcision is unknown, but its wide ethnic and geographic distribution and the use of the stone knife before the metal knife leaves no doubt as to its remote antiquity. The only groups where its practice has not been proved are the Indo-Germanic, the Mongols, and the Finno-Ugrians. The ancient Egyptians circumcised between the ages of 6 and 12. The Ethiopians, the Jews, and other peoples did it shortly after birth. But the majority of the groups that practice circumcision perform it in puberty. In all cases, it is an initiation rite for the individual's acceptance into society that determines his position in the group as well as his rights and obligations.

In the monotheistic conception it signals the covenant between the Lord and Abraham and the Pentateuch tells how the Lord orders that all males be circumcised eight days after birth. But Ishmael, son of Abraham and the Egyptian slave Hagar, was then 13. This explains the delayed ritual circumcision of the Ishmaelites, descendants of Abraham in that line.

When Pythagoras went to study in the Egyptian temples (530 B.C.), he had to submit to circumcision in order to be accepted. The *Encyclopaedia Britannica* (1966) states that the tomb discovered in Saqqara in Egypt depicts on one of its walls scenes of a boy held by the wrists by a man standing behind him while the priest leans over to perform the circumcision. It adds that this practice was already established in Egypt 4,000 years before Christ, which is not strange, since it is now practiced by cultures more primitive than the highly developed one in ancient Egypt. It seems that at the beginning it was mostly limited to the priestly classes and only later taken up by the warriors, the nobility, and the royalty.

In any case, we cannot ignore that circumcision constitutes an attenuated form of castration that came about as a decrease in much crueler aggressive behaviors which included above all the slaughter of the firstborn. There is no doubt that it replaced the killing of the firstborn and the primitive actual castration to the same extent that the parents' loving and preserving tendencies were gradually consolidated. We insist that it is important to bear in mind that the superior culture developed in ancient Egypt is the one that has most ostensibly recorded circumcision in its ancient historical documents; at the same time, the universal existence of circumcision in the least developed primitive tribes must also be taken into account.

Although circumcision is the most universal and widespread of them, there are other practices that reveal filicidal mutilation inflicted by parents, sometimes as an expression of the culture that symbolizes them. These include the most diverse types of incisions, perforations, partial or total extirpations, cauterizations, compressions, stretching, elongations, and so on. The cranial deformations are the best documented, since archeological skeletons clearly indicate their existence. In them, we can observe deformations produced by the pressure of small splints or other plane surfaces applied permanently to the child's head or circular deformations caused by the application of constrictive bands around the skull. The Mayans considered crossed eyes a sign of beauty and provoked this anomaly by placing an object between the baby's eyes. In China from the T'ang dynasty until 1911, many women wore very tight bandages on their feet from infancy to keep them from growing, in order to have very tiny "golden lily" feet. Thus, they hoped to achieve this aesthetic ideal which was a rationalization of a castratory displacement. Bodily deformations such as the induction of obesity and mortifying modifications of the skin, hair, skull, nose, lips, teeth, eyes, ears and neck, the breast, trunk and extremities, and the fingers and feet, form a varied series of mutilations and tortures that are no less cruel than mental ones. However, the most frequent are the genital mutilations of which there is also a remarkable variety. We have already dealt with circumcision in general and we can add to this a subincision of the urethra on the undersurface of the penis in different parts, from the urinary meatus to the scrotum, a common practice in the initiation of Australian aborigines (Spiegel 1969) as well as in other peoples.

The customary castration of one testicle, called monorchectomy, is also a common ritual in diverse African and Australian peoples, and has been studied especially in the Ponape Islands of Micronesia. We have already mentioned bilateral castration and we could go on with a strange series of practices including incrustations in the urethra or in other parts of the genitals. We cannot omit frequent feminine mutilations such as the clitoridectomy, infibulation, dilatation and stretching of the major and minor labia of the genitals. The partial sacrifices originating in ritually organized sadistic and masochistic wishes are quite frequently practiced on children and are forms instituted at the dawn of the lives of these boys and girls.

Among these historical and anthropological facts, forms of mental murder are no less important: mortification, humiliation, neglect, and abandonment. These have been insufficiently understood because they are less objective and are often products of the psychopathological structures of parents and of entire societies that do not become aware of the brutal meaning of attitudes that are difficult to perceive. Abandonment, lack of consideration for the need for love and for human warmth, for understanding and companionship—in terms of permanence, quantity and quality—is what leads especially to the deepest mental disturbances. But we shall take up this important topic at a more appropriate time, since we must now attend to the extension of a basic formulation that will ensure the most complete understanding of this one.

The abuse of children as the basis of the educational process has an extremely long history and is one of the most difficult practices to eradicate. From ancient Sumeria where the schools already had their "whip man" to contemporary Great Britain, the corporal punishment of children has been institutionalized. It was eliminated from English state schools only in 1969 and throughout most of the world it is considered an "educational procedure." Thus, just as in Sumeria the schoolchildren's punisher was called the "whip man," in Great Britain he was called the "whipper."

Before concluding this subject, we cannot fail to mention the influence that criminal exploitation of children has had on the industrial age. Thus, in the English factories at the turn of the century, children as young as 4 years old worked in the factories and from the age of 8 worked in the coal mines for sixteen hours a day. They were often placed in irons to restrict their movements and to keep them from running away from their workplaces. Consequently, premature death was the rule and they reached 20 years of age only exceptionally. The cruelest of all the trades was that of the chimneysweep (Radbill 1968):

> Restless and skinny, with a natural tendency to climb, they were forced to go up the narrow chimnies to scrape off the soot. No job was more detestable for a child. They worked day and night, frequently abused during their work by hard-hearted masters and were the object of all kinds of violence. People were insensitive to their sufferings. If a woman felt moved by an accident that happened to one of these children in her house, her protection was considered suspicious. The poor things wasted away quickly, both physically and mentally. They were not only victims of cancer of the scrotum, described by Percival Pott and called cancer of the chimney, but also succumbed to the advance of lung consumption. [p. 12]

We have left out the long list of murders of their children perpetrated by important historical figures. A classic example is

Ivan the Terrible, who killed his son the czarevich in a fit of rage.
Iphigenia dies by her father's hand and Jephthah also sacrifices his
daughter for different reasons. Examples abound and the inves-
tigator interested in discovering the denied truth underlying the
conflict between generations can confirm its authenticity.

6

Jesus and Filicide

Jesus is the extraordinary precursor who came forth two thousand years ago to denounce the nature of the holocaust that the sociocultural process demands: the sacrifice of the son of man.

Our intention at this time is to analyze the essential features of his doctrine from a strictly psychological viewpoint, leaving aside theological or religious discussions. We will center our analysis on the teachings attributed to Jesus and on some aspects of fundamental importance for those who are interested in studying filicide and its millennial history.

Any attempt to undertake a study based on all the wealth of valuable literature on the person and works of Jesus would be an arduous and exhausting task. Therefore, we shall refer only to the Gospels, since they are considered faithful versions of the events and theories pertaining to the Nazarene; of these, we shall analyze only some fragments that relate precisely to the sacrifice of children denounced by Jesus in his universal message.

THE CIRCUMSTANCES SURROUNDING THE ORIGIN OF THE MYSTIC HERO

Just as with the origin of the hero, the birth of Jesus is surrounded with dark foreboding. The threat of murder, decreed by Herod, hangs over him. This threat only reiterates a recurrent historical fact: the sentence condemning all the male children, in the case of Abraham by order of Nimrod, and also of all the Jewish boys by order of the pharaoh when Moses was born. The slaughter of children is repeated when the Exodus from Egypt is organized and the firstborn are condemned to death by the angel of death. Furthermore, these mass murders of children recorded throughout history show the constancy of the death threat that hangs over children because of their parents' conflicts in all epochs.

In another text (Rascovsky 1971) we have referred to the fact that all heroes, among whom we must include the great visionaries like Jesus, always have as a prerequisite a childhood during which they are harried by persecutory anxieties resulting from the filicidal attitude of their parents or equivalents. These equivalents may be represented by the king, by the queen, by the tyrant and, more often, by the hero's own king-father, as in the case of Oedipus. Rank (1981) offers us remarkable information on this phenomenon and Freud (1939a) has referred to these concepts in *Moses and Monotheism: Three Essays*. We will only transcribe the initial facts in this universal situation:

> The hero is the child of the *most aristocratic* parents; usually son of a king. His conception is preceded by difficulties, such as abstinence or prolonged barrenness or his parents having to have intercourse in secret owing to external prohibitions or obstacles. During the pregnancy, or even earlier, there is a prophecy (in the

form of a dream or oracle) cautioning against his birth, threatening danger to his father. As a result of this, the newborn child is condemned to death or to *exposure*, usually by the orders of *his father or of someone representing him* . . . [*Standard Edition* 23: 10–11]

It is important to demonstrate the dynamics of the origin of this circumstance, since they explain the endopsychic or mental origin of the lofty and exceptional possibilities of the hero's condition, as well as his mystical exaltation. The genetic mechanism producing the heroic condition is the precocious intensification of persecutory anxieties provoked by the equally persecutory or fatally threatening attitude of his parents or their substitutes. This amount of intense aggression, passively absorbed from the beginning of childhood development, provokes, on one hand, the hero's identifications and consequent aggressive, active behavior. On the other hand, it provokes the intense regression which leads to his immersion in mysticism and to the depth of his insight with extraordinary broadening of his intuitive knowledge. The latter circumstance can be seen in Jesus, not only in the paternal abandonment which he proclaims in his last moment on the cross, but also in the persecution decreed by Herod. The newborn Jesus must be taken to Egypt to save him from the massacre in Bethlehem. He only returns to Israel after the death of Herod who personifies the bad, persecutory father:

Matthew 2:16–23: Then Herod, when he saw that he was mocked of the wise men, was exceedingly wroth, and sent forth, and slew all the children that were in Bethlehem and in all the coasts thereof, from two years old and under, according to the time which he had diligently inquired of the wise men.

17 Then was fulfilled that which was spoken by Jeremiah the prophet, saying,

18 In Rama was there a voice heard,
lamentation and weeping, and great mourning,
Rachel weeping for her children,
and would not be comforted,
because they are not.

19 But when Herod was dead, behold, an angel of the Lord appeareth in a dream to Joseph in Egypt, saying,

20 Arise, and take the young child and his mother, and go into the land of Israel: for they are dead which sought the young child's life.

21 And he arose, and took the young child and his mother, and came into the land of Israel.

22 But when he heard that Archelaus did reign over Judaea in the room of his father Herod, he was afraid to go thither: notwithstanding, being warned of God in a dream, he turned aside into the parts of Galilee.

23 And he came and dwelt in a city called Nazareth, that it might be fulfilled which was spoken by the prophets, He shall be called a Nazarene.

THE INFANCY AND CHILDHOOD OF JESUS

The Gospels tell us little of Jesus' later childhood. Only in Luke is there a reference to it:

Luke 2:40–50: And the child grew, and waxed strong in spirit, filled with wisdom; and the grace of God was upon him.

41 Now his parents went to Jerusalem every year at the feast of the passover.

42 And when he was twelve years old, they went up to Jerusalem, after the custom of the feast;

43 and when they had fulfilled the days, as they returned, the child Jesus tarried behind in Jerusalem; And Joseph and his mother knew not of it.

44 But they, supposing him to have been in the company, went a day's journey; and they sought him among their kinsfolk and acquaintance.

45 And when they found him not, they turned back again to Jerusalem, seeking him.

46 And it came to pass, that after three days they found him in the temple, sitting in the midst of the doctors, both hearing them and asking them questions;

47 And all that heard him were astonished at his understanding and answers.

48 And when they saw him, they were amazed; and his mother said unto him, Son, why hast thou thus dealt with us? behold, thy father and I have sought thee sorrowing.

49 And he said unto them, How is it that ye sought me? wist ye not that I must be about my Father's business?

50 And they understood not the saying which he spake unto them.

How could we interpret the meaning of the so-called "hidden life" of Jesus, which includes all his childhood? Is it perhaps that all of Jesus' life expresses the entire mental life of the child in which his condemnation, mortification, and suffering are perpetuated as the highest expression of the sacrifice of children? Long after that initial event, Jesus appears before John:

> *Matthew 3:13-15*: Then cometh Jesus from Galilee to Jordan, unto John, to be baptized of him.

> 14 But John forbade him, saying, I have need to be baptized of thee, and comest thou to me?

> 15 And Jesus, answering, said unto him, Suffer it to be so now; for thus it becometh us to fulfil all righteousness. Then he suffered him.

The version by Mark adds a connotation to the meaning of baptism: it is rebirth into a new, reparatory order, which gives rise to an exalted expression of parental love:

> *Mark 1:9-11*: And it came to pass in those days, that Jesus came from Nazareth of Galilee, and was baptized of John in Jordan.

> 10 And straightway coming up out of the water, he saw the heavens opened, and the Spirit, like a dove, descending upon him;

> 11 And there came a voice from heaven, saying Thou art my beloved Son, in whom I am well pleased.

This expresses the supreme human aspiration: *to be a beloved child giving total satisfaction to the one who loves it.* Could we possibly ignore the symbolization of the mother's breast in the shape of a divine dove? This beginning is the source of all reparation and all hope, and the creed of love as the most powerful therapeutic force will be the essential motif in the Nazarene's preaching.

Now the period of trial in the desert begins, and after forty days and forty nights of fasting[1] during which he overcomes the temptations of the devil, he returns to Galilee where John has been imprisoned.

JESUS AS A THERAPIST

Jesus goes to Capernaum and begins to preach and to catechize there. His prestige grows, especially because of his success as a therapist.

> *Matthew 4:23-25*: And Jesus went about all Galilee, teaching in their synagogues, and preaching the gospel of the kingdom, and healing all manner of sickness, and all manner of disease among the people.
>
> 24 And his fame went throughout all Syria; and they brought unto him all sick people that were taken with divers diseases and torments and those which were possessed with devils, and those which were lunatic, and those that had the palsy; and he healed them.
>
> 25 And there followed him great multitudes of people from Galilee and from Decapolis, and Jerusalem, and from Judaea and from beyond Jordan.

---

[1]The correlation between the forty days Jesus spent in the desert and the first forty postnatal days of the newborn is remarkably interesting for psychology. We have written elsewhere on this special period in the mother–child unit that ends at the close of the puerperal period when the father comes into the child's emotional life, which goes from the dyadic situation with the mother to the triangular situation with the father and the mother. See A. and M. Rascovsky (1967).

Jesus' initial preaching is oriented towards individual and collective healing and salvation, insisting on the supreme effect of love and the need for working through guilt and mourning by accepting our most painful psychic motivations. This acceptance, which would lead to reparation as the final integration of everything, is summed up in the notion of repentance.

For this reason, his words are directed to the humble, to those who suffer, to the children, to those who go on forever being children. His blessing is offered to the poor in spirit, to those who mourn, to the meek, to those who hunger and thirst for justice, to the merciful, to the pure in heart, to the peacemakers, to those who are persecuted for righteousness' sake, and to those who are persecuted for his cause, which is the cause of the son who is sacrificed in every sense.

His teaching is of justice and love; in the exaltation of the humble we can see the exaltation of the child, the definitive source of grace and hope.

> *Matthew 5:13-17:* Ye are the salt of the earth; but if salt have lost its savour, wherewith shall it be salted? It is thenceforth good for nothing, but to be cast out, and to be trodden under foot of men.
>
> *14* Ye are the light of the world. A city that is set on an hill cannot be hid.
>
> *15* Neither do men light a candle, and put it under a bushel, but on a candlestick; and it giveth light unto all that are in the house.
>
> *16* Let your light so shine before men, that they may see your good works and glorify your Father which is in heaven.
>
> *17* Think not that I am come to destroy the law, or the prophets; I am not come to destroy but to fulfil.

Jesus introduces a basic modification in the contemporary concepts of justice and of struggle, essentially against the gerontocratic imposition of the distorted law that failed to respect children's rights and needs. We must remember the dominion at that time of Roman law, according to which the two voluntary acts of generating and extinguishing a child's life were united so that the former authorized the latter. The twelve tablets of Romulus of ancient Rome demonstrate that filicide was a widespread practice and that the law gave the Roman citizen absolute power over the life and death of his offspring. The *Patria Potestas* granted the right to sell, kill, offer to the gods, subordinate to any occupation, and *devour* one's children. Thus, the Justinian Institutes (Lee 1956) boasted that: "The legal power which we hold over our children is particular to each Roman citizen, since no other men exist who possess it" (p. 80).

Among historians, Lecky (quoted in Sumner 1906) denounced infanticide as the "atrocious vice of the Roman Empire" (p. 315). Constantine reduced the filicidal severity of the law, but was unable to stop the sale of newborn babies on the slave market, a commerce that continues and is secretly condoned even today. It is interesting to note that it was also Constantine who authorized the entry of Christianity into the Empire. The growing valuation of children and the acceptance of their rights were the direct result of Jesus' influence.

THE ACCEPTANCE OF AGGRESSION, THE INTRODUCTION OF DEPRESSIVE WORKING THROUGH, AND THE INTERGENERATIONAL CONFLICT

At the height of the Roman Empire with its rigid patriarchal concepts—to which those of the Jewish patriarchy must be added—Jesus appears with his new and revolutionary justice. Together with the defense of children, there are diverse profound and subtle messages. One of the most remarkable of these is the acceptance of the aggressive component in the object relation or, better yet, the appeal for absorption of the aggressive components in the object relation. In modern psychological terms, this means overcoming the paranoid nature of the subject's conception of the object by integrating loving and aggressive tendencies in an inseparable whole. It is an appeal for understanding and acceptance of children's innate aggression, the same aggression that helps them to establish their initial relationship with their parents. In effect, the depressive integration that creates a capacity for reparation depends on our awareness of aggression against our loved objects and of the consequent guilt.

> *Matthew 5:38–42:* Ye have heard that it hath been said, *"An eye for an eye, and a tooth for a tooth."*
>
> 39 But I say unto you, that ye resist not evil; but whosoever shall smite thee on thy right cheek, turn to him the other also.
>
> 40 And if any man will sue thee at the law, and take thy coat, let him have thy cloak also.
>
> 41 And whosoever shall compel thee to go a mile, go with him twain.
>
> 42 Give to him that asketh thee, and from him that would borrow of thee turn not thou away.

This teaching connotes unconditional insistence on both the loving and aggressive meanings involved in any object relation and proposes a totally new formula for the valuation of affective relationships:

Matthew 5:43-46: Ye have heard that it hath been said, Thou shalt love thy neighbor, and hate thine enemy;

44 But I say unto you, Love your enemies, bless them that curse you, do good to them that hate you, and pray for them which despitefully use you, and persecute you;

45 That ye may be the children of your Father which is in heaven; for he maketh his sun to rise on the evil and on the good, and sendeth rain on the just and on the unjust.

46 For if ye love them which love you, what reward have ye? do not even the publicans the same?

Jesus, who foresees the persecutions that his preaching against despotic institutions and his revolutionary love for truth will provoke, expresses his antigerontocratic position and his protest against these parents, inciting the people to rebel against them:

Matthew 10:34-36: Think not that I am come to send peace on earth; I came not to send peace, but a sword.

35 For I am come to set a man at variance against his father, and the daughter against her mother, and the daughter in law against her mother in law.

36 And a man's foes shall be they of his own household.

In his preaching, Jesus devotes himself most especially to defending children and exalts his attitude against bad parents. He also places the responsibility for their children's disturbances on these parents.

These concepts are expressed in his allusions to trees and their fruit, cloaked in the language of parables he commonly used:

Matthew 12:33–35: Either make the tree good, and his fruit good; or else make the tree corrupt, and his fruit corrupt; for the tree is known by his fruit.

34 O generation of vipers! how can ye, being evil, speak good things? for out of the abundance of the heart the mouth speaketh.

35 A good man out of the good treasure of heart bringeth forth good things; and an evil man out of the evil treasure bringeth forth evil things.

THE VALUATION OF CHILDREN

His supreme valuation of children is reaffirmed when his disciples ask him who is the greatest in the Kingdom of Heaven:

Matthew 18:1–6: At the same time came the disciples unto Jesus, saying, Who is the greatest in the kingdom of heaven?

2 And Jesus called a little child unto him, and set him in the midst of them,

3 And said, Verily I say unto you, Except ye be converted and become as little children, ye shall not enter into the kingdom of heaven.

4 Whosoever therefore shall humble himself as this little child, the same is greatest in the kingdom of heaven.

5 And whoso shall receive one such little child in my name, receiveth me.

6 But whoso shall offend one of these little ones which believe in me it were better for him that a millstone were hanged about his neck, and that he were drowned in the depth of the sea.

The affirmation of his fundamental esteem for children is reiterated:

> *Matthew 19:13–15:* Then were there brought unto him little children, that he should put his hands on them, and pray; and the disciples rebuked them.
>
> 14 But Jesus said, Suffer little children, and forbid them not, to come unto me; for of such is the kingdom of heaven.
>
> 15 And he laid his hands on them, and departed thence.

THE SACRIFICE OF THE CHILD

Jesus has foreseen that the sacrifice of the son of man will fall upon him. In his first prediction he says:

> *Mark 8:31:* And he began to teach them, that the Son of man must suffer many things, and be rejected of the elders, and of the chief priests, and scribes, and be killed . . .

Later he says for the second time:

> *Mark 9:31:* For he taught his disciples, and said unto them, The Son of man is delivered into the hands of men, and they shall kill him; and after that he is killed, he shall rise the third day.

And for the third time:

> *Mark 10:32:* And they were in the way going up to Jerusalem; and Jesus went before them; and they were amazed; and as they followed, they were afraid. And he took again the twelve, and began to tell them what things should happen unto him.

33 Saying, Behold, we go up to Jerusalem; and the Son of man shall be delivered unto the chief priests, and unto the scribes, and they shall condemn him to death, and shall deliver him to the Gentiles;

34 And they shall mock him, and shall scourge him, and shall spit upon him, and shall kill him. . .

THE INTERGENERATIONAL STRUGGLE

We cannot omit Jesus' allusion to the bad mother through the symbolism of the fig tree that fails to nourish and is consequently condemned to sterility. Thus, the factors that will lead to the rebellion against the filicidal gerontocracy build up and, when it is imminent, Jesus foresees the great tribulations the intergenerational struggle will provoke:

> *Mark 13:11-13*: But when they shall lead you, and deliver you up, take no thought beforehand what ye shall speak, neither do ye premeditate; but whatsoever shall be given you in that hour, that speak ye; for it is not ye that speak, but the Holy Ghost.
>
> *12* Now the brother shall betray the brother to death, and the father the son; and children shall rise up against their parents, and shall cause them to be put to death;
>
> *13* And ye shall be hated of all men for my name's sake; but he that shall endure unto the end, the same shall be saved.

After these great trials he foretells the coming of the son of man: that is, the triumph and liberation of children, once the generational yoke has been destroyed.

Mark 13:24–27: But in those days, after that tribulation, the sun shall be darkened, and the moon shall not give her light,

25 And the stars of heaven shall fall, and the powers that are in heaven shall be shaken.

26 And then shall they see the Son of man coming in the clouds, with great power and glory.

27 And then shall he send his angels, and shall gather his elect from the four winds, from the uttermost part of the earth, to the uttermost part of heaven.

The affirmation of the betrayal that the son of man experiences is placed upon Judas Iscariot and is predicted in this way:

Matthew 26:20–25: Now when the even was come, he sat down with the twelve.

21 And as they did eat, he said, Verily I say unto you, that one of you shall betray me.

22 And they were exceeding sorrowful, and began every one of them to say unto him, Lord, is it I?

23 And he answered and said, He that dippeth his hand with me in the dish, the same shall betray me.

24 The Son of man goeth as it is written of him; but woe unto that man by whom the Son of man is betrayed! It had been good for that man if he had not been born.

25 Then Judas, which betrayed him, answered and said, Master, is it I? He said unto him, Thou hast said.

THE DENIAL OF FILICIDE

In his prediction of Judas' betrayal, is there perhaps a prophetic admonition against those who betray, mistreat, and sell out their children? But parents do not become aware of their negative attitudes on account of the intensity of the systematic denial of the sacrifice of children. Jesus, who takes the holocaust fully upon himself, predicts human denial of filicide through Peter's words:

> Mark 14:26–31: And when they had sung an hymn, they went out into the Mount of Olives.
>
> 27 And Jesus saith unto them, All ye shall be offended because of me this night; for it is written, I will smite the shepherd, and the sheep shall be scattered.
>
> 28 But after that I am risen, I will go before you into Galilee.
>
> 29 But Peter said unto him, Although all shall be offended, yet will not I.
>
> 30 And Jesus saith unto him, Verily I say unto thee, that this day, even in this night, before the cock crow twice, thou shalt deny me thrice.
>
> 31 But he spake the more vehemently, If I should die with thee, I will not deny thee in any wise. Likewise also said they all.

Afterwards Jesus suffers his agony, the intense suffering of the son of man, and then his arrest and betrayal that signals the beginning of his passion. In the version according to Mark, when they all flee and abandon Jesus, a young man appears covered only with a cloth; when he is seized he succeeds in escaping naked, leaving the cloth behind. Is this perhaps an allusion to the son of man saved by the sacrifice that Jesus takes upon himself in the name of all men and through projective identification in the Communion? Might his very nakedness represent man's helplessness even after he has been saved?

Mark 14:50–52: And they all forsook him, and fled.

51 And there followed him a certain young man, having a linen cloth cast about his naked body; and the young men laid hold on him;

52 And he left the linen cloth, and fled from them naked.

The difficulty in accepting evidence of the sacrifice of children or, in other words, the intense denial needed to keep from becoming aware of filicidal forces, can be seen explicitly in Jesus' warning to Peter, confirmed by subsequent events:

Mark 14:66–72: And as Peter was beneath in the palace, there cometh one of the maids of the high priest;

67 And when she saw Peter warming himself, she looked upon him, and said, And thou also wast with Jesus of Nazareth.

68 But he denied, saying, I know not, neither understand I what thou sayest, And he went out into the porch; and the cock crew.

69 And a maid saw him again, and began again to say to them that stood by, This is one of them.

70 And he denied it again. And a little after, they that stood by said again to Peter, Surely thou art one of them; for thou art a Galilean, and thy speech agreeth thereto.

71 But he began to curse and to swear, saying, I know not this man of whom ye speak.

72 And the second time the cock crew. And Peter called to mind the word that Jesus said unto him, Before the cock crow twice, thou shalt deny me thrice. And when he thought thereon, he wept.

Then Jesus is brought before Pilate and, after being crowned with thorns, is mortified on the road to the cross with atrocities and calumnies before and after the crucifixion. Finally, Jesus dies and is later resurrected.

At the moment of his sacrifice, Jesus proclaims his utmost longing for his father's love and exalts the meaning of his generational heritage.

John 17:1–10: These words spake Jesus, and he lifted up his eyes to heaven, and said, Father, the hour is come; glorify thy Son, that thy Son also may glorify thee;

2 As thou hast given him power over all flesh, that he should give eternal life to as many as thou hast given him.

3 And this is life eternal, that they might know thee the only true God, and Jesus Christ, whom thou hast sent.

4 I have glorified thee on the earth; I have finished the work which thou gavest me to do;

5 And now, O Father, glorify thou me with thine own self, with the glory which I had with thee before the world was.

6 I have manifested thy name unto the men which thou gavest me out of the world; thine they were, and thou gavest them me; and they have kept thy word.

7 Now they know that all things whatsoever thou hast given me are of thee.

8 For I have given unto them the words which thou gavest me; and they have received them, and have known surely that I came out from thee, and they have believed that thou didst send me.

9 I pray for them; I pray not for the world, but for them which thou hast given me; for they are thine;

10 And all mine are thine, and thine are mine; and I am glorified in them.

Jesus' final words on the cross acquire transcendent meaning within his preaching. This is the central question in everyone's personal calvary when we are condemned to suffer our parents' desertion to various degrees. Jesus expresses the fundamental longing and pain of the son of man, of all parents' children who, when faced with the absence of the object, ask the primordial and painful question: "Why have you abandoned me?"

Matthew 27:45–46: Now from the sixth hour there was darkness over all the land unto the ninth hour.

46 And about the ninth hour Jesus cried with a loud voice, saying, "Eli, Eli, lama sabach-tha-ni? that is to say, "My God, my God, why hast thou forsaken me?

IDENTIFICATION WITH THE FATHER AND THE PROCESS OF IDENTITY

In the light of modern knowledge about the processes of identification and of acquisition of identity, it is most interesting to see how Jesus discussed these processes. In his "Speech on the Son's Work," in the Gospel according to John, he describes the concept of identification and the acquisition of identity from the relationship with the father.

John 5:19–24: Then answered Jesus and said unto them, verily, verily, I say unto you, The Son can do nothing of himself, but what he seeth the Father do; for what things soever he doeth, these also doeth the Son likewise.

20 For the Father loveth the Son, and showeth him all things he doeth; and he will shew him greater works than these, that ye may marvel.

21 For as the Father raiseth up the dead, and quickeneth them; even so the Son quickeneth whom he will.

22 For the Father judgeth no man, but hath committed all judgment unto the Son;

23 That all men should honour the Son, even as they honour the Father, He that honoureth not the Son, honoureth not the Father which hath sent him.

24 Verily, verily, I say unto you, He that heareth my word, and believeth on him that sent me, hath everlasting life, and shall not come into condemnation; but is passed from death unto life.

Identification through oral introjection is defined more clearly in the institution of the Eucharist. Thus, Jesus offers his disciples equivalents of himself to be eaten in the Passover supper; this reproduces the totemic model of the Jewish Passover which in turn provides the model for family meals with the children. In the middle of the Passover supper, along with the Jewish rituals (blessings to Jehovah said over the bread and wine that replace the sacrifice of Isaac with the Passover lamb), Jesus preaches the return to the original truth, to the primordial sacrifice of the son, he himself suffering the holocaust and being eaten:

> Matthew 26:26–29: And as they were eating, Jesus took bread, and blessed it, and brake it, and gave it to the disciples, and said, Take, eat; this is my body.

27 And he took the cup, and gave thanks, and gave it to them, saying, Drink ye all of it;

28 For this is my blood of the new testament[2] which is shed for many for the remission of sins.

29 But I say unto you, I will not drink henceforth of this fruit of the vine, until that day when I drink it new with you in my Father's kingdom.

Thus, Jesus shows that the sacrifice of the son lies behind the displacement onto the sacrificial animal and the persistence of the meaning of the sacrifice which Abraham begins to execute. The working through of all this process is another obvious expression of the struggle for integration by the son torn apart by the sacrifice.

THE DENUNCIATION OF THE FILICIDAL FATHER

On the other hand, Jesus denounces the filicidal father in a very explicit way:

John 8:39–45: They answered and said unto him, Abraham is our father. Jesus saith unto them, "If ye were Abraham's children, ye would do the works of Abraham.

40 But now ye seek to kill me, a man that hath told you the truth, which I have heard of God; this did not Abraham.

41 Ye do the deeds of your father. Then said they to him, We be not born of fornication; we have one Father, even God.

---

[2]The covenant is the pact made with the Lord at the price of the sacrifice of Isaac, the son, which Jesus then takes upon himself.

42 Jesus said unto them, If God were your Father, ye would love me; for I proceeded forth and came from God; neither came I of myself, but he sent me.

43 Why do ye not understand my speech? Even because ye cannot hear my word.

44 Ye are of your father the devil, and the lusts of your father ye will do. He was a murderer from the beginning, and abode not in the truth, because there is no truth in him. When he speaketh a lie, he speaketh of his own for he is a liar, and the father of it.

45 And because I tell you the truth, ye believe me not.

Overcoming by means of love is the farewell commandment and the supreme greatness of Jesus' message:

John 13:34-35: A new commandment I give unto you, That ye love one another; as I have loved you, that ye also love one another.

35 By this shall all men know that ye are my disciples, if you have love one to another.

CONCLUSIONS RELATING TO FILICIDE

We will now present some conclusions on Jesus as a forerunner of concepts of filicide. Since we consider this to be his most transcendent teaching, we shall emphasize the expressions that relate directly to this theme. Thus, for example:

"The son of man is betrayed."

Who but his parents could betray the son of man? We consider that the conditions created by human society and intensified by the monotheistic conception conspire against any positive unity between parents and their children and that they have led the hierarchy of power in the parental generation to institute permanent systems of child sacrifice. Jesus denounces these systems quite specifically. His holocaust is the living demonstration of that denunciation. On the other hand, the Nazarene reveals his absolute knowledge of the meaning of the child's sacrifice in sociocultural development, seeking its solution in the exaltation of love.

The last words of Jesus on the cross are also an exhortation against all kinds of abandonment of children. It is an appeal for consideration towards children and respect for all their needs of identification based on the presence and loving assistance of their parents, who underestimate their children's need for affection.

"Why hast thou forsaken me?"

This lament just before death reveals that life is impossible without the loving presence of one's parents, that it is also indispensable in the first moments of life and, though to a lesser degree, in all the others. Abandonment in all its diverse forms, so destructive for the child, can also be seen when the parents' presence lacks the affectionate protection or the minimum love necessary for life.

"Before the cock crow twice, thou shalt deny me thrice."

Here Jesus shows his extraordinary understanding of the most widespread mechanism for perpetuating the sacrifice of children: denial. Thus, the process does not become conscious and can be carried on indefinitely. Denial also serves to conceal the abuse and mortification of children and, consequently, to go on inflicting them.

"Suffer little children, and forbid them not, to come unto me."

We have already said that Jesus preaches the valuation of children. It is another aspect of his anti-filicidal struggle and of his anti-gerontocratic preaching, which becomes even more explicit when he discusses the problems of the struggle between the generations.

"Love one another."

This is the most valuable formula for overcoming hatred. But the capacity for loving is based on the child's first relationship with his mother and his father, on their satisfaction with their beloved child. This satisfaction provides the model that structures love in that child, in the future adult, in mankind.

Finally, the father's homicidal condition is also made explicit:

> You are of your father the devil, and your will is to do your father's desires. He was a murderer from the beginning, and has nothing to do with the truth, because there is no truth in him; when he lies, he speaks according to his own nature, for he is a liar and the father of lies. [John 8:44]

This meditation on the lie of the homicidal father brings up a question: Could it be a direct allusion to the denial of aggressive attitudes toward children?

But the recognition of this negative aspect of the father does not imply ignorance of the existence of the loving and protecting tendencies that make life and happiness possible for children.

PART II

FILICIDE IN LITERATURE

7

Oedipus Rex by Sophocles[1]

Freud selected this tragedy by Sophocles as an example of the universality of parricide and incest in the unconscious psyche. His exemplification was considered the most perfect synthesis of the essential conflicts of the human condition. Although it retains all its value on the manifest level, it is lacking in the teleological sense and therefore invites us to search for deeper causes. It is in the strata preceding the genital conflict that we find the motivations leading to the unfolding of the tragedy. When we take psychic development back to its pregenital beginnings, we encounter the vicissitudes of the oedipal struggle at the oral level; consequently, we inevitably come across the latent factors underlying the manifest aspect of parricide and incest. In the foreground we see the bad parents, Laius and Jocasta, whose

[1]This chapter was co-authored by Matilde Rascovsky.

impulses to mutilate, kill, and desert Oedipus determine the subsequent steps that destiny prepares and the story weaves together.

Oedipus reaches maturity and commits the crimes motivated by his previously organized structure. Who today could allege that the tragedy came about suddenly, ignoring the background of the complemental series that configures it? Sophocles begins with the climactic moment of the family organization included in everyone's unconscious and leads us step-by-step to disentangle the complicated knot; as if it were a psychoanalytic treatment, the playwright shows us where the complex causes of human destiny lie, pointing out the most decisive aspects of the struggle between the generations. This monumental narrative offers us multifaceted lessons with its remarkable details on the myriad aspects of the eternal foundations of the good and bad relationship between parents and their children.

At the tragedy's climax, Oedipus falls from his royal grandeur and is accused and abused as author of the worst crimes in the eyes of the gods: parricide and incest. Later he leaves, blind, denigrated, and exiled from his state by his own children, wandering throughout Hellas in search of a place that might accept him. In this dramatic atmosphere, the most terrible curses and self-reproaches rain down on him. Oedipus feels that, from within, his residual parents—his conscience—accuse him relentlessly, driving him mercilessly to his miserable exile.

Following the conscious revelation of his tragedy (Sophocles, *Oedipus The King* 1954) and the commiseration of the chorus, the messenger from Corinth describes Jocasta's suicide and Oedipus' pain:

> And then she groaned and cursed the bed in which
> she brought forth husband by her husband, children
> by her own child, an infamous double bond.

How after that she died I do not know,—
for Oedipus distracted us from seeing.
He burst upon us shouting and we looked
to him as he paced frantically around,
begging us always: Give me a sword, I say,
to find this wife no wife, this mother's womb,
this field of double sowing whence I sprang
and where I sowed my children! As he raved
some god showed him the way—none of us there.
Bellowing terribly and led by some
invisible guide he rushed on the two doors,—
wrenching the hollow bolts out of their sockets,
he charged inside. There, there he saw his wife
hanging, the twisted rope around her neck.
When he saw her, he cried out fearfully
and cut the dangling noose. Then, as she lay,
poor woman, on the ground, what happened after,
was terrible to see. He tore the brooches—
the gold chased brooches fastening her robe—
away from her and lifting them up high
dashed them on his own eyeballs, shrieking out
such things as: they will never see the crime
I have committed or had done upon me!
Dark eyes, now in the days to come look on
forbidden faces, do not recognize
those whom you long for—with such imprecations
he struck his eyes again and yet again
with the brooches. And the bleeding eyeballs gushed
and stained his beard—no sluggish oozing drops
but a black rain and bloody hail poured down. [pp. 66–67]

Only many years later, after having suffered from over-whelming melancholia during his long pilgrimage, Oedipus recovers his psychic equilibrium and answers Creon (Sophocles, *Oedipus at Colonus* 1954):

O arrogance unashamed! Whose age do you
Think you are insulting, mine or yours?
The bloody deaths, the incest, the calamities
You speak so glibly of: I suffered them,
By fate, against my will! It was God's pleasure,
And perhaps our race had angered him long ago.
In me myself you could not find such evil
As would have made me sin against my own.
And tell me this: if these were prophecies
Repeated by the oracles of the gods,
That father's death should come through his own son,
How could you justly blame it upon me?
On me, who was yet unborn, yet unconceived,
Not yet existent for my father and mother?
If then I came into the world—as I did come—
In wretchedness, and met my father in fight,
And knocked him down, not knowing that I killed him
Nor whom I killed—again, how could you find
Guilt in that unmeditated act?
As for my mother—damn you, you have no shame,
Though you are her own brother, in forcing me
To speak of that unspeakable marriage;
But I shall speak, I'll not be silent now
After you've let your foul talk go so far!
Yes, she gave me birth—incredible fate!—
But neither of us knew the truth; and she
Bore my children also—and then her shame.
But one thing I do know: you are content
To slander her as well as me for that;
While I would not have married her willingly
Nor willingly would I ever speak of it.
No: I shall not be judged an evil man,
Neither in that marriage nor in that death
Which you forever charge me with so bitterly.—
Just answer me one thing:

If someone tried to kill you here and now,
You righteous gentleman, what would you do,
Inquire first if the stranger was your father?
Or would you not first try to defend yourself?
I think that as you like to be alive
You'd treat him as the threat required; not
Look around for assurance that you were right.
Well, that was the sort of danger I was in,
Forced into it by the gods. My father's soul,
Were it on earth, I know would bear me out. [pp. 123–125]

This clarifying passage taken from *Oedipus at Colonus* shows us that Freud's judgment of the murder of Laius was not only biased, underestimating the crime committed against Oedipus, but also omitted the circumstances that Sophocles later described in *Oedipus at Colonus*. In the latter tragedy, Oedipus denounces all the infamy that has been heaped on him.

There is a clear ethical lesson in this tragedy referring to the relationship between generations, because the conflict begins with filicide. The fateful relationship with the bad parents leads Oedipus to actively commit the crime that he first had to suffer passively. That is, the parricide and the incest are responses to the filicide, committed by Laius and Jocasta, to which he is exposed even before he is born.

But Oedipus also shows us a positive and affectionate relationship with his good parents or, in other words, with the good aspects of his parents as represented by Polybus and Merope, the rulers of Corinth who took him in and brought him up and for whom Oedipus feels deep affection and respect. Thus, he replies to Jocasta (Sophocles, *Oedipus The King* 1954):

Polybus was my father, king of Corinth,
and Merope, the Dorian, my mother.

I was held greatest of the citizens
in Corinth till a curious chance befell me
as I shall tell you — curious indeed,
but hardly worth the store I set upon it.
There was a dinner and at it a man,
a drunken man, accused me in his drink
of being bastard. I was furious
but held my temper under for that day.
Next day I went and taxed my parents with it;
they took the insult very ill from him,
the drunken fellow who had uttered it.
So I was comforted for their part, but
still this thing rankled always, for the story
crept about widely. And I went at last
to Pytho, though my parents did not know.
But Phoebus sent me home again unhonoured
in what I came to learn, but he foretold
other and desperate horrors to befall me,
that I was fated to lie with my mother,
and to show to daylight an accursed breed
which men would not endure, and I was doomed
to be murderer of the father that begot me.
When I heard this I fled, and in the days
that followed I would measure from the stars
the whereabouts of Corinth — yes, I fled
to somewhere where I should not see fulfilled
the infamies told in that dreadful oracle.
And as I journeyed I came to the place
where, as you say, this king met with his death.
Jocasta, I will tell you the whole truth.
When I was near the branching of the crossroads,
going on foot, I was encountered by
a herald and a carriage with a man in it,
just as you tell me. He that led the way
and the old man himself wanted to thrust me

out of the road by force. I became angry
and struck the coachman who was pushing me.
When the old man saw this he watched his moment,
and as I passed he struck me from his carriage,
full on the head with his two pointed goad.
But he was paid in full and presently
my stick had struck him backwards from the car
and he rolled out of it. And then I killed them
all. If it happened there was any tie
of kinship twixt this man and Laius,
who is then now more miserable than I,
what man on earth so hated by the Gods,
since neither citizen nor foreigner
may welcome me at home or even greet me,
but drive me out of doors? And it is I,
I and no other have so cursed myself.
And I pollute the bed of him I killed
by the hands that killed him. Was I not born evil?
Am I not utterly unclean? I had to fly
and in my banishment not even see
my kindred nor set foot in my own country,
or otherwise my fate was to be yoked
in marriage with my mother and kill my father,
Polybus who begot me and had reared me.
Would not one rightly judge and say that on me
these things were sent by some malignant God?
O no, no, no—O holy majesty
of God on high, may I not see that day!
May I be gone out of men's sight before
I see the deadly taint of this disaster
come upon me. [pp. 45–46]

The earlier defense of his good parents, which led him to
leave Corinth never to return, is expressed further on when the

messenger arrives to announce the death of Polybus and his right
to the Corinthian throne (Sophocles, *Oedipus The King*, 1954):

> *Oedipus*: Ha! Ha! O dear Jocasta, why should one
> look to the Pythian hearth? Why should one look
> to the birds screaming overhead? They prophesied
> that I should kill my father! But he's dead,
> and hidden deep in earth, and I stand here who never laid a hand
> on spear against him,
> unless perhaps he died of longing for me,
> and thus I am his murderer. But they,
> the oracles, as they stand—he's taken them
> away with him, they're as dead as he himself is,
> and worthless. [p. 51]

And later:

> *Oedipus*: O no! Once on a time Loxias said
> that I should lie with my own mother and
> take on my hands the blood of my own father.
> And so for these long years I've lived away
> from Corinth; it has been to my great happiness;
> but yet it's sweet to see the face of parents.
>
> *Messenger*: This was the fear which drove you out of Corinth?
>
> *Oedipus*: Old man, I did not wish to kill my father.
>
> *Messenger*: Why should I not free you from this fear, sir,
> since I have come to you in all goodwill?
>
> *Oedipus* : You would not find me thankless if you did.
>
> *Messenger*: Why, it was just for this I brought the news,—
> to earn your thanks when you had come safe home.

Oedipus: No, I will never come near my parents.

Messenger: Son,
it's very plain you don't know what you're doing.

Oedipus: What do you mean, old man? For God's sake, tell me.

Messenger: If your homecoming is checked by fears like these.

Oedipus: Yes, I'm afraid that Phoebus may prove right.

Messenger: The murder and the incest?

Oedipus: Yes, old man;
that is my constant terror.

Messenger: Do you know
that all your fears are empty?

Oedipus: How is that,
if they are father and mother and I their son?

Messenger: Because Polybus was no kin to you in blood.

Oedipus: What, was not Polybus my father?

Messenger: No more than I but just so much.

Oedipus: How can
my father be my father as much as one that's nothing to me?

Messenger: Neither he nor I
begat you.

Oedipus: Why then did he call me son?

Messenger: A gift he took you from these hands of mine.

Oedipus: Did he love so much what he took from another's hand?

Messenger: His childlessness before persuaded him.

Oedipus: Was I a child you bought or found when I
was given to him?

Messenger: On Cithaeron's slopes
in the twisting thickets you were found. [pp. 52–54]

It is his beloved parents whom Oedipus tries to protect
when he exiles himself from Corinth and promises never to
return to avoid the fulfillment of the oracle's prediction. This is
the model that organizes exogamy. Through the good parents,
Polybus and Merope, his exit from the family home is encour-
aged as soon as the conflict arises. At the same time and on the
other hand, Laius and Jocasta are the parents who condemn him
to maintain his endogamy and to the impossibility of overcoming the conflict in which Oedipus has become enmeshed.
For this reason, the fixation provoked by the bad parents leads
Oedipus to go back to Thebes where his ill fate will be inexorably
fulfilled.

There is another example that confirms Oedipus' response
to the kindly actions he has received. When he kills his father in
self-defense at the crossroads as his father attempts to murder
him for the second time, he also strikes out at the other members
of the party and kills all of them except one: the same shepherd
who took pity on Oedipus when his parents ordered him to kill
the child on Mount Cithaeron. Thus, instead of killing Oedipus,
the shepherd saves his life and gives him to the messenger from
Corinth, who in turn gives him to the rulers of that country.
Oedipus saves the good object who rescued him and who
eventually will testify to the circumstances of his crime.

The tragedy starts as the beginning of the working through
of Oedipus' former actions that have remained unconscious. In
due course, the manic defenses that he has built up to conceal the
process slowly fall to pieces. The first to fall is the denial of the
traumatic facts of the beginning of Oedipus' life, followed by the
fall of his idealization and omnipotence. Once these denials have

been torn down, the deeper processes come to the surface: Oedipus is first and foremost an ill-fated, persecuted child, a child sent away to be killed by order of his criminal parents. The oracle's condemning prediction is not limited to announcing his parents' ill will toward him long before his birth; when he is born his parents, besides mutilating him by piercing his feet, order a shepherd to kill him or to abandon him when he is three days old. These circumstances create the persecutory fixation point to which he later regresses.

His parents' initial desertion and the consequent disturbance of an appropriate introjection of them leads the ego to lose its capacity for developing defenses that would allow gradual working through of the anxiety. This enormous anxiety that threatens to destroy the ego is inhibited or countered by the use of extreme manic defenses, especially denial. But the excessive use of denial leads to the failure of the subsequent process of repression.

The use of denial instead of repression is the salient mechanism in Oedipus since what is essential in the drama is his inability to repress the parricide and incest that are instead acted out. This action involves uncontrollable hate toward the parents who abandoned him. However, during his early development Oedipus maintains his psychic equilibrium by denying the existence of his bad parents and by resorting to a typical family romance by means of idealization displaced to the sovereigns of Corinth who support this process with their kindly behavior. This goes on until denial and idealization are broken through when Oedipus learns that Polybus and Merope are not his parents. Then his threatened psychic equilibrium leads him to regress to his earliest fixations. As we have already said, this is the meaning of his return to Thebes where, with renewed denial and full of omnipotence, he acts out his unrepressed aggression toward his father. Following primitive patterns, he identifies with the aggressor and, replete with manic triumph, kills his father at the crossroads. He charges on with uncontrollably impetuous omnipotence and comes up against a displaced image of his mother incarnated in the fearful Sphinx, murderer of young Thebans. This time it is he, condemned to be murdered by his mother, who triumphs over the homicidal mother.

This must be seen as a splitting of the figure of the persecutory mother. Insofar as the Sphinx is the suffocating image of the criminal mother, Jocasta acquires the meaning of the same image in an idealized form. This dissociation keeps Oedipus from becoming aware of the unity of this persecutory figure and consequently he continues his relationship with the idealized bad object, placing the death tendencies in the Sphinx and the erotic tendencies in Jocasta. In the beginning there was a dissociation of the parental couple between Jocasta–Laius and Polybus–Merope; it is now a dissociation only of the maternal figure, which indicates even deeper regression. Maintaining the denial, Oedipus then marries her and immediately puts his manic defenses to work, always basically at the price of denial. These defenses allow him to maintain his psychic equilibrium until the moment at which the tragedy begins to reach its climax.

The tragedy begins when denial and manic defenses can no longer be supported by such an impoverished ego. This impoverishment is seen in its projection to Thebes: the poverty, the sterility, and the plague afflicting it. Thus, Thebes represents Oedipus himself since, from the beginning, the idealization, omnipotence, and dissociation of the ego itself have been broken down, keeping him from being conscious of what is happening. Also, the denigration of his objects, represented again by Thebes, has reached an extreme and begins to be unbearable. The suppliants tell him so, hounding him as urgent external and psychic realities, showing him the calamities and plagues afflicting Thebes.

As investigation into the murder of Laius proceeds and the veil of denial is lifted, Tyresias arrives at the scene. Tyresias[2] is the dissociated, denied, and projected part of Oedipus' ego that perceives the painful psychic reality and appears on stage in order to join the rest of it. This reintegration takes place through constant struggle and includes fleeting persecutory relapses. His efforts to deny the conflict and his guilt lead Oedipus to act: he sends Creon to consult the oracle. His feverish action continues, looking for people in the external world to accuse of the crimes in order to make them depositories for his own denied criminal parts. For this reason, when Tyresias, after much vacillation, finally tells him that he is Laius' murderer, Oedipus in a renewed attempt at projection turns the accusation against Tyresias, just as he later does against Creon.

But external and psychic reality pressure him increasingly, seeking to influence his obstructed perception. Finally, the testimonies of reality presented by the messenger from Corinth and by the shepherd can no longer be denied. The shepherd received Oedipus from Jocasta herself when he was barely three days old and he, moved by pity, let the messenger from Corinth take him away. It is the same shepherd who, years later, escaped alive when Oedipus killed Laius and all the rest of his retinue.

While Oedipus is gaining awareness that the man he killed

---

[2]Roheim (1952) has written: "Tyresias and Oedipus are two aspects of the same person. Therefore, they are the only two persons who know who could have committed the crime, and the dialogue between them is between the repression (Oedipus) and the return of the repressed (Tyresias). We would say between the denied and the return of the denied" (p. 531).

is his father Laius, the messenger announces that Polybus, his idealized good father, has died. At this moment the dissociation between the persecutory and the idealized father is broken. In the face of the irrefutable statements of the messenger and the shepherd, Jocasta commits suicide, thus putting an end to the idealized part of the filicidal mother, at the moment when the shepherd says that she gave him the child for him to kill.

Once the defenses that kept Oedipus from seeing his horrendous reality are torn down, persecutory anxieties rush in that are so overwhelming that they push him to another act of desperation, this time of the melancholic type: he puts out his eyes with Jocasta's brooch, again obeying the pattern of submission to the aggressions of the mother who pierced his feet when he was born. When Oedipus puts out his eyes, the dissociation between him and Tyresias is cancelled and his ego again takes upon itself what it had before placed in the sightless seer. Now, it is he who is sightless.

Oedipus' loss of his eyes is generally interpreted as a displacement of the genital castration to which the superego has condemned him for his incestuous relationship. Deeper than this, the loss of external vision is related to his acquisition of internal vision, a characteristic of the seer Tyresias as well.

When Oedipus abjures his acts, he renounces his external vision and in compensation strengthens his inner vision, like Tyresias. The alternation and antagonism between outer and inner vision is another aspect of his ego's extreme splitting; it is expressed in this culminating event of the tragedy.

In the messenger's version we can see the beginning of the process of repression: (Sophocles, *Oedipus The King* 1954)

> . . . dashed them on his own eyeballs, shrieking out
> such things as: they will never see the crime

I have committed or had done upon me!
Dark eyes, now in the days to come look on
forbidden faces, do not recognize
those whom you long for . . . [pp. 66 –67]

Once the manic defenses have fallen, the melancholic self-reproaches begin (Sophocles, *Oedipus The King* 1954):

Oedipus: Take me away, and haste—to a place out of the way!
Take me away, my friends, the greatly miserable,
the most accursed, whom God too hates
above all men on earth! [p. 69]

Thus, he again suffers the abuse and hatred of his progenitors who now work from within. Then, he submits even further to his parents' wishes. Thus, he repeats:

Curse on the man who took
the cruel bonds from off my legs, as I lay in the field.
He stole me from death and saved me,
no kindly service.
Had I died then
I would not be so burdensome to friends. [p. 69]

And he adds:

Then I would not have come
to kill my father and marry my mother infamously.
Now I am godless and child of impurity,
begetter in the same seed that created my wretched self.
If there is any ill worse than ill,
that is the lot of Oedipus. [p. 69]

But Oedipus goes on living and the melancholic process continues in *Oedipus at Colonus*. Thebes, projection of a part of Oedipus, cannot shake off its conflicts, immersed as it is in fratricidal struggle, and the ongoing unhappiness impedes any depressive and reparatory working through.

All to the contrary, Athens, under its sovereign Theseus, who was dearly loved by his father Aegeus, enjoys the peace and prosperity that, according to the oracle, would be gained by the death of Oedipus.

Before dying in the kingdom of the son of the good father, Oedipus learns of the oracle's prophecy from his daughter Ismene (Sophocles, *Oedipus the King* 1954):

> *Oedipus*: You have some hope then that [the gods] are concerned With my deliverance?
>
> *Ismene*: I have, father.
> The latest sentences of the oracle . . .
>
> *Oedipus*: How are they worded? What do they prophesy?
>
> *Ismene*: That you shall be much solicited by our people Before your death – and after – for their welfare
>
> *Oedipus*: And what could anyone hope from such as I?
>
> *Ismene*: The oracles declare their strength's in you –
>
> *Oedipus*: When I am finished, I suppose I am strong!
>
> *Ismene*: For the gods who threw you down sustain you now. . . .
>
> *Oedipus*: What good am I to them outside the country?
>
> *Ismene*: It is merely that if your burial were unlucky,
> That would be perilous for them. [pp. 96–97]

In the tragedy, Oedipus must disappear without a trace. The oracle has announced that from his anonymous tomb he will give peace and prosperity to the land that receives him. In the same way, filicide, parricide, and incest must be totally repressed in order to ensure the peace and progressive prosperity of each human being. The Oedipus complex must remain hidden after it has existed and has been intensely experienced in the first six years of life. But the condition for its repression is that the intensity of the stimulating and especially the aggressive acts of the parents must not exceed what is acceptable and susceptible to working through with the contribution of affectionate and tender forces from the loving and positive parents. The repressed existence of filicide, parricide, and incest is the essential foundation of human development, but its unrepressed expression leads to uncontrollable acts and criminal behavior, criminal behavior which, as in the case of *Oedipus the King*, always originates in the parents' attitude.

8

Dostoyevsky and Filicide[1]

There is a central event in Dostoyevsky's life in which we can recognize, if not full paternity, at least a fundamental motivation in the genesis of his last and definitive work: *The Brothers Karamazov.* That event was the death of Alyosha, his youngest child. In the year 1878, when the boy was 3, he suffered his first epileptic seizure, as a result of which he died without regaining consciousness.

Dostoyevsky's grief and guilt were boundless. He accused himself of having transmitted his illness to his son, feeling responsible for his death. In his last work we shall find innumerable manifestations of that grief and remorse. Thus, Mitya Karamazov exclaims: "We are all responsible for all." That death reactivated the intense generational conflict and its climax in Dostoyevsky's relationship with his children and, on a deeper level, with his terrible father. *The Brothers Karamazov* is a final working-through of his drama. Guilt and the need for expiation are the feelings that dominate this work; it shows us how, through creative work, Dostoyevsky managed to mitigate and to

[1]This chapter was co-authored by Matilde Rascovsky.

overcome his overwhelming grief. He died in 1881, a few months after the three years it took him to write *The Brothers Karamazov*.

As a basis for this hypothesis, we must first point out the resurrection of the dead child's name in the central and noblest character of the novel: Alyosha Karamazov. This name is found again in another passing and meaningful character, Alyosha, the deceased 3-year-old child of a peasant woman who in her desperation seeks consolation in the same convent Alyosha Karamazov wishes to enter as a novice. The name appears once again in the phonetic similarity of the name Ilusha, the boy whose death inserts a subplot into the larger novel.

Can we then consider that *The Brothers Karamazov* was written as an attempt to work through the mourning for the pathetic death of Dostoyevsky's child? To what extent did guilt and torment over his child's death lead Dostoyevsky to create in fiction the contrary retaliatory murder of the father? Can it be that in the process of his melancholia he thought that the father, Dostoyevsky himself, should have died instead of the son? Or must we add that perhaps his childhood history and the death of his own father, who was murdered, form the cumulative elements that motivate this narrative? There is a powerful argument that supports this hypothesis: the fact that Dostoyevsky gave his own name, Fyodor, to the most execrable character in the novel, the father of the Karamazov brothers. We must consider that these motivations, rather than conflicting, coincide.

The conflict between parricide and filicide develops throughout the plot. Hidden behind the manifest and superficial fact of the murder of the father, we shall find the latent and profound drama: the murder of the sons through constant mortification, abandonment, and neglect. In the novel, as happens in real life, the child is accused of a crime he has not committed. Also, as in real life, justice fails to take into account

the true crime or crimes: the abandonment, abuse, and mortification to which Fyodor Karamazov, as a symbol of humanity
itself, has subjected his sons.

The novel is divided into four parts and an epilogue. The
crucial theme is constituted when the Karamazov brothers, now
adults, are reunited with their father. The resentments, demands, and consequent conflicts between them are centralized
in the arguments between the father and his eldest son, Mitya,
who reclaims the inheritance his mother has left him. At the
same time, father and son are rivals for the woman Mitya loves,
whom his father tries to win away from him with promises of
money. At this point the father is murdered and the circumstances surrounding the crime develop. The jury's verdict condemning the innocent son closes the novel.

This work is unfinished in a way. From Dostoyevsky's notes
we know that he had planned to include it in a longer work that
was to be called *The Life of a Sinner* in which the main protago-
nist would be Alyosha, his beloved son and favorite hero,
presented as the visionary whose life, it is said, will be a Calvary
before he attains peace through religion. Dostoyevsky's project
for the future was to write a book about Jesus, evidently following up on his ideas about the sacrificed son.

Although Freud (1928, *Standard Edition* 21) wrote that *The
Brothers Karamazov* was the most accomplished novel ever
written and that one of the chapters was "one of the high points
of universal literature," he felt and clearly expressed his reluc-
tance to comment on it and to write the preface for the German
translation of the complete works of Dostoyevsky requested from
him by editors René Fullop and Müller Eckstein.

In 1926 he began to write the preface that he would entitle
"Dostoyevsky and Parricide," finishing and publishing it only in
1928 under pressure from Eitingon, who sent him the complete

correspondence of the great Russian novelist in an attempt to stimulate Freud to write. The essay provoked severe criticism from Reik and also from Ernest Jones (1964). For the latter, Freud had not gone further than the manifest contents, since the theme of parricide was on the surface. For his part, Reik criticized the moralistic point of view taken by Freud. We will come back to this criticism and will attempt to discover the latent contents of *The Brothers Karamazov*, which both Jones and Reik found lacking in Freud's text.

Although the novel itself refers to the murder of Fyodor Karamazov, the author has not been able to omit the background of the crime: the birth and painful childhood of the accused brothers-sons, developing the theme of guilt, its origin, and expiation throughout the novel. To do this, the tale begins with the story of the infancy of the four brothers, all sons of the same father, but of three different mothers. Fyodor Karamazov, the father, is, as we have already said, the projection of an aspect of Fyodor Dostoyevsky. He is described as a psychopathic personality, a buffoon, and a maliciously depraved individual who is only interested in satisfying his desires without the least consideration for others. He manages to marry first a rich noblewoman, with whom he has his first son, Dmitri. But when the child is only 3 years old, the mother, tired of her lamentable marriage, runs away with another man, abandoning her child. A servant couple, Grigory and Marfa, pitying the child's helplessness, take him in. Dmitri then lives in the servants' cottage, ignored by his father until a relative of his mother takes him to Moscow to school. Mitya (the diminutive of Dmitri) is 4 when, after the death of his ill and degraded mother, his father again marries, this time a poor orphan who had already attempted suicide. The licentious life and abuse of Fyodor Karamazov finally lead his second wife to psychosis and death, leaving two sons, Ivan and Alyosha, at that time aged 7 and 4, respectively. They are also ignored and abandoned by their father and taken in by the same servant couple until a relative protects them, taking them to Moscow. The brothers only meet again as adults when they get together with the rest of the family in their father's house.

The fourth son is Smerdyakov, the son unrecognized by his father, whose mother, a poor idiot whom Fyodor raped, dies when giving birth to the baby one night in Karamazov's bath house. The child is taken in by Grigory and Marfa and becomes the cook and confidant of his father.

We shall now attempt to sketch a brief summary of the novel's plot. Fyodor Karamazov is living in his suburban house, attended by his servants, Grigory and Marfa, and by his illegitimate and epileptic son, Smerdyakov who, as we have said, works as his cook. The novel begins with the stormy arrival, on different dates, of the three legitimate sons, who have all interrupted their studies, though on the verge of finishing them, to return to their father's house. The first to arrive is Alyosha, prompted by the desire to visit his mother's tomb. As soon as he arrives, he establishes an intense relationship with Father Zossima, the spiritual leader of a monastery, which after a time Alyosha decides to enter as a novice. Later, Mitya, the only son of the first marriage, and Ivan, the elder of the sons of the second marriage, arrive, and the four brothers meet together with their father for the first time.

Mitya, agitated and resentful, comes to claim his mother's inheritance that his father has stolen from him under various pretexts. From the outset there is a dispute over Gruschenka, a loose woman whom Mitya loves and with whom the old man falls in love, to the point of fighting with his son over her. Ivan, afraid of what might happen between his father and Mitya, tries to mediate between them, but is at the same time in love with Mitya's fiancée.

Mitya is described as impulsive and rash, the one most identified with his father's character. Ivan seems to represent the intellectual of the period, a spirit tortured by the social ills he sees, aloof from the church and a fighter for human rights. Alyosha, the youngest, on the other hand represents mystical and conciliatory sweetness. The illegitimate son, Smerdyakov, who is the only one who has remained in his father's house, is the one who will commit the crime.

Why has the epileptic Dostoyevsky made the epileptic son the criminal? Is it perhaps the persecutory guilt that arises in the form of melancholic self-reproaches for having destroyed the object of his love, his son, also reactivating the emotions associated with the murder of his own father? Is it his defense against the crime committed by the epileptic son, the most humiliated and denigrated of the sons, with whom Dostoyevsky has identified?

The novel takes place in a short period of time and presents a situation of constant threat between the father and his sons. In a culminating moment, in their eagerness to clear up the problem, the entire family and their close friends meet in the cell of Father Zossima who directs the monastery where Alyosha lives. At this meeting, which we later analyze in detail, the oedipal conflict between father Fyodor and his son Mitya surfaces immediately. The son accuses his father of having stolen his mother's inheritance with tricks and of trying to take away his lover Gruschenka by seducing her with money. The father in turn accuses his son of having abused an old employee of his, seizing him by the beard, dragging him out into the street and beating him publicly, only because he worked for Fyodor. He also reproaches him for seeing a loose woman like Gruschenka, while being betrothed to and able to marry a woman of his own class. It is around this oedipal situation that the events leading to the crime develop. The murder is planned in great detail by Smerdyakov who believes he is thus carrying out the secret wishes of Ivan, who has seduced him with his anticlerical ideology and attacks on authority. In order to accomplish it, he draws Ivan away from the father's house, convincing him that he should take a trip. Then, he tells Mitya that his father has offered Gruschenka three thousand rubles to marry him and at the same time he confides the way that Smerdyakov is to knock for the father to open the door in case Gruschenka arrives at the house and accepts the offer. Thus, he prepares the means for Mitya, furious, to fall upon his father, or if he himself commits the crime, for all the evidence to point to Mitya. On the night of the crime, he pretends to suffer a severe epileptic fit and apparently stays in bed, unconscious.

Meanwhile, Mitya arrives that same night at Gruschenka's house and finds that she has gone out. The servant girls, frightened by his anger, do not dare confess that Gruschenka has gone to the nearby town to meet a military man she had an affair with years before and whom she never stopped loving in spite of having left him. When he does not find Gruschenka, Mitya supposes that she has accepted his father's offer and runs out in a fury to look for her. He climbs over the garden fence and his father, hearing the noise, thinks it is Gruschenka and calls out to her, which makes Mitya understand that his beloved is not there. When he attempts to leave and again climb over the fence he meets Grigory, the servant, who has been awakened by the cries and tries to stop him because he thinks that Mitya has killed his father, to the point that he accuses him of parricide. In his attempt to escape, Mitya pushes the servant and hits him with an object he has in his hand. Horrified when he sees him fall down bloodied, he flees without knowing whether he has killed Grigory. Then he returns to Gruschenka's house, where the servants tell him the truth. He runs out seeking his lover, bent on seeing her for the last time before killing himself. But when he finds her, things turn out differently. Her relationship with the military man has failed and Gruschenka confesses her love for Mitya and her desire to formalize their relationship. At this moment the court official arrives and accuses Mitya of his father's murder. Mitya thinks at first that he is referring to the death of Grigory and accepts his guilt; but later he discovers his error and knows that he is innocent of the crime of which he is accused. The oedipal conflict ends in this way: at the moment in which Mitya attains the love of the woman he also loves, both the external authority and his own superego accuse and condemn him; he submits to both agencies.

The last part of the central scheme of the novel centers on the trial and conviction. Ivan goes mad when he learns that he has been the unwilling instigator of the crime. Smerdyakov, who has confessed to Ivan that he was the only murderer, hangs himself, since the idealized relationship with Ivan has ended and he is overwhelmed by intense guilt feelings. Once this witness has disappeared, no one accepts Ivan's accusation of Smedyakov. Ivan, ill and desperate over the uselessness of his defense, gives himself up to a permanent delusion and, in spite of the speech of the lawyer who tries to demonstrate Mitya's innocence, in spite of the general belief that the accused will be declared innocent, the jury decides he is guilty and condemns him to twenty years of forced labor in Siberia.

This general outline of the work, which we present to refresh the reader's memory, is also meant to highlight the unjust accusation of parricide against Mitya, for which he is condemned. This is one of the saddest aspects of human ethics: the perpetual accusation of the child for crimes he or she has never committed and the projection onto the child of crimes committed by the parents.

Might it have been Dostoyevsky's intention, as Freud considers in his article, to condemn not only parricide but even the desire to commit it? Or more deeply, was it to denounce human injustice that is blinded and terrible when someone, by rebelling against the instituted paternal authority, threatens to break down the psychic and social integrity that has been achieved by constant projection of the guilt onto the children? The emergence of this theme in the novel–the rebellious son sacrificed–mobilizes latent tensions; and the oedipal problem, with its essentially filicidal components, takes center stage.

Freud centered his analysis of the novel on the oedipal problem–the son's jealousy of his father–ambivalence–parricide. He also identified Fyodor Karamazov with Mihail, Dostoyevsky's father, a brutal and miserly man who was murdered by his serfs whom he abused and tortured. The murder of Dostoyevsky's father was the *consequence* of the continual abuse of the *serf-sons* by their master-father and indicates the degree to which Mihail Dostoyevsky was cruel and despotic toward his sons. Freud failed to give sufficient weight to the father's criminal attitude when he interpreted the oedipal conflict, following the classical terms of the son's envy of his father, the ambivalence, the homosexuality, and the consequent death wishes. What Freud denies is the total relation between this situation and the father's previous attitude of abandonment, denigration, negligence, and abuse of his sons. Although Fyodor's death is fully justified in the novel, the same is not true of the condemnation of Mitya, which is a tremendous judicial error. Further, he has not only been declared guilty and sentenced but also, psychically

defeated, he submits passively, overwhelmed by the real persecutory situation, by his guilt feelings and because of submission
to the superego, an internal residue of the brutality of his father
and of the society that he represents.

In his paper, Freud studied Dostoyevsky's personality from
four vantage points: as a poet, as a neurotic, as a moralist, and as
a sinner. Reik (1945) pointed out that he had left out a very
important aspect, that of the psychologist. As a poet, Freud
situated Dostoyevsky on a par with Shakespeare, but his judgment is excessively severe when he judges him from the moral
point of view. For Freud, a person is moral when he is able to
repress and renounce to his desires; repentance would only be a
means to make homicide possible. This induced him to situate
Dostoyevsky among criminals, while taking into account the
redeemable aspects of his personality through the characters of
his works. Freud also thinks that his sadomasochistic structure
led him to be irritable, irascible, and intolerant towards the
people he loved, or to turn this aggression against himself,
becoming a submissive, guilt-ridden masochist. Freud also discusses "his perverse instinctive disposition" and Dostoyevsky's
epilepsy, which he analyzes in terms of hysteroepilepsy or severe
hysteria, adding that the neurosis had already begun in infancy
in the form of melancholia with hypochondriacal fears of being
buried alive. In these attacks and fears of death, Freud sees the
realization in his own self of the death he wishes for his father,
and he affirms that the son wants to take the father's place, both
because he loves and admires him and also because he hates and
wishes to get rid of him. That is the same theme as in the manifest
contents of Oedipus the King by Sophocles, except that in the
Greek drama everything happens without Oedipus' knowing
that the characters are his parents or, as happens in Hamlet,

where the desires of the son appear displaced to another character who carries out what he himself dreams of doing.

We have analyzed elsewhere (Rascovsky 1967) the filicidal aspects of Sophocles' play, ignored or denied in Freud's interpretation of the tragedy, and we have said that the basic factor promoting the acting out or the crime of Oedipus or of Karamazov, resulting in the impossibility of organizing the repression of parricidal tendencies, is always the persecutory exacerbation that stems from the parents' filicidal impulses. These tendencies are not only expressed as murder or death threats against the Oedipus-son, but also in multiple forms of abandonment, punishment, mutilation, and submission. Our purpose has been to point out that the filicidal tendencies of the parents must *always* be included in the oedipal conflict, tendencies that are constantly denied and that provoke parricidal wishes in the children as a secondary consequence, as an irrevocable identification.

In this context, Dostoyevsky's relationship with his internalized father is most revealing and appears in the novel in the conflicts that arise between Karamazov and his sons. For this reason, before going on to analyze the novel, we shall briefly summarize Dostoyevsky's biography, since in his last work there are many events that refer only too directly to his own life.

Mihail Andreyevich Dostoyevsky, Fyodor's father, was the son of a pastor who had decided he too should enter the Church. But he managed to follow his vocation, medicine. He ran away from home and participated in the Franco-Russian war as an army doctor. Later, he was given a position as a doctor in the Mariskaya hospital, then a hospital for the poor.

Mihail was despotic and cruel to everyone, even to his own family; and, although he suffered periodic depressive fits, when he recovered he returned to his role as tyrant. Although he did not physically abuse his children, his mute fury was even more terrible. Singularly stingy, he exercised rigid control over all who lived around him and he was in constant fear of being robbed or cheated. Aside from these paranoid manifestations, he also suffered from jealous delusions. The Dostoyevsky family lived next to the hospital, separated only by a fence. In spite of his father's prohibition, Fyodor liked to chat with the inmates and throughout his childhood he had daily contact with those suffering masses alienated from society, with those miserable and abused people.

There were three brothers: Mihail, Fyodor, and Andrey. When their mother died, Fyodor, who was then 16, was sent with Mihail to study at the military engineering school in Moscow. For the first time, Fyodor was able to observe the oppressed life of the Russian peasants, their condition as serfs. He saw them beaten like animals and witnessed the sordid scenes that he would later paint in his novels. This cruelty of man toward man increased the sad and grief-ridden feelings of his childhood that contributed to his tendency to depressive nervous crises, hypochondria, and epilepsy; at the same time, it drove him to fight ideologically for a more concerned and just society. His father, disconsolate over his wife's death, lived at that time in a country property where he sank into alcoholism and became even more cruel and miserly.

Fyodor survived in very poor and miserable living conditions. On one occasion, lacking the most basic means of subsistence while continuing his studies, he writes the following in a letter to his father (Troyat 1960)

My good and beloved father. Do not believe that your son, in asking you for financial help, asks for something superfluous . . . I have a head, I have arms. If I could manage alone I would not ask you for even a kopeck and I would become used to poverty. But dear pappa, remember that at this moment I am in a service . . . and I must, like it or not, adapt to the rules of the society in which I live. Right now camp life requires at least forty roubles for each student. I do not include in this sum tea or sugar, even though they are indispensable when one is numbed by the rain in a camp tent after doing extenuating maneuvers, worn out by the cold . . . One can fall ill, something that happened to me last year. But taking into account your annoyance I will do without the tea. I only ask you for enough to buy plain boots. . . . [pp. 45–46]

The father's answer is demonstrative of his stinginess in spite of his wealth:

I myself have nothing to wear. I haven't had a suit made in four years, I haven't a kopeck for myself. However, I will send you thirty-five roubles . . . spend them intelligently . . . because I will not be able to send you more. [p. 46]

In a letter to his brother Mihail, Fyodor writes:

You complain of your poverty . . . during the maneuvers I haven't had a kopeck in my pocket . . . I got sick from the cold, it rained all the time and we had no shelter . . . and from hunger too, because I had nothing to pay for a sip of hot tea with. I don't know if my melancholic ideas will ever go away. [p. 46]

At the same time Fyodor was asking his father for money to subsist on, his father was murdered by his serfs, weary of his cruelty, miserliness, and abuse. According to most of his biographers, when Dostoyevsky learns of his father's death he has his first attack of epilepsy.

In Moscow, Dostoyevsky devotes three years to reading the great Russian and foreign writers. He was drawn to the tragic aspect of life, especially the sad existence of helpless and lowly people; although he was educated in a conservative milieu, he felt attracted by a circle of writers more interested in political and social problems than in literary ones. In 1848, he joins an even more radical group. Thus, at the end of a meeting in which he speaks out against censorship and demands the abolition of restrictions and reform of the laws, Dostoyevsky is arrested. He shows no sign of submission and demands the right to free discussion of political ideas and the liberation of the serfs. In 1849, at age 28, he is condemned to death and considered a dangerous revolutionary. After the famous simulated execution by firing squad, his sentence is reduced to 8 years of forced labor in Siberia. In 1857, when he has served his sentence, he marries a widow with a child, but the marriage fails. Authorized to return to Saint Petersburg in 1859, Dostoyevsky is no longer the violent revolutionary militant nor what Turgenev said of him: "the most malignant Christian." Confinement and isolation have seemingly increased his intense persecutory anxieties that lead him regressively to submit to order, authority, religion, and the masochistic compulsion to gamble. Finally, he becomes a fanatic defender of the czar. However, in his literary work he is always a leftist writer, acclaimed by young people because of his anti-gerontocratic convictions.

In 1867, three years after his wife's death, he marries again and because of his new wife's ability to organize things, his economic situation improves notably. They have a daughter who dies when she is 2 months old and then another. Then two sons are born: Fyodor in 1871 and in 1875 Alexey, the favorite, who dies when he is 3 during his first attack of epilepsy.

At the end of his life, Dostoyevsky sees a period of revolutionary unrest in Russia, but he is already in the conservative camp and even accepts a position as director of a reactionary newspaper. In his last days, he believes that his country's destiny is to resolve European contradictions.

Returning to the study of his major work, we observe that the drama of the Karamazov family is unleashed, just as in *Oedipus the King* and in *Hamlet*, when the sons return home. They all return because they have bonds, however disturbed, with their families, but at the same time have fundamental differences from them. We could add that they return to seek the love that is owed to them and to respond to the hate with which they were nourished. In this imperative return we see the ego deterioration in their personalities that will lead them, through diverse pathological manifestations, to the drama and its consequences. It is evident that the ruptures in the processes of identification, as well as in the active identifications with the bad attitudes of the parents they have experienced passively, explain the essence of the plot. The lack of good or positive identifications and the excess of bad or negative identifications are the factors leading to the tragedy. The description of the conflicts resulting from the meeting between Karamazov and his adult sons is extraordinarily valuable and places Dostoyevsky among the great predecessors of contemporary psychology and sociology.

In effect, what happens when a father lacking any capability as such, irresponsibly assumes that role? Fyodor Karamazov feels threatened by his sons, whom he sees as competitors to be feared. Their arrival dismantles the precarious equilibrium of the symbiosis beteween Fyodor and Smerdyakov, his trusted epileptic son, depositary of his illness. This upset provokes the reactivation of psychic anxieties in which persecution, envy, and jealousy predominate. Although it is he, Fyodor, who cheats his sons out of the inheritance of their respective mothers, he himself feels cheated by them because of his massive projection. He wants to deny and ignore the existence of his sons now, just as he did when they were children. But once the symbiosis with Smerdyakov is broken, that is, once the depositary is lost, the father reacts manically, trying to compete with Mitya, his eldest son, for the love of the lover-mother, represented this time by Gruschenka. In consequence, he fails.

We have already shown how the oedipal conflict takes shape during the first meeting in father Zossima's cell. A character who witnesses the scene comments:

> A father is jealous of his son's relations with a woman of loose behaviour and intrigues with the creature to get his son into prison! [p. 70]

Old Fyodor reacts, blindly and omnipotently threatening his son:

> "if you were not my son I would challenge you this instant to a duel . . . with pistols, at three paces . . . across a handkerchief. . ."

> Dmitri frowned painfully, and looked with unutterable contempt at his father. "I thought . . . I thought . . . that I was coming to my native place with the angel of my heart, my betrothed, to cherish his old age, and I find nothing but a depraved profligate, a despicable clown!"

> "A duel!" yelled the old wretch again . . .

> "Why is such a man alive?" Dmitri, beside himself with rage, growled in a hollow voice . . . "Tell me, can he be allowed to go on defiling the earth?" . . . and pointed at the old man.

> "Listen, listen, monks, to the parricide!" cried Fyodor . . . [p. 70]

This scene ends abruptly when Father Zossima gets up suddenly, moves towards Dmitri, and, as a sign of compassion, foreseeing his future suffering, bows down at Dmitri's feet till his forehead touches the floor:

"Forgive me, all of you! . ."

Dmitri stood for a few moments in amazement . . . what did it mean? Suddenly he cried out aloud, "Oh God!" hid his face in his hands, and rushed out of the room. [p. 71]

In this first confrontation and presentation of the conflict in Zossima's cell, something meaningful happens. When the family is together prior to Mitya's arrival, a group of women despairing over the deaths of their children request to see Zossima, seeking consolation in his words. The first of them to speak is, as we mentioned before, a poor melancholic peasant who has lost her little 3-year-old Alyosha. We have also said that both the name and the age are the same as those of Dostoyevsky's own dead child (Dostoyevsky 1966):

"What are you weeping for?"

"It's my little son I'm grieving for, Father. He was 3 years old—3 years all but 3 months. For my little boy, Father. I'm in anguish, for my little boy. He was the last one. We had four . . . I buried the first three without grieving overmuch, and now I have buried the last I can't forget him. He seems always standing before me. He never leaves me. He has withered my heart . . . I lay out all that is left of him, all his little things. I look at them and wail."

"And if only I could look upon him one little time, if only I could peep at him one little time [remember that Alyosha Dostoyevsky died without regaining consciousness], without going up to him, without speaking . . . If only I could hear him pattering with his little feet about the room just once, only once . . . if only I could hear his little feet I should know him! But he's gone, Father, he's gone, and I shall never hear him again." [p. 47–48]

Zossima tries to console the woman with religious faith:

"I shall pray for the peace of your child's soul. What was his name?"

"Alexey, Father."

"A sweet name. After Alexey, the man of God?" [p. 49]

The second woman grieves over the absence or perhaps death of her son from whom she has had no news for a year. The next interview is with a woman who feels guilty for the death of her husband, because she wished for it when he was ill:

"I am a widow these three years . . . I had a hard life with my husband . . . He lay ill . . . And then the thought came to me." [p. 50]

Zossima replies:

"All things are atoned for, all things are saved by love . . . Go, and fear not . . ." He got up and looked cheerfully at a healthy peasant woman with a tiny baby in her arms. [p. 51]

Such are the first episodes in the novel in which the child's death and the grief, the remorse, and the guilt feelings appear frankly, though expressed in displaced form. But the pleasant opposite connotation is also revealing in the cheerfulness produced in Zossima by the sight of the good mother represented by the "healthy peasant woman with a tiny baby in her arms." When Father Zossima returns to his cell where all the Karamazovs are awaiting him, the dispute between father and son comes up again, culminating in his bowing down before Mitya as described above. We cannot but associate the prediction of Mitya's future sufferings with the account of the death of Alexey, the little 3-year-old son of the disconsolate woman, and also with the words of Father Zossima when he says good-bye to Alyosha Karamazov at the end of this interview, encouraging him to leave the refuge he has sought in the monastery:

> "You will see great sorrow, and in that sorrow you will be happy . . . in sorrow seek happiness." [p. 73]

Thus, on the deepest level and on a parallel with what is apparently the main theme of the novel—the murder of the father—there is another theme, the basic one: the tragedy and pain of the children, of the sons, which is the basic nucleus of the work. The social theme and its psychological contents are especially evident and astonishingly sensitive in the passages in which Dostoyevsky addresses the problem of suffering children. The highest expression of this appears when Ivan Karamazov protests against a society that punishes and kills its sons and rejects a church that promises the joys of eternity while in this world there are children who are miserable.

Ivan, son of a psychotic mother and the elder son from Fyodor's second marriage, has lost faith in the Orthodox Church that, according to him, has twisted Christ's message of love and the original Christian faith. Thus, he says to Alyosha:

> "I meant to speak of the suffering of mankind generally, but we had better confine ourselves to the sufferings of children . . . I

won't speak of grown-up people [because], besides being disgusting and unworthy of love, they have a compensation—they've eaten the apple and know good and evil, and they have become 'like god' . . . But the children haven't eaten anything, and are so far innocent . . . you will understand why I prefer to speak of them. If they, too, suffer horribly on earth, they must suffer for their fathers' sins, they must be punished for their fathers, who have eaten the apple . . . The innocent must not suffer for another's sins, and especially such innocents! . . . Children while they are quite little . . . are so remote from grown-up people; they are different creatures, as it were, of a different species. . . . A well-educated cultured gentleman and his wife beat their own child with a birch-rod, a girl of seven. I have an exact account of it. The papa was glad that the birch was covered with twigs. 'It stings more,' said he, and so he began stinging his daughter. I know for a fact there are people who at every blow are worked up to sensuality, to literal sensuality, which increases progressively at every blow they inflict. They beat for a minute, for five minutes, for ten minutes, more often and more savagely. The child screams. At last the child cannot scream, it gasps, 'Daddy! daddy!' " [pp. 215–218]

Ivan goes on with his account. The father is brought to justice for having whipped his little daughter; a lawyer defends his rights and the judges absolve him. The public roars with delight when they see he is acquitted and that the rights over children have been defended.

And Ivan adds:[2]

---

[2]In a letter, Dostoyevsky notes: "All that my hero says in the text I am sending you is based on reality . . . All the anecdotes on children are authentic and have been published in the newspapers, and I can tell you in which ones. I have invented nothing. All Ivan's argument to Alyosha is based on contemporary and historic fact."

"But I've still better things about children. I've collected a great, great deal about Russian children, Alyosha. There was a little girl of 5 who was hated by her father and mother, 'most worthy and respectable people, of good education and breeding'. You see, I must repeat again, it is a peculiar characteristic of many people, this love of torturing children, and children only . . . they are very fond of tormenting children, even fond of children themselves in that sense. It's just their defenselessness that tempts the tormentor, just the angelic confidence of the child who has no refuge and no appeal, that sets his vile blood on fire. In every man, of course, a demon lies hidden—the demon of rage, the demon of lustful heat at the screams of the tortured victim . . . This poor child of 5 was subjected to every possible torture by those cultivated parents. They beat her, thrashed her, kicked her for no reason till her body was one bruise. Then, they went to greater refinements of cruelty—shut her up all night in the cold and frost in a privy, and because she didn't ask to be taken up at night (as though a child of 5 sleeping its angelic, sound sleep could be trained to wake and ask), they smeared her face and filled her mouth with excrement, and it was her mother, her mother did this. And that mother could sleep, hearing the poor child's groans! Can you understand why a little creature, who can't even understand what's done to her, should beat her little aching heart with her tiny fist in the dark and cold, and weep her meek resentful tears to dear, kind God to protect her? . . . the whole world of knowledge is not worth that child's prayer to 'dear, kind God'!" [pp. 218–219]

Finally, Ivan asked Alyosha to listen to him, in spite of the suffering that this may cause him, and recounts the following episode: A general who felt he had power over the life and death of his serfs learned that a small child had accidentally hurt his favorite hound's paw when he threw a stone. Indignant, he ordered the child taken:

He was taken – taken from his mother and kept shut up all night. Early that morning the general comes out on horseback, with the hounds, his dependents, dog-boys, and huntsmen, all mounted around him in full hunting parade. The servants are summoned for their edification, and in front of them all stands the mother of the child. The child is brought from the lockup. It's a gloomy cold, foggy autumn day, a capital day for hunting. The general orders the child to be undressed . . . he shivers, numb with terror, not daring to cry. "Make him run", commands the general. "Run! run!" shout the dog-boys. The boy runs. "At him!" yells the general, and he sets the whole pack of hounds on the child. The hounds catch him, and tear him to pieces before his mother's eyes! [pp. 219–220]

What should be done with the general? The atheistic Ivan asks the religious Alyosha:

"To be shot for the satisfaction of our moral feelings?.."

"To be shot," murmured Alyosha, lifting his eyes to Ivan with a pale, twisted smile.

"Bravo!" cried Ivan delighted. [p. 220]

Another meaningful episode for the study of the filicidal aspects underlying the oedipal conflict takes place when Mitya is accused of his father's death, precisely at the moment in which the situation with Gruschenka is cleared up and their relationship is to be formalized. Then, the official appears, accusing Mitya of his father's murder. Mitya, thinking that he means the death of the servant Grigory, whom he has struck, recriminates himself for his action and accuses himself. Once the mistake has been cleared up, he denies having murdered Karamazov in a confused situation created by Gruschenka who, thinking Mitya is guilty, accuses herself of having provoked the drama between father and son.

Fatigued by the interrogation and by the ill-treatment of the police, Mitya falls asleep and has the following dream:

> He was driving somewhere in the steppes . . . through snow and sleet. He was cold . . . the peasant drove him smartly . . . Not far off was a village, he could see the black huts, and half the huts were burnt down, there were only the charred beams sticking up. And as they drove on, there were peasant women drawn up along the road, a lot of women . . . all thin and wan, with their faces a sort of brownish colour, especially one at the edge, a tall, bony woman . . . with a long thin face. And in her arms was a little baby crying. And her breasts seemed so dried up that there was not a drop of milk in them. And the child cried and cried, and held out its little bare arms, with its little fists blue from cold.
>
> "Why are they crying? Why are they crying?" Mitya asked, as they dashed . . . by.
>
> "It's the babe," answered the driver, "the babe weeping."
>
> "But why is it weeping? . . . Why are its little arms bare? Why don't they wrap it up?"
>
> "The babe's cold, its little clothes are frozen and don't warm it."
>
> "But why is it? Why?" foolish Mitya still persisted.
>
> "Why, they're poor people, burnt out. They've no bread . ." "No, no," Mitya, as it were, still did not understand. "Tell me why is it those poor mothers stand there? Why are people poor? Why is the babe poor? . . . Why don't they hug each other and kiss? Why don't they sing songs of joy? Why are they so dark from black misery? Why don't they feed the babe? . . ." And he felt that a passion of pity, such as he had never known before, was rising in his heart, and he wanted to cry, that he wanted to do something

for them all, so that the babe should weep no more, so that the dark-faced, dried-up mother should not weep. . . .

Mitya is awakened by the justice official:

"What! Where?" he exclaimed opening his eyes and sitting up on the chest, as though he had revived from a swoon . . . Nikolay Parfenovitch was standing over him, suggesting that he should sign the testimony.

He went to the table and said that he would sign whatever they liked. "I've had a good dream, gentlemen," he said in a strange voice, with a new light, as of joy, in his face. Then the "Commital" was read to him and he was informed that he would be sent to prison in Moscow as long as the trial lasted, to which Mitya answered:

"Stay," . . . "Gentlemen, we're all cruel, we're all monsters, we all make men weep, and mothers, and babes at the breast, but of all . . . I am the lowest reptile! . . . I understand now that such men as I need a blow, a blow of destiny to catch them as with a noose, and bind them by a force from without . . . But the thunderbolt has fallen. I accept the torture of accusation, and my public shame, I want to suffer and by suffering I shall be puri-fied . . . I accept my punishment, not because I killed him, but because I meant to kill him, and perhaps I really might have killed him. . . ." [pp. 459–460]

Mitya submits. Both external authority and his superego accuse him. He is tried for parricide. However, in his dream, in his "good dream," the persecutory situation that originated his conflict is clear: there is his dry, burnt mother, his desolate infancy, and the suffering that never became conscious. In prison, the process of his melancholia advances. Identified with the hungry babe in whom he recognizes himself, he feels obliged to sacrifice himself, accepting the pain and punishment in order to redeem the other babes from guilt.

For this reason he says:

> "It's for the babe I'm going [to Siberia] . . . I didn't kill father, but I've got to go . . . Why was it I dreamed of that 'babe' at such a moment? . . . That was a sign to me at that moment. It's for the babe I'm going. Because we are all responsible for all. For all the 'babes,' for there are big children as well as little children. All are 'babes.' I go for all, because someone must go for all. I didn't kill father, but I've got to go. I accept it. [p. 534]

Mitya, taken to prison and unjustly sentenced, thus pathologically works through the mourning both for his father's death and for his own ego—the babe—and because of the increased severity of his superego, becomes more moral and mystical.

The trial is the exposition of the struggle between the generations. The accused in the dock are the sons and the accusers are the persecutory parents, those who defend their privileges and the principle of authority, those who judge. Only the defense lawyer, brought especially from Moscow, attempts to vindicate the rights of the children to be treated as individuals and to be freed from paternal domination.

Dostoyevsky, through the accusing attorney, focuses on what has happened to the Karamazov family as a miniature of what was happening in Russia at mid-19th century, with the upset of the rigid principles on which the czarist society was based and the breakdown of the old paternalistic strata as a result of scientific progress and judicial changes.

With the apparent desire to understand the events that led dissident youth to rebel in the midst of complete ideological and social chaos, which led to the exhaustion of what had until then

been considered reason and judgment, Dostoyevsky retrospec-
tively analyzes the character of the protagonists involved in the
Karamazov drama. To justify the accusation against Mitya, he
reviews the present and past circumstances of the life of the
accused that should naturally have led him to kill his father, so
that the prosecutor becomes the accuser of a society that abandons and abuses its children, pushing them into delinquency
and crime. Although his conscious purpose is to accuse the son
being judged, the problem of parental responsibility and the
parental function comes up and is debated more than the guilt of
the accused. Thus, through the prosecutor, Dostoyevsky
presents a study of the father's personality:

> A petty knave, a toady and buffoon, of fairly good, though
> undeveloped intelligence, he was, above all, a moneylender . . .
> His abject and servile characteristics disappeared, his malicious
> and sarcastic cynicism was all that remained . . . He saw nothing
> in life but sensual pleasure . . . He had no feelings for his duties as
> a father. He ridiculed those duties. He left his little children to the
> servants, and was glad to be rid of them, forgot about them
> completely. The old man's maxim was *après moi le déluge!* . . . he
> was content, he was eager to go on living in the same way for
> another twenty or thirty years. He swindled his own son and
> spent his money, his maternal inheritance, on trying to get his
> mistress from him . . . I can well understand what resentment he
> had heaped up in his son's heart against him . . . Am I unjust,
> indeed, in saying that he is typical of many modern fathers? Alas!
> many of them only differ in not openly professing such cynicism,
> for they are better educated, more cultured, but their philosophy
> is essentially the same as his. [p. 630]

Then, the prosecutor makes a detailed summary of the
characteristics of the four brothers and their unhappy fates.
When he ends his condemning speech the prosecutor

. . . looked as though he were feverish, he spoke of the blood that cried for vengeance, the blood of the father murdered by his son, with the base motive of robbery! He pointed to the tragic and glaring consistency of the facts . . . "remember that at this moment you are in a temple of justice. Remember that you are the champions of our justice, the champions of our holy Russia, of her principles, her family, everything that she holds sacred!" [p. 653]

After the prosecutor's speech, the attorney for the defence begins his speech. In the first part of his exposition, he sarcastically refutes all the arguments and proof against Mitya. Then he affirms that none of the evidence would stand up under the least criticism. Thus, he takes up the episodes formerly narrated and gives them a different interpretation, invoking the argument that "psychology is a knife that cuts both ways and it depends on who it is that uses it." He centers the defense on the oedipal problem: the father who abandons and robs has no paternal rights, is no longer a father. Then he accuses Smerdyakov, the sickest of the brothers and the representative of the sickest part of Dostoyevsky and of the Karamazov family. He states that he is the one who has the most reasons for wishing the old man dead. The same reasons given by the prosecutor which should have led Mitya to kill his father are used by the defense attorney in order to place the blame on the uncontrollable epileptic part of the sons, represented by Smerdyakov.

The defense attorney says that Smerdyakov

". . . resented his parentage, was ashamed of it, and would clench his teeth when he remembered that he was the son of 'stinking Lizaveta.' Believing himself to be the illegitimate son of Fyodor Pavlovitch (there is evidence of this) he might well have resented his position, compared to that of his master's legitimate sons . . . they had the inheritance, while he was only the cook." [pp. 667–668]

When he asks why Smerdyakov did not confess his crime before hanging himself, the defense attorney says that he must have felt not remorse but "despair" and, turning again to what Mitya would have wished to find when he returned home after twenty-three years and what actually happened:

"He was met by cynical taunts, suspicions, and wrangling about money . . . and at last he saw his father seducing his mistress from him with his own money. Oh, gentlemen of the jury, that was cruel and revolting! And that old man was always complaining of the disrespect and cruelty of his son. He slandered him in society, injured him, calumniated him, bought up his unpaid debts to get him thrown into prison." [p. 672]

The defense ends his speech with a study on what a "real father" should be like:

"Yes, it's a fearful thing to shed a father's blood . . . who has loved me . . . grieved over my illness from childhood up, troubled all his life for my happiness, and has lived in my joys, in my successes. To murder such a father—that's inconceivable. Gentlemen of the jury, what is a father—a real father? . . . in the present case, the father, Fyodor Pavlovitch Karamazov, did not correspond to that conception of a father . . . That's the misfortune. And indeed some fathers are a misfortune. Let us examine this misfortune . . . ." [p. 672]

Dostoyevsky's profound vision of human nature through his characters, their passions, and their anxieties, as well as his

deep psychological understanding of the genesis of these conflicts, show his remarkable sensitivity for psychic knowledge.
The parental functions are admirably described when the defense attorney tries to destroy the accusation of parricide put
forward by the prosecutor:

> " . . the father is not merely he who begets the child, but he who
> begets it and does his duty by it . . . The youth involuntarily
> reflects: . . . Why am I bound to love him, simply for begetting me
> when he has cared nothing for me all my life after? . . . 'Father,
> tell me, why must I love you? Father, show me that I must love
> you', and if that father does not [show him good reason], there's
> an end to the family tie. He is not a father to him, and the son has
> a right to look upon him as a stranger, and even an enemy. Our
> tribune, gentlemen of the jury, ought to be a school of true and
> sound ideas . . . Fathers, provoke not your children to wrath . . .
> Otherwise we are not fathers, but enemies of our children, and
> they are not our children . . . How can we blame children if they
> measure us according to our measure? . . . such a father as old
> Karamazov cannot be called a father and does not deserve to be.
> Filial love for an unworthy father is an absurdity, an impossibil-
> ity. Love cannot be created from nothing. . ." [pp. 673–674]

At the beginning of this chapter, we mentioned that there
is a subplot inserted into the novel's main plot. This is the story
of another child, another substitute for Alyosha, this time called
Ilusha. As you may remember, in Father Zossima's cell old
Fyodor accuses Mitya of having abused one of his employees,
Captain Snegiryov, a captain who had been thrown out of the
army and who worked for the old man against Mitya. On one
occasion, seeing him in a tavern, Mitya grows furious and,
seizing him by the beard, drags him a long way, throwing him
out into the street. This episode takes place before the despairing

eyes of Ilusha, his 9-year-old son, who in anguish begs someone
to help his humiliated father. No one responds to his cries for
help and everyone laughs at them mockingly. Thus begins the
story of Ilusha, which develops parallel to the main theme of the
novel. The characters are children and they apparently have
little bearing on the theme of the Karamazovs. The correlations
with the main plot are seen only through Alyosha Karamazov
and his relationship with the children. In dealing with this
subject, Dostoyevsky becomes immersed in the pain of childhood life with a certain grieving voluptuousness; he protests the
suffering of children and evokes, perhaps in secret, the decisive
moments of his own childhood.

Why does Dostoyevsky include this story of the death of
small, tortured Ilusha alongside the theme of parricide and the
Karamazovs? Undoubtedly, he means to show us that behind
the crime and death of the father there is suffering and destruction inflicted on the children. In the novel, the jury condemns
Mitya on the same day Ilusha is buried, thus closing the book.

In the story of Ilusha, we can see that the child's reaction to
his father's submission and lack of response in the episode with
Mitya is to direct his rage and pain against his schoolmates who
mock him. He is a child offended in the person of his father and,
in an interplay of projections and identifications with him, he
draws away from his companions. Shortly after, he falls ill and
never recovers. Dostoyevsky's accusation against the filicidal
family and society is obvious in his description of the home and
the people who surround Ilusha:

The captain, the father:

There was something angular, flurried and irritable about him.
Though he had obviously just been drinking, he was not drunk.
There was extraordinary impudence in his expression, and yet,

strange to say, at the same time there was fear. He looked like a man who had long been kept in subjection and had submitted to it . . . there was a sort of crazy humour, at times spiteful and at times cringing. . . .[p. 180]

The family included the mother, crazy and crippled, a daughter of 20, a hunchback with deformed feet, another daughter, sharp and aggressive, and Ilusha, 9 years old. They all lived in one unhealthy room, crowded with things and with people resigned to their fate.

The three windows, which consisted each of four tiny greenish mildewy panes, gave little light, and were closed shut, so that the room was not very light and rather stuffy . . . [there] was a string running across the room, and on it there were rags hanging. There was a bedstead against the wall on each side, right and left, covered with knitted quilts . . . The opposite corner was screened off by a curtain or a sheet hung on a string. Behind this curtain . . . a bed made up on a bench and a chair . . . The boy lay covered by his coat and an old wadded quilt . . . he was in a fever. [pp. 180–182]

This child, ill and abused because of his father, made the object of derision of his companions because of his "horrible little suit, his outgrown pants, and his shoes with holes," feels eaten up by guilt, remorse, and a desperate eagerness to repair a cruel prank of his companions who, together with him, have given a dog a ball of bread with a pin inside. The dog howls and turns round and round before the horrified Ilusha and then disappears. From that moment the child suffers constantly from delirium while his companions search desperately for the dog. Ilusha says crying: "I'm ill, father, because I killed Zhutchka, God has punished me!"

The prank played on the dog had been suggested by Smerdyakov. Again, a child is made to bear the guilt for an attitude induced by the epileptic adult, who represents the perverse and aggressive aspects of the father; although his ambivalence in the conflict with his father, depreciated and humiliated in public, had led him to act aggressively with the dog, the child now identifies with the victim, falls ill, and dies. Everyone tries in vain to make him forget about the dog. All that seems to bring him relief is to see his companions, once his enemies and now reconciled with him, around his poor cot, trying to make him forget his grief. He is tolerant and tries not to show his distaste when he sees his father trying to entertain him by telling funny stories or imitating people, all of which brings out his worst traits as a submissive buffoon. Finally, the child recovers a friend he was proud of, who has apparently found Zhutchka, the lost dog, and has brought it to him. Ilusha feels immense joy, but he is so weak that he can only manage to unite in his embrace his father, who weeps foreseeing the end is near, and his dear friend:

> "Father, father! How sorry I am for you! . . . Father, don't cry, and when I die get a good boy, another one . . . choose one of them all, a good one, call him Ilusha and love him instead of me. . ." [p. 506]

It is the small son who comforts the father, a miserable, incapable drunk, a failure. Now the child has to be a father to his own father.

> " . . and father, bury me by our big stone, where we used to go for our walk, and come to me there . . . in the evening. . ."

> His voice broke . . . seeing them all crying . . . "Father will cry, be with father," Ilusha had instructed his companions before dying. [p. 506]

Just as in the Karamazov house the sons buried the father as an expression of the superficial and manifest contents, this subplot within the novel reveals the latent and deep contents: the father who cries and buries his son. Ilusha dies at the moment Mitya is condemned. When Alyosha leaves the courtroom, the bells announcing the funeral can be heard.

In the novel, the sons are apparently condemned for having killed the father, but this very condemnation repeats the filicide whose latent contents can be seen in the death of Ilusha. Dostoyevsky's manifest project was to describe parricide, but he was unable to escape his need to confess the latent contents of all parricide: filicide, the death of Ilusha. This interrelation explains the simultaneous presentation of the two plots: the murder of the father as a corollary of the original murder of the son.

The novel ends in fact with Ilusha's burial, as if the story of this tortured child had condensed the reasons for the work. The sequence of the two final chapters is even clearer. In the first of these, Mitya, already condemned by the jury, accepts the possibility of escaping during the trip to Siberia in order to go on living with his beloved Gruschenka. The plan has been prepared by Ivan and Katya, his ex-fiancée, who in her jealousy of the love between Mitya and Gruschenka had at the last moment provided the evidence condemning Mitya: a letter her fiance had written to her when he was drunk in which he threatened to kill his father, Fyodor, if he failed to give him the money he owed him. Once again, as in the case of Oedipus, it is the figure of the mother-wife who condemns.

Katya and Gruschenka meet in Mitya's cell and accuse each other. Gruschenka says:

"We are full of hatred, my girl, you and I! As though we could forgive one another!" [p. 692]

Katya leaves, promising to save Mitya, and her last words before leaving the cell refer not to her ex-fiance but to Ilusha's burial:

> "Listen: I can't go with you to the funeral now. I've sent them flowers." And rushing Alyosha: "You are late as it is—the bells are ringing for the service." [p. 693]

Thus, at the end of the work, Dostoyevsky unites Mitya, the dissociated son sacrificed, condemned for a crime he did not commit, and Ilusha, the son who carries the guilt and offenses incurred by his father and who dies sacrificed by him. After the burial, Alyosha says good-bye to Ilusha's companions, saying:

> "You must know that there is nothing higher and stronger and more wholesome and good for life in the future than some good memory, especially a memory of childhood, of home. People talk to you a great deal about your education, but some good, sacred memory, preserved from childhood, is perhaps the best education. If a man carries many such memories with him into life, he is safe to the end of his days, and if one has only one good memory left in one's heart, even that may sometime be the means of saving us." [p. 699]

In his work, *Dostoyevsky and Parricide*, Freud strengthened the foundation he had laid in *Totem and Taboo* referring to a conception of the origins of society that has prevailed to the present in both psychology and sociology. This conception considers that the basic structure of human organization is based on the murder of the father and names parricide specifically as the principal and original crime of mankind and also of the individual, this being the main source of guilt feelings.

Freud analyzes the tragedy of the Karamazov brothers in this context. It is remarkable that the man who laid the foundations for contemporary psychology and contributed most to the knowledge of the human mind has adopted such a partial position with respect to Dostoyevsky. When Jones and Reik criticized this text, he excused himself by confessing his lack of interest in reading Dostoyevsky, being tired of seeing human pain in his analytic work.

This excuse is not on the same level as his thinking or his works, and it is obvious that he was unable to reach the depth of the central nucleus of the theme of *The Brothers Karamazov*: filicide, since he used this work essentially as a basis for his concepts on parricide. This explains why he ignored the important Russian social problem of the 19th century as well as the real reasons that lead to parricide. The murder of the father is a secondary phenomenon. What really matters throughout the plot of *The Brothers Karamazov* is the struggle between the generations and the perverse and negative action of parents in a paternalistic society with strongly repressive characteristics as described in diverse examples and dramatized by Karamazov and his four sons. The very essence of the work, from which the title is taken, is the destruction of the children. Further, it is not simply literary fiction but is also, as we have said, related to Dostoyevsky's own drama, to his own life. Thus, it is also an attempt to work through what was perhaps the most dramatic event of the last years of the author's life: the death of his little son Alyosha; the author has displaced the defining aspects of his own life stemming from his relationship with his father and his brothers onto this tragedy.

We cannot go on to consider the rest of the multitude of arguments, reasons, and examples offered by Dostoyevsky to denounce the universal sacrifice of the child in *The Brothers*

Karamazov. We would have to dedicate another text to the discussion of all these facts and meanings: Ivan's story of "The Great Inquisitor" stands out.

In conclusion, we wish to emphasize the final fate of the severely hurt Karamazov offspring, in other words, the results of the pathetic organization that dictates the definitive fates of the children. Thus, Mitya, condemned by justice, suffers a consequent increment in his persecutory anxieties, further elaborating his already intense guilt feelings and mourning in a pathological way. He gives up fighting and accepts his punishment as a way of achieving his redemption for a crime he only wished to commit. Ivan follows the model of the melancholic mother who killed herself, and in the process of identifying with her, goes mad. Alyosha, in an intermediate position, suffers from equivalents of epilepsy in the form of fainting spells and finds the way to work through his conflicts in his passive-masochistic submission to religion. Smerdyakov, the only son who does not leave his father's house, is the extreme case. He suffers his first epileptic fit after corporal punishment. Later, he not only commits the crime against his father but also against himself. When he can find no relief for his guilt feelings, once the idealized relationship with Ivan breaks down when the latter repudiates him, he finally hangs himself.

This extraordinary creation, used by Freud to typify parricide, leads us to pinpoint with obvious precision the most important filicidal aspects causing the oedipal situation. In Dostoyevsky we hear the child's voice, the children's voices, denouncing the father, the parents, as causing the miserable life of all humanity and its ills: the epilepsy that attacked Smerdyakov, the tuberculosis that led to little Ilusha's death, and the dark, persecutory guilt that marked the unfortunate destinies of the other three Karamazov brothers. This work was perhaps the expression of Dostoyevsky's greatest grief, his deepest protest, and his shrillest cry, the last one, foretelling the end of his life. He died when his cry began to die out and became a stream of blood flowing from his mouth, caused by a hemorrhage that no one could stop, just as no one could stop his immortal, profound lament.

9

"The Monkey's Paw" by W. W. Jacobs[1]

In the varied world of the short story, of which excellent anthologies have been compiled, one story is so outstanding that it is included in most of these collections. This is equally true for those anthologies compiled in the most diverse regions of the globe, since this remarkable story has been translated from the original English into nearly all languages having a significant literary production. "The Monkey's Paw" is considered a classic of horror and has been dramatized many times. In effect, no reader can escape the moving impact it produces to a degree rarely experienced with other literary works.

What is the ingredient in this tale that produces such a singular effect, something inherent to the very essence of the uncanny? The analysis we are about to do will show that this

---

[1]W. W. Jacobs, an English humorist, was born in 1863 and died in 1943. "The Monkey's Paw" was first published in *The Lady of the Barge* in 1902.

horrifying ingredient is filicide, the author's masterly skill leading us to experience it with extraordinary keenness.

Although stories about the murder of children always provoke an uncanny effect, few of them are able to produce a shock of such intensity. True or fictional stories depict parents having their children executed, murdering them, or trying to kill them themselves: Laius in the Oedipus tragedy, Abraham and Isaac in the biblical story, Czars Ivan the Terrible and Alexander, and so on. But in this story by Jacobs the conflict underlying the father–son rivalry and the father's ambivalence are developed with exceptional depth and verisimilitude, reaching the reader's unconscious structures extremely effectively. Through the identification he experiences with the words he takes in, the reader relives the fundamental and archaic human tragedy, either in the role of son or daughter or in that of real or potential parent.

Because the story is brief, we shall reproduce it before going on to analyze its latent meanings.

THE MONKEY'S PAW

Without, the night was cold and wet, but in the small parlor of Laburnam Villa the blinds were drawn and the fire burned brightly. Father and son were at chess, the former, who possessed ideas about the game involving radical changes, putting his king into such sharp and unnecessary perils that it even provoked comment from the white-haired old lady knitting placidly by the fire.

"Hark at the wind," said Mr. White, who, having seen a fatal mistake after it was too late, was amiably desirous of preventing his son from seeing it.

"I'm listening," said the latter, grimly surveying the board as he stretched out his hand. "Check."

"I should hardly think that he'd come tonight," said his father, with his hand poised over the board.

"Mate," replied the son.

"That's the worst of living so far out," bawled Mr. White, with sudden and unlooked-for violence; "of all the beastly, slushy, out-of-the-way places to live in, this is the worst. Pathway's a bog, and the road's a torrent. I don't know what people are thinking about. I suppose because only two houses in the road are let, they think it doesn't matter."

"Never mind, dear," said his wife soothingly; "perhaps you'll win the next one."

Mr. White looked up sharply, just in time to intercept a knowing glance between mother and son. The words died away on his lips, and he hid a guilty grin in his thin grey beard.

"There he is," said Herbert White, as the gate banged to loudly and heavy footsteps came toward the door.

The old man rose with hospitable haste, and opening the door, was heard condoling with the new arrival. The new arrival also condoled with himself, so that Mrs. White said, "Tut, tut!" and coughed gently as her husband entered the room, followed by a tall, burly man, beady of eye and rubicund of visage.

"Sergeant-Major Morris," he said, introducing him.

The sergeant-major shook hands, and taking the proffered seat by the fire, watched contentedly while his host got out whisky and tumblers and stood a small copper kettle on the fire.

At the third glass his eyes got brighter, and he began to talk, the little family circle regarding with eager interest this visitor from distant parts, as he squared his broad shoulders in the chair and spoke of wild scenes and doughty deeds; of wars and plagues and strange peoples.

"Twenty-one years of it," said Mr. White, nodding at his wife and son. "When he went away he was a slip of a youth in the warehouse. Now look at him."

"He don't look to have taken much harm," said Mrs. White politely.

"I'd like to go to India myself," said the old man, "just to look round a bit, you know."

"Better where you are," said the sergeant-major, shaking his head. He put down the empty glass, and sighing softly, shook it again.

"I should like to see those old temples and fakirs and jugglers," said the old man. "What was that you started telling me the other day about a monkey's paw or something, Morris?"

"Nothing," said the soldier hastily. "Leastways nothing worth hearing."

"Monkey's paw?" said Mrs. White, curiously.

"Well, it's just a bit of what you might call magic, perhaps," said the sergeant-major off-handedly.

His three listeners leaned forward eagerly. The visitor absent-mindedly put his empty glass to his lips and then set it down again. His host filled it for him.

"To look at," said the sergeant-major, fumbling in his pocket, "it's just an ordinary little paw, dried to a mummy."

He took something out of his pocket and proffered it. Mrs. White drew back with a grimace, but her son, taking it, examined it curiously.

"And what is there special about it?" inquired Mr. White as he took it from his son, and having examined it, placed it upon the table.

"It had a spell put on it by an old fakir," said the sergeant-major, "a very holy man. He wanted to show that fate ruled people's lives, and that those who interfered with it did so to their sorrow. He put a spell on it so that three separate men could each have three wishes from it."

His manner was so impressive that his hearers were conscious that their light laughter jarred somewhat.

"Well, why don't you have three, sir?" said Herbert White cleverly.

The soldier regarded him in the way that middle age is wont to regard presumptuous youth. "I have," he said quietly, and his blotchy face whitened.

"And did you really have the three wishes granted?" asked Mr. White.

"I did," said the sergeant-major, and his glass tapped against his strong teeth.

"And has anybody else wished?" inquired the old lady.

"The first man had his three wishes. Yes," was the reply; "I don't know what the first two were, but the third was for death. That's how I got the paw."

His tones were so grave that a hush fell upon the group.

"If you've had your three wishes, it's no good to you now, then, Morris," said the old man at last. "What do you keep it for?"

The soldier shook his head. "Fancy, I suppose," he said slowly. "I did have some idea of selling it, but I don't think I will. It has caused enough mischief already. Besides, people won't buy. They think it's a fairy tale; some of them, and those who do think anything of it want to try it first and pay me afterward."

"If you could have another three wishes," said the old man, eyeing him keenly, "would you have them?"

"I don't know," said the other. "I don't know."

He took the paw, and dangling it between his fore-finger and thumb, suddenly threw it upon the fire. White, with a slight cry, stooped down and snatched it off.

"Better let it burn," said the soldier solemnly.

"If you don't want it, Morris," said the old man, "give it to me."

"I won't," said his friend doggedly. "I threw it on the fire. If you keep it, don't blame me for what happens. Pitch it on the fire again, like a sensible man."

The other shook his head and examined his new possession closely. "How do you do it?" he inquired.

"Hold it up in your right hand and wish aloud," said the sergeant-major, "but I warn you of the consequences."

"Sounds like the *Arabian Nights*," said Mrs. White, as she rose and began to set the supper. "Don't you think you might wish for four pairs of hands for me?"

Her husband drew the talisman from his pocket, and then all three burst into laughter as the sergeant-major, with a look of alarm on his face, caught him by the arm.

"If you must wish," he said gruffly, "wish for something sensible."

Mr. White dropped it back into his pocket, and placing chairs, motioned his friend to the table. In the business of supper the talisman was partly forgotten, and afterward the three sat listening in an enthralled fashion to a second instalment of the soldier's adventures in India.

"If the tale about the monkey's paw is not more truthful than those he has been telling us," said Herbert, as the door closed behind their guest, just in time for him to catch the last train, "we shan't make much out of it."

"Did you give him anything for it, father?" inquired Mrs. White, regarding her husband closely.

"A trifle," said he, coloring slightly. "He didn't want it, but I made him take it. And he pressed me again to throw it away."

"Likely," said Herbert, with pretended horror. "Why, we're

going to be rich, famous, and happy. Wish to be an emperor, father, to begin with; then you can't be henpecked."

He darted round the table, pursued by the maligned Mrs. White armed with an antimacassar.

Mr. White took the paw from his pocket and eyed it dubiously. "I don't know what to wish for, and that's a fact," he said slowly. "It seems to me I've got all I want."

"If you only cleared the house, you'd be quite happy, wouldn't you?" said Herbert, with his hand on his shoulder. "Well, wish for two hundred pounds, then; that'll just do it."

His father, smiling shamefacedly at his own credulity, held up the talisman, as his son, with a solemn face, somewhat marred by a wink at his mother, sat down at the piano and struck a few impressive chords.

"I wish for two hundred pounds," said the old man distinctly.

A fine crash from the piano greeted the words, interrupted by a shuddering cry from the old man. His wife and son ran toward him.

"It moved," he cried, with a glance of disgust at the object as it lay on the floor. "As I wished, it twisted in my hand like a snake."

"Well, I don't see the money," said his son as he picked it up and placed it on the table, "and I bet I never shall."

"It must have been your fancy, father," said his wife, regarding him anxiously.

He shook his head. "Never mind, though; there's no harm done, but it gave me a shock all the same."

They sat down by the fire again while the two men finished their pipes. Outside, the wind was higher than ever, and the old man started nervously at the sound of a door banging upstairs. A silence unusual and depressing settled upon all three, which lasted until the old couple rose to retire for the night.

"I expect you'll find the cash tied up in a big bag in the middle of your bed," said Herbert, as he bade them good night, "and something horrible squatting up on top of the wardrobe watching you as you pocket your ill-gotten gains."

He sat alone in the darkness, gazing at the dying fire, and seeing faces in it. The last face was so horrible and so simian that he gazed at it in amazement. It got so vivid that, with a little uneasy laugh, he felt on the table for a glass containing water to throw over it. His hand grasped the monkey's paw and with a little shiver he wiped his hand on his coat and went up to bed.

II

In the brightness of the wintry sun next morning as it streamed over the breakfast table he laughed at his fears. There was an air of prosaic wholesomeness about the room which it had lacked on the previous night, and the dirty, shrivelled little paw was pitched on the sideboard with a carelessness which betokened no great belief in its virtues.

"I suppose all old soldiers are the same," said Mrs. White. "The idea of our listening to such nonsense! How could wishes be granted in these days? And if they could, how could two hundred pounds hurt you, father?"

"Might drop on his head from the sky," said the frivolous Herbert.

"Morris said the things happened so naturally," said his father, "that you might if you so wished attribute it to coincidence."

"Well, don't break into the money before I come back," said Herbert, as he rose from the table. "I'm afraid it'll turn you into a mean, avaricious man, and we shall have to disown you."

His mother laughed, and following him to the door, watched him down the road; and returning to the breakfast table, was very happy at the expense of her husband's credulity. All of which did not prevent her from scurrying to the door at the postman's knock, nor prevent her from referring somewhat shortly to retired sergeant-majors of bibulous habits when she found that the post brought a tailor's bill.

"Herbert will have some more of his funny remarks, I expect, when he comes home," she said, as they sat at dinner.

"I dare say," said Mr. White, pouring himself out some beer; "but for all that, the thing moved in my hand; that I'll swear to."

"You thought it did," said the old lady soothingly.

"I say it did," replied the other. "There was no thought about it; I had just—What's the matter?"

His wife made no reply. She was watching the mysterious movements of a man outside, who, peering in an undecided fashion at the house, appeared to be trying to make up his mind to enter. In mental connection with the two hundred pounds, she noticed that the stranger was well dressed and wore a silk hat of glossy newness. Three times he paused at the gate, and then walked on again. The fourth time he stood with his hand upon it, and then with sudden resolution flung it open and walked up the path. Mrs. White at the same moment placed her hands behind her, and hurriedly unfastening the strings of her apron, put that useful article of apparel beneath the cushion of her chair.

She brought the stranger, who seemed ill at ease, into the room. He gazed at her furtively and listened in a preoccupied fashion as the old lady apologized for the appearance of the room, and her husband's coat, a garment which he usually reserved for the garden. She then waited patiently for him to broach his business, but he was at first strangely silent.

"I—was asked to call," he said at last, and stooped and picked a piece of cotton from his trousers. "I come from Maw and Meggins, the factory."

The old lady started. "Is anything the matter?" she asked breathlessly. "Has anything happened to Herbert? What is it? What is it?"

Her husband interposed. "There, there, mother," he said hastily. "Sit down, and don't jump to conclusions. You've not brought bad news, I'm sure, sir;" and he eyed the other wistfully.

"I'm sorry—" began the visitor.

"Is he hurt?" demanded the mother wildly.

The visitor bowed in assent, "Badly hurt," he said quietly, "but he is not in any pain."

"Oh, thank God!" said the old woman, clasping her hands. "Thank God for that! Thank—"

She broke off suddenly as the sinister meaning of the assurance dawned upon her and she saw the awful confirmation of her fears in the other's averted face. She caught her breath, and turning to her slower-witted husband, laid her trembling old hand upon his. There was a long silence.

"He was caught in the machinery," said the visitor at length in a low voice.

"Caught in the machinery," repeated Mr. White, in a dazed fashion, "yes."

He sat staring blankly out at the window, and taking his wife's hand between his own, pressed it as he had been wont to do in their old courting-days nearly forty years before.

"He was the only one left to us," he said, turning gently to the visitor. "It is hard."

The other coughed, and rising, walked slowly to the window. "The firm wished me to convey their sincere sympathy with you in your great loss," he said, without looking round. "I beg that you will understand I am only their servant and merely obeying orders."

There was no reply; the old woman's face was white, her eyes staring, and her breath inaudible; on the husband's face was a look such as his friend the sergeant-major might have carried into his first action.

"I was to say that Maw and Meggins disclaim all responsibility," continued the other. "They admit no liability at all, but in consideration of your son's services, they wish to present you with a certain sum as compensation."

Mr. White dropped his wife's hand, and rising to his feet, gazed with a look of horror at his visitor. His dry lips shaped the words, "How much?"

"Two hundred pounds," was the answer.

Unconscious of his wife's shriek the old man smiled faintly, put out his hands like a sightless man, and dropped, a senseless heap, to the floor.

III

In the huge new cemetery, some two miles distant, the old people buried their dead, and came back to a house steeped in shadow and silence. It was all over so quickly that at first they could hardly realize it, and remained in a state of expectation as though of something else to happen—something else which was to lighten this load, too heavy for old hearts to bear.

But the days passed, and expectation gave place to resignation—the hopeless resignation of the old, sometimes miscalled apathy. Sometimes they hardly exchanged a word, for now they had nothing to talk about, and their days were long to weariness.

It was about a week after that the old man, waking suddenly in the night, stretched out his hand and found himself alone. The room was in darkness, and the sounds of subdued weeping came from the window. He raised himself in bed and listened.

"Come back," he said tenderly. "You will be cold."

"It is colder for my son," said the old woman, and wept afresh.

The sound of her sobs died away on his ears. The bed was warm, and his eyes heavy with sleep. He dozed fitfully, and then slept until a sudden wild cry from his wife awoke him with a start.

"*The paw!*" she cried wildly. "The monkey's paw!"

He started up in alarm. "Where? Where is it? What's the matter?"

She came stumbling across the room toward him. "I want it," she said quietly. "You've not destroyed it?"

"It's in the parlor, on the bracket," he replied, marvelling. "Why?"

She cried and laughed together, and bending over, kissed his cheek.

"I only just thought of it," she said hysterically. "Why didn't I think of it before? Why didn't *you* think of it?"

"Think of what?" he questioned.

"The other two wishes," she replied rapidly. "We've only had one."

"Was not that enough?" he demanded fiercely.

"No," she cried triumphantly; "we'll have one more. Go down and get it quickly, and wish our boy alive again."

The man sat up in bed and flung the bedclothes from his quaking limbs. "Good God, you are mad!" he cried, aghast.

"Get it," she panted; "get it quickly, and wish—Oh, my boy, my boy!"

Her husband struck a match and lit the candle. "Get back to bed," he said unsteadily. "You don't know what you are saying."

"We had a first wish granted," said the old woman feverishly; "why not the second?"

"A coincidence," stammered the old man.

"Go and get it and wish," cried his wife, quivering with excitement.

The old man turned and regarded her, and his voice shook. "He has been dead ten days, and besides he—I would not tell you else, but—I could only recognize him by his clothing. If he was too terrible for you to see then, how now?"

"Bring him back," cried the old woman, and dragged him toward the door. "Do you think I fear the child I have nursed?"

He went down in the darkness, and felt his way to the parlour, and then to the mantelpiece. The talisman was in its place, and a horrible fear that the unspoken wish might bring his mutilated son before him ere he could escape from the room seized upon him, and he caught his breath as he found that he had lost the direction of the door. His brow cold with sweat, he felt his way round the table, and groped along the wall until he found himself in the small passage with the unwholesome thing in his hand.

Even his wife's face seemed changed as he entered the room. It was white and expectant, and to his fears seemed to have an unnatural look upon it. He was afraid of her.

"*Wish!*" she cried, in a strong voice.

"It is foolish and wicked," he faltered.

"*Wish!*" repeated his wife.

He raised his hand. "I wish my son alive again."

The talisman fell to the floor, and he regarded it fearfully. Then he sank trembling into a chair as the old woman, with burning eyes, walked to the window and raised the blind.

He sat until he was chilled with the cold, glancing occasionally at the figure of the old woman peering through the window. The candle-end, which had burned below the rim of the china candlestick, was throwing pulsating shadows on the ceiling and walls, until, with a flicker larger than the rest, it expired. The old man, with an unspeakable sense of relief at the failure of the talisman, crept back to his bed, and a minute or two afterward the old woman came silently and apathetically beside him.

Neither spoke, but lay silently listening to the ticking of the clock. A stair creaked, and a squeaky mouse scurried noisily through the wall. The darkness was oppressive, and after lying for some time screwing up his courage, he took the box of matches, and striking one, went downstairs for a candle.

At the foot of the stairs the match went out, and he paused to strike another; and at the same moment a knock, so quiet and stealthy as to be scarcely audible, sounded on the front door.

The matches fell from his hand and spilled in the passage. He stood motionless, his breath suspended until the knock was repeated. Then he turned and fled swiftly back to his room, and closed the door behind him. A third knock sounded through the house.

"*What's that?*" cried the old woman, starting up.

"A rat," said the old man, in shaking tones—"a rat. It passed me on the stairs."

His wife sat up in bed listening. A loud knock resounded through the house.

"It's Herbert!" she screamed. "It's Herbert!"

She ran to the door, but her husband was before her, and catching her by the arm, held her tightly.

"What are you going to do?" he whispered hoarsely.

"It's my boy; it's Herbert!" she cried, struggling mechanically. "I forgot it was two miles away. What are you holding me for? Let go. I must open the door."

"For God's sake, don't let it in," cried the old man, trembling.

"You're afraid of your own son," she cried, struggling. "Let me go. I'm coming, Herbert; I'm coming."

There was another knock, and another. The old woman with a sudden wrench broke free and ran from the room. Her husband followed to the landing, and called after her appealingly as she hurried downstairs. He heard the chain rattle back and the bottom bolt drawn slowly and stiffly from the socket. Then the old woman's voice, strained and panting.

"The bolt," she cried loudly. "Come down. I can't reach it."

But her husband was on his hands and knees groping wildly on the floor in search of the paw. If he could only find it before the thing outside got in. A perfect fusillade of knocks reverberated through the house, and he heard the scraping of a chair as his wife put it down in the passage against the door. He heard the creaking of the bolt as it came slowly back, and at the same moment, he found the monkey's paw, and frantically breathed his third and last wish.

The knocking ceased suddenly, although the echoes of it were still in the house. He heard the chair drawn back, and the door opened. A cold wind rushed up the staircase, and a long loud wail of disappointment and misery from his wife gave him courage to run down to her side, and then to the gate beyond. The street lamp flickering opposite shone on a quiet and deserted road.

THE LATENT MEANING

We shall now analyze the development of our horrifying tale.

To begin with, it is noteworthy that the author establishes the confrontation between father and son from the very outset of the story. He situates the three essential characters of the tragedy in this confrontation: that is, the oedipal triangle consisting of the father, the mother, and the son. The skillful narration has dramatized the exposition of this rivalry in the best symbol of war: the game of chess. It not only suggests the initial circumstances of the plot, but also insinuates the dynamics of the future situation of the generations, which is the son's survival and the father's defeat by time.

The reaction to this universal condition, unacceptable in this case, is seen in the father's

sudden and unlooked-for violence

displacing his wrath to the road.[2] His wife, who senses his envy, the rivalry, and the hidden reason behind this complaint about the road, tells him then by way of compensation not to be upset:

---

[2]One interpretation of the symbolism of the pathway that has become "a bog" leads us to the female genitals, in this case those of the wife-mother.

"perhaps you'll win the next one."

This moment in the plot imperceptibly signals the culminating circumstance that triggers Mr. White's profound emotional regression.

> Mr. White looked up sharply, just in time to intercept a knowing glance between mother and son. The words died away on his lips, and he hid a guilty grin in his thin grey beard.

Now we see full regression. And consequently, a knock on the door is heard immediately and Sergeant-Major Morris comes onto the scene; he is an exotic and archaic character who revives magic and witchcraft, a residue of ancient, primitive, and barbaric morals. He is doubtless the ancient double who comes from Mr. White's own unconscious. Then Mr. White introduces his wife, his son, and the picturesque character, who immediately heightens his own excitement with three glasses of whiskey.

In this dialogue with his manic double, White refers to his own youth when he ambiguously speaks of Morris:

> "when he went [to India] he was a slip of a youth"

He is, therefore, he himself at his own son's age, an image he accepts in the unconscious envious competition that he is growingly entering into with Herbert; he openly insists:

> "I'd like to go to India myself,"

which means: many years ago I was like my son and I want to be like him now! But at the same time, the trip to India signifies the magical trip around the world of his first days of life, since the question immediately arises, in the form of a dialogue with Sergeant Morris, which is actually a dialogue with himself:

> "What was that you started telling me the other day about a monkey's paw or something, Morris?"

After a few questions, the magical spell is affirmed:

> "Well, it's just a bit of what you might call magic, perhaps," said the sergeant-major off-handedly."

The depth of the regression is expressed by the nature of the object that carries the spell: the monkey's paw, alluding to the prehuman ancestor and to the animistic, phallic overvaluation of the fetish. Therefore, together with the recovery of the ancestor, both primitive affects and phallic-omnipotent instinctual expressions also appear; the magical resources will be placed in the service of ancient omnipotence of thought and manic wish fulfillment.

All the protagonists of the tragedy are brought under the spell and caught up in Mr. White's regression. Mr. White announces this state of mind through his double, the sergeant:

> "It had a spell put on it by an old fakir. . . . He wanted to show that fate ruled people's lives, and that those who interfered with it did so to their sorrow. He put a spell on it so that three separate men could each have three wishes from it."

This announcement signifies the affirmation of the fateful power of the unconscious and the grave consequences that result from opposing the disposition of the generations, that is, the natural fate of those who are destined to die before their children. It also means that no one can destroy the growing vigor of the offspring that parallels the decadence of their progenitors without consequently suffering the corresponding catastrophic guilt. Throughout all the rest of the tale, this inner dialogue continues between the aspects of Mr. White that are adapted to reality and his manic-regressive aspects. The drama he experiences urges him to leave aside the omnipotent fulfillment of his wishes, while his oedipal resentment and the search for hallucinatory elimination of his rival cause him to insist on possessing the fetish. The struggle between these two tendencies is expressed both by the sergeant's attitude when he throws the monkey's paw on the fire in the attempt to get rid of it and its curse and by that of Mr. White, who thwarts this measure by exultantly retrieving it. At this point, Mr. White is already "possessed," immersed in omnipotent wish fulfillment. He has taken over the magical powers that had until then been the property of the sergeant (his repressed double), and embarks on the fulfillment of the wishes he never overcame in his rivalry with his son for the possession of the wife-mother. After the sergeant has left, having taught him the regressive ritual, Mr. White becomes the depository of the omnipotent magical process, while at the same time attempting manically to deny his terror in the face of the demons that are returning.

At this time, a banal conversation between father and son renews the allusion to the wife-mother:

"Why, we're going to be rich, famous, and happy. Wish to be an emperor, father, to begin with; *then you can't be henpecked.*"

This is the beginning of the sinister wish with all its latent meaning. And it is the son himself who masochistically insinuates it:

"If you only cleared the house, you'd be quite happy, wouldn't you?" said Herbert, with his hand on his shoulder. "Well, wish for two hundred pounds, then";[3]

This wish, which is the nucleus of the drama, deserves detailed analysis. Its manifest meaning clearly implies getting final possession of the house by paying the mortgage on it. But getting the two hundred pounds also implies the concomitant death of the son. Thus we see that the possession of the house conceals the final possession of the wife-mother through elimination of the rival, along with all the unresolved primitive meanings. The wish both expresses rational contents and reveals the latent contents of this unconscious possession, which appears to be threatened from the beginning when the son wins the chess match. Although Herbert was able to checkmate his father with his generational privilege, there is now a manic attempt at opposition by killing the son by the means the author has provided: the acceptable wish for two hundred pounds that conceals the latent and unconfessed wish to kill the son.

It is useful to follow the plot on two levels: the manifest and the latent. The emotional effect achieved by the author also resides in the constant, though never antagonistic, parallelism between the two desires, the rational and the irrational—that is, between the house and the wife-mother, between the two hundred pounds and the death of the son-rival, between the filicidal predominance expressed in the father's first wish and the second reparatory one at the mother's insistence and the final, unmanifest consummation of the third one, which represents the return of the father's primitive filicidal wish.

---

[3]We cannot ignore the symbolic meaning of the sum chosen, which refers to the female sexual attributes: the number 2 is the universal symbol for the woman.

The story dwells for a time on the struggle between the predominance of the logical process and the overwhelming emergence of the unconscious wish. This balance is broken with the first wish. For this reason, the magical invocation creates a commotion:

> A fine crash from the piano greeted the words, interrupted by a shuddering cry from the old man. His wife and son ran toward him.

This commotion signals the breakdown of the logical process and of the sociocultural varnish, because magical thought has become real experience. By now, all is fully submerged in regression and the events to come occur as a function of the archaic feelings that arise when the repressive mechanism fails. The son observes fatefully:

> "Well, I don't see the money . . . and I bet I never shall."

In effect, events reveal that money (the father's potency in his relationship with the wife-mother) and the son's life are regressively experienced as incompatible, and this incompatibility is evident when the check for two hundred pounds arrives together with the unhappy news.

On the first night, after the first wish, the author sketches Mr. White's hallucinations, whose simian allegories indicate another allusion to the "ancestral monkey overwhelming Mr. White" in his regression.

> He sat alone in the darkness, gazing at the dying fire, and seeing faces in it. The last face was so horrible and so simian that he gazed at it in amazement. It got so vivid that, with a little uneasy

laugh, he felt on the table for a glass containing water to throw over it. His hand grasped the monkey's paw, and with a little shiver he wiped his hand on his coat and went up to bed.

We are now in the second part of the story. Regression has apparently been overcome in the winter sunlight. But we see that it is lurking in Mr. White's mind when he says:

> "Morris said the things happened so naturally . . . that you might if you so wished attribute it to coincidence."

The struggle between the logical process and the magic process emerges again in the disagreement between White and his wife:

> . . . returning to the breakfast table, [she] was very happy at the expense of her husband's credulity . . . "Herbert will have some more of his funny remarks, I expect, when he comes home," she said. . . .
>
> "I dare say," said Mr. White . . . "but for all that, the thing moved in my hand; that I'll swear to."
>
> "You thought it did," said the old lady soothingly.
>
> "I say it did," replied the other. "There was no thought about it; I had just—What's the matter?"

The magic process takes hold when the stranger enters with the tragic news and the dreadful check. After the terrible opening scene:

> "He was caught in the machinery," said the visitor at length in a low voice.

"Caught in the machinery," repeated Mr. White, in a dazed fashion, "yes."

He sat staring blankly out at the window, and taking his wife's hand between his own, pressed it as he had been wont to do in their old courting days nearly forty years before.

"He was the only one left to us," he said, turning gently to the visitor. "It is hard."

This concise paragraph suggests that they have had other children who died and that Herbert was the only survivor. Immediately after the announcement of the loss of all his offspring, Mr. White is offered the reward:[5]

"Mr. White dropped his wife's hand, and rising to his feet, gazed with a look of horror at his visitor. His dry lips shaped the words, "How much?"

"Two hundred pounds," was the answer.

Unconscious of his wife's shriek, the old man smiled faintly, put out his hands like a sightless man, and dropped, a senseless heap, to the floor.

We shall now go on to the third and last part. After the description of the intensity of the melancholic process that follows the dreadful drama and the loss of the sense of future that represents the loss of the son, we see how the manic defense emerges, this time from the mother:

---

[5]The factory whose machines killed Herbert may in this case symbolize the social institutions that consummate filicide; that is, social mechanisms like wars to which youths are sent to be killed. Society (the factory) is also seen here rewarding "the parents who sacrificed their children."

The sound of her sobs died away on his ears. The bed was warm, and his eyes heavy with sleep. He dozed fitfully, and then slept until a sudden wild cry from his wife awoke him with a start.

"*The paw!*" she cried wildly. "The monkey's paw!"

He started up in alarm. "Where? Where is it? What's the matter?"

She came stumbling across the room toward him. "I want it," she said quietly. "You've not destroyed it?"

"It's in the parlor, on the bracket," he replied, marvelling. "Why?"

She cried and laughed together, and bending over, kissed his cheek.

"I only just thought of it," she said hysterically. "Why didn't I think of it before? Why didn't *you* think of it?"

"Think of what?" he questioned. .

"The other two wishes," she replied rapidly. "We've only had one."

"Was not that enough?" he demanded fiercely.

"No," she cried triumphantly; "we'll have one more. Go down and get it quickly, and wish our boy alive again."

The man sat up in bed and flung the bedclothes from his quaking limbs. "Good god, you are mad!" he cried, aghast.

"Get it," she panted; "get it quickly, and wish—Oh, my boy, my boy!"

Her husband struck a match and lit the candle. "Get back to bed," he said unsteadily. "You don't know what you are saying."

It is now the father who uses the logical process against the fantasy of magic fulfillment on the mother's part. The unconscious impulse that imploded in the father is satisfied with the son's death and no longer pressures with as much force as the mother's longing for her son does:

> "He has been dead ten days, and besides he—I would not tell you else, but—I could only recognize him by his clothing. If he was too terrible for you to see. . ."

> "Go and get it and wish," cried his wife, quivering with excitement. "Do you think I fear the child I have nursed?"

However, in spite of his logical opposition and conscious desire to escape from the sight of his mutilated son:

> "He found himself in the passage with the unwholesome thing in his hand."

The unconscious magic part of him has carried out the wishes of his wife, with whom he identifies in the desire to repair the son. But the struggle between the two processes continues:

> "Wish!" she cried, in a strong voice.

> "It is foolish and wicked," he faltered.

> "Wish!" repeated his wife.

> He raised his hand. "I wish my son alive again."

Once again, omnipotence and regression flood him with terror, which is relieved when the magical invocation is not fulfilled. But when he goes to get a candle and the match he intends to use to find it goes out, both his contact with reality and also the truce break down. When the knock on the door announces the possible magic fulfillment, he drops the matches and flees to his room. The knocks continue in spite of his failed attempts at denial, and as the feeling that his resuscitated mutilated son is arriving grows imminent, he trembles with terror and again tries to oppose his son's life. White searches for the monkey's paw:

If he could only find it before the thing outside got in . . .

Until he finds it and:

frantically breathed his third and last wish.

The author does not make explicit this last wish, maintaining the prohibition against naming the filicidal wish that throughout the story has not been expressed as such.

The knocks cease and with them the last beat of the son's heart, now finally silenced. White can then run down to his wife and to the gate and find the road quiet and deserted—that same road that the son's triumph had transformed into a bog. His desires for his son's death have finally been fully consummated, thus satisfying his envy and the infantile wish that he never overcame for exclusive possession of the wife-mother.

Meanwhile, the reader has temporarily become the "possessed," the depository of the tragedy that has taken place, previously resting latently at the back of his own unconscious and now reactivated. The story's entire configuration fits in perfectly with the history of the species and is repeated in each individual, so that once again the great persecutory threat emerges, filling the reader with anxiety. The return of this old anxiety in the face of the murderous father, the return of "something which ought to have remained hidden but has come to light" (Freud 1919, p. 241), is what gives this exceptional tale such extremely uncanny meaning.

PART III

THOUGHTS ON
FILICIDE TODAY

Direct filicide or the murder of the offspring and all the diversity of its attenuated forms: neglect, abuse, denigration, mutilation, and abandonment, are increasing throughout our contemporary world, along with the progressive development of the sociocultural process. Surprising information from many scientific disciplines reveals the magnitude this phenomenon has acquired nowadays and challenges us to verify the authenticity of statistical data and individual case histories, clinical or criminological, and at the same time to deepen our study of the institutionalized forms of abuse of minors, of the mortification inflicted on them from the beginning of their lives so as to impose cultural norms through the educational system, of the utilization of the child as depository of the parents' conflicts and unbalance and, even more so, of collective phenomena consisting in the immolation of infanto-juvenile legions in the name of diverse pretexts and idealizations.

We assign equal importance to the psychological study of

the inner child each of us carries within. Though we may not be parents, we are all certainly someone's child and our psyche preserves the same parent–child organization we acquired at the beginning of our childhood development. That inner child in each of us suffers the same destructive impact that the sociocultural process inflicts on the offspring, provoking total or partial damage to our own ego from within through the action of the superego. Further, when this inner child passively suffers aggression from the superego, it tends to identify with the aggressor and to project and perpetuate the filicidal action on its own actual children. We are all involved in a system that becomes patent and flagrant when the immolation or mutilation of the offspring is too overt to be denied. But when the evidence of sacrifice grows too obvious, denial is displaced to the concealment of the real reason, calling on concepts and reasons that mask the reality of the parents' sadistic and envious impulses. As an example, the primitives said that if crops were to be good it was necessary to sacrifice a certain number of children to appease the gods who controlled the earth's fertility. Today we know that these gods are a displacement of the figure of the parents who were, after all, responsible for the thirst for their children's blood they attributed to the divinity.[1]

This process and others like it have intensified so drastically throughout the world that we are fully justified in asking the question so often repeated: Can human life continue when it is threatened from its very beginning? This threat engenders a whole chain of epiphenomena and responses that are expressed sooner or later in the brutal explosion of contemporary violence.

The climate of violence during infancy is evident in a

---

[1]Mars was initially a fertility god, later becoming the god of war.

criminal's description of the environment in which he grew up (Parker 1962):

> Violence is something like the common language, something a person like me grew up with. Something I began to use at a very early age as part of the daily scene of my childhood. I don't reject it or feel that kind of innate disgust that you feel. As far back as I can remember, I've always seen violence used around me. My mother would beat up her kids, all my brothers and sisters would hit my mother or the other kids, the man downstairs would hit his wife, etc. [p. 93]

Perhaps today's violence is no more brutal than in other times, but today we possess destructive means that could bring about the apocalyptic future so often predicted.

Murder of the progeny has been committed since time immemorial, as this book documents, but our times are characterized, partly by the increment in covert massive filicidal acts, and partly by the fearful destructive capacity of modern technology.

THE MURDER OF CHILDREN

Reviewing contributions from various scientific disciplines, we first consider the data provided by criminology. Although crime touches few individuals, these data greatly interest us, since they not only reveal the great frequency of filicide but also show us how to investigate the attenuated forms that go unnoticed because they escape public control by means of a family-imposed secret.

In the United States (Hoover 1966), statistics reveal that in

1966 one in every twenty-two crimes was committed against a child by the child's own parents. Similar data were recorded in Denmark (Harder 1967) where in 1967 half of the victims of crime were children and eighty-five percent of those infanticides were committed by their own parents.

Although the figures provided by criminological statistics are shocking because they do not allow any denial of the phenomenon, the findings of other disciplines are more valuable because of their eloquence. For example, pediatrics has made an important discovery: the *battered child syndrome*, which described by Helfer, Kempe and their school (Kempe et al. 1962), which has led to intensive work in researching and understanding the problem, at least in this branch of medicine. This initiative in facing the problem is one of the positive facts that we must highlight in an otherwise discouraging panorama.

It would be useful at this point to transcribe an article from *The New York Times* quoted by Bakan (1971, p. 45):

> The particular case investigated by the Judicial Relations Committee involved little Roxanne Felumero, the repeatedly abused three-year-old who was found dead in the East River not long ago, bruised and battered, the pockets of her clothes weighted with rocks. Her step-father, accused of previously beating the little girl, has been charged with the vicious crime.

> The findings by the committee that "if the Family Court and the complex of public and private agencies operating within it had functioned more effectively, Roxanne Felumero would probably not have met her tragic death" goes beyond this particular case to expose an incredible pattern of slipshod practices and procedures that have apparently become the norm. The committee's excellent report points up institutional inefficiencies that endanger the health and life of every child in the city needing society's protection.

This need is, unfortunately, a wide one. Nearly a thousand child abuse cases were reported to the State Department of Social Services last year, a figure that officials note is but the tip of a vast and ugly iceberg. It represents a 30 percent increase over the year before. In thirty-six of the reported cases, children were killed. In others the injuries they received caused permanent damage. Viciously brutal beatings by parents, step-parents, and guardians have often left children permanently crippled, blind, and retarded.

The horrible abuse continues. Among the cases this year, in addition to Roxanne Felumero, is that of an eighteen-month-old baby in the Bronx who was hanged by her wrists and savagely whipped with a belt, then cut down and left to lie on the bathroom floor for almost two days suffering from a broken arm. In Manhattan, a four-year-old died of starvation and neglect. Etc., etc., etc.

The sheer horror of these situations, the utter helplessness and vulnerability of the children cry out for immediate action on the judicial committee's recommendations. . . .

There is hardly a more heinous crime than the brutal abuse of children by adults to whom they look for love and protection. Society has been shamefully late in coming to their protection—cruelty to animals was condemned in New York before cruelty to children—and it has been unconscionably lax in erecting adequate safeguards. The judicial committee in its soul-searching report indicts the courts and supporting agencies—and it indicts society as well.

Similar reports come from other countries having the same cultural level. The results of the investigation carried out by the prosecutor Infelisi (1971) in Rome in early 1971 are perhaps even more pathetic. The prosecutor made surprise inspections of the

276 orphanages and similar institutions in that city, escorted by 1,500 national guardsmen to verify in an absolutely impartial manner the sinister situation reported in these establishments housing three or four thousand minors (Invernizzi 1971).

Prosecutor Infelisi's report moved Italy and the world deeply because of the severity of the punishments inflicted on thousands of defenseless children. It was published in the Rome newspapers on March 6, 1971, together with the news that the governor had named a watchdog committee. Of the twenty-one guardian judges who, as substitute parents, should have protected the children and prevented the constant abuses committed by the authorities who ran the orphanages, nineteen confessed that they had never visited these establishments. The other two had done so only occasionally. The governor himself, ultimately responsible for the minors' guardianship, had no idea of the facts; ironically, only a few days before, he had publicly congratulated Father Leonardo, considered the main culprit in the ill-treatment and criminal abuse of the children in his care. The knowledge of these facts corroborated what had happened three years before in an institute for abnormal children in Grotta Ferrara run by the ex-nun, Diletta Pagliuca, who was proved to have kept the minors chained in subhuman conditions that caused the death of at least ten of them.

These investigations are evidence of the lifting of the millennial denial and the growing recognition of children's rights through the denunciation of physical abuse, which must be followed up with the denunciation of mental abuse.

It is noteworthy that the discovery of the cause of the *battered child syndrome* resulted from the observations of radiologists. In effect, when first Caffey (1946) and later Silverman and colleagues (1953) tried to explain the strange cases of children who had fractures of the long bones and swelling and hemorrhages inside the skull between the brain and the protective membranes, they understood, after much effort, that these lesions could only be caused by the violently destructive action of the parents or their substitutes. This was finally confirmed by the patient work of pediatricians and other child care professionals in the hospitals, private clinics, and institutes in the United States, and also later in other countries. Today, there is greater awareness of habitual abuse by parents; and physical abuse of children has come to be considered a severe and widespread medical and social problem that can cause irreversible damage to the physical and mental health of these children, even leading to their death. According to Helfer and Kempe (1968):

> More children under five die as a consequence of the abuse of their parents or of those who take care of them than as a consequence of tuberculosis, whooping cough, poliomyelitis, scarlatina, diabetes, rheumatic fever and appendicitis, all together. [p. iv]

In the descriptions of the *battered child syndrome*, the types of lesions vary from bruises and superficial wounds like skin irritations, burns, and fractures, to various internal lesions and even severe trauma to the brain and the central nervous system, amputations, and intentional starvation. The lesions result from simple disciplinary measures or from sudden outbursts of temper exacerbated by alcohol, as well as from premeditated criminal attacks.

In the preface to their book on the battered child, Helfer and Kempe (1968) tell us:

> Tens of thousands of children were severely battered or killed in the United States in 1967. This book is written about and for

these children. Who are they, where do they come from, why were they beaten and, most important—what can we do to prevent it? [p. vii]

Although the first radiological observations of Caffey (1946) were reported as far back as 1946, only sixteen years later, in 1962, did Kempe and colleagues (1962) publish, in the *Journal of the American Medical Association* the denunciation of the *Battered Child Syndrome*. This simple fact gives us an idea of the intensity of the millennial denial of those charged with the protection and care of the young. Only in 1962 did this aberration, as ancient as the existence of mankind, reach the awareness of physicians worldwide.

There is a reference to an earlier situation reported by Radbill (1968) that shows the same negligence and lack of consideration for the suffering of children:

Although children inspire humanity's tenderest emotions, cruelty toward them has always prevailed. Fontana reports the history of Mary Ellen, a little girl abused by her adoptive parents. They punished her constantly and she was severely undernourished. The religious social workers were unable to persuade the local authorities to initiate legal action against the parents. The rights of parents to punish their children were still sacred and there was no law that could be invoked to protect children. But the religious social workers were not discouraged. They resorted to the Society for the Prevention of Cruelty to Animals (ASPCA), which took immediate action. In this way they were able to free Mary Ellen from her parents' abuse, since the child belonged to the animal kingdom and was consequently under the protection of the laws that prohibit cruelty to animals. [p. 13]

The above situation occurred before the foundation in 1871 of the society against cruelty to children.

The murder of children in modern times reached its culmination in Nazi Germany where it was institutionalized under the most flimsy criminal pretexts (Wertham 1971):

The children sentenced to death were sent to a "children's division" located first in Goerden and later in Eichberg, Idstein, Steinhof and Eglfing. Most of them were poisoned with strong doses of luminal and other drugs administered with spoons as if they were medicines or else well mixed with the food. Death came several days and sometimes weeks later. In practice, the orders to kill the children multiplied with time and they included children with "deformed ears," those who wet the bed and those who were totally healthy but considered "difficult to educate." The children placed under the authority of the Commission of the Reich were mostly very small. . . . Later they used the method called "child euthanasia," which consisted in literally and deliberately starving them to death in the "children's division." A great many children died in this way. . . . In autumn, 1939, Ludwig Lehner, a student of psychology who later became a teacher in a public school, was authorized, with other persons, to visit the state hospital in Eglfing-Haar. . . . In the children's ward there were about 25 children nearly starved to death, whose ages varied between one and five years: Doctor Pfanmuller, director of the establishment, explained the procedure used: "We do not use poison or injections," he said. "Our method is much simpler and more natural." And saying this, the fat and smiling hospital director lifted from his bed a skeletal and whimpering child, holding him up in the air like a dead rabbit. He later explained that the children were not suddenly deprived of food, but their rations were reduced gradually. "The case of this child," he explained, "is a matter of two or three days more."

This scene is certainly worse than those described by Dante. And the punishment could only be dantesque. In 1948, Doctor Pfanmuller was accused before a jury of having ordered at least 120 children killed and of having committed several of these crimes himself. In fact, it was proved that he killed several children with injections. He was sentenced to six years in prison, of which he served only two. This means he served only six days in prison for each child killed. [pp. 172–173]

The number of children horribly abused by their parents was reported in 1971 to be 110,000 per year in Federal Germany (Rowe 1971). In 1947, forty-seven children lost their lives at their parents' hands under various pretexts that in the reader's eyes take on sinister meaning because, in a way, they remind him or her of similar real or fantasied experiences in his or her own childhood. Children perceive and also have fantasies of their parents' filicidal tendencies. Parents' angry threats and even jokes are experienced as real threats by children and are stored in their unconscious, "forgotten" as such. These figures have not improved in the last twenty-five years, and are similar, with quantitative variations, in all Western countries. As a further illustration of our thesis, we have only to mention the high rate of child mortality due to malnutrition and starvation observed today in many Asian, African, and American countries, as well as deaths caused by negligence in hygiene and in everything related to the care and protection of children.

WAR

Although both the murder of children and the *battered child syndrome* with all its series of symptoms are eloquent proof of the magnitude and persistence of filicide in modern society, the study of the unconscious motivation of war is even more important due to the increasing number of deaths it causes.[2] Bouthoul (1951) has pointed out that war is organized homicide that has been legalized, to which we have added that it is a system for the permanent sacrificial murder of the offspring (Rascovsky 1970). In this sense, Bouthoul has anticipated two conceptions: (1) war is "deferred infanticide" (p. 298) and (2) it exercises a stabilizing social function.

Among the diverse causes of war, an important one is the need to perpetuate human sacrifice in the form of the holocaust of the children with all of the primitive sociocultural meanings it implies. According to the enlightening studies of Fornari (1966), war is one of the highly organized methods for holding collective paranoid anxiety at an acceptable level by elaborating and projecting guilt onto the enemy. Thus, the enemy becomes the

---

[2]According to the report presented by the Soviet Professor Emilianov (1972) to the Conference of Non-governmental Organizations on Disarmament in Geneva, September, 1972: "From 1820 to 1859, 800,000 persons died in 92 wars. Between 1860 and 1900, 4.6 million persons died in 106 conflicts and, in the first 50 years of this century, 42.5 million died in 117 wars" (figures taken by Emilianov from British sources). These figures leave no doubt that deaths resulting from war are increasing. The figures given by Dr. John Seaman (1971) are also interesting. Dr. Seaman assisted refugee children in Calcutta during the recent war in Pakistan. He thinks that half a million of them will die before the end of the year (1971). In the Salt Lake camp alone, near Calcutta, three thousand children died in three months and, to the date of this report, no less than a total of one hundred thousand children had died. Dr. Nevin Scrimshaw, an American specialist in nutrition who accompanied Senator Kennedy on his tour of the refugee camps in India, also estimated that approximately 300,000 children would die unless appropriate measures were rapidly taken. Although these statistics are outdated, recent newspaper articles show that child mortality that results from the direct or indirect effects of war has not abated.

depository for a dissociated part of the person who is seeking a solution for his or her own inner conflict. Further, and paradoxically, another function of war is to fuel an increment in persecutory anxiety by intimidating and submitting the individual to the group. War holds a death threat over the young, who must totally submit to the army and displace their emotional ties from their families to the community. It also effectively murders a sector of society, and those members of the young generation who refuse to submit are subjected to destructive intimidation and sometimes prosecution. The frequency of wars is also related to the sociocultural process. It is easy to observe that war is more frequent where cultural development is greater.

Although filicide is an obvious and permanent phenomenon occurring in innumerable circumstances, it continues to be a nearly unknown concept, while the dialectically opposite phenomenon of parricide is, all to the contrary, exaggerated. This emphasis on the parricidal tendencies increases the persecutory guilt with which children are oppressed, with the addition of a melancholic connotation that intensifies the submission that is desired. In the same way, the sadism and cruelty toward children exercised by their parents and by social institutions are denied, and the rage of parents or their substitutes, such as society or the gods, is justified by attributing hypothetical iniquities to the children. The truth is that the children's aggression is a response provoked or instigated by their persecutors. We must conclude, therefore, that insistence on the accusation of parricide is another form of filicidal action. Thus, the fantasies and denigrating or abusive acts of the parents are transformed into feelings of guilt that are then placed onto the children.

In the case of war, those who are sent to be sacrificed on the battlefield become delinquents if they attempt to desert in order to save their lives. On the other hand, they are honored if they identify with the parental attitude and kill young enemies who have, like themselves, been sent to their deaths. Infraction or desertion of the rite of initiation represented by the military service leads to the loss of civil rights, that is, the rights of adults in the community. There is no longer any doubt that in contemporary society conscription and war are the most widespread modern expression of the rite of initiation that demands the sacrifice of the developing generation. We do well in emphasizing that the procedure traditionally used to impose instinctive prohibitions has been to frighten the children, reinforced by the murder of some of them. This is the source of a strong moral connotation that implies insisting on the innocence of the gerontocracy and accusing the children. Parents hide or deny their aggression and lead their child to idealization—a process that follows denial of filicide—thus building up a unifying structure that condemns the entire new generation to sacrifice. This gerontocracy is today camouflaged by a symbolic abstraction: the fatherland, glorified by those who voluntarily give up their lives for it, although such voluntary service is actually a disguised demand for sacrifice. Submission, incorporated into the child's mind by centuries of intimidation, has now finally taken root. This intimidation is transmitted and experienced in many ways during childhood development, the most common of these being what is called "education."

The primitive rites of initiation have been transferred to a systematic organization of war that periodically breaks out so that one part of youth can be sent to its death, once it has reached near-adult development. Thus, the youths take the place of the parents who are threatened by the war that they themselves have organized. It seems that at this point, envy of the new generation's growing vigor plays an active role. The decision to go to war has never been made by the generations who participate in it, but by the filicidal minds at the pinnacle of the gerontocracy. This is even clearer in today's wars because the youths, obliged to blindly obey the laws, have acquired greater awareness. The statesmen who impose the decision to wage war personify the paranoic regression of the masses, perhaps because they possess a larger number of pathological traits of the persecutory type, including senile decadence.

In recent years an extraordinary rebellion has taken place and has become an important social statement. We are referring to the rebellion of contemporary youth groups directed especially against war and characterized by diverse anti-gerontocratic aspects. This reaction has created a defensive fraternity that involves a broad sector of the world and is expressed especially in the universities, particularly in countries with the greatest cultural development: the United States, France, England, Germany, Japan, and so on. One of the most positive protests is expressed in the slogan: "Make love, not war." But the rebellion is demonstrated not only by general nonconformity with arbitrary authority but also by resistance to fighting in war. One of the most pathetic slogans of the youth rebellion says this: "War is good business, invest your son." In publications by these youths, we read their accusations of the parents who send their sons to die in war with the help of the State, using the paranoic technique of patriotic idealization. They consider the persecutory parents to be idealized as the fatherland or the earth. These public demonstrations by contemporary youth show their sensitive understanding of the real sacrifice that war represents and of its deep, hidden meanings. The lack of submission of the new generations and the superficial arguments, the increase in paranoic exaltation in the face of the atomic threat, the boom in information resulting from improved communications systems, and the publicizing of psychoanalytic knowledge have made the profound understanding of war possible. The struggle between the generations that has come to public attention incites us to investigate the true origin of the genetic question. Thus, we turn once again to the Oedipus conflict in our efforts to improve understanding of the fundamental problems that lead to violence[3] in parent–child relationships.

In this sense, Atkins (1968) thinks that

> Just as revolution must be taken as an expression of parricide, periodic wars between nations are an extreme manifestation of parental aggression. The massacre of youth reaches its final and most devastating form and the blind kings of all the family groups have occasion to carry out their filicidal aggressions, while at the same time denying them. [p. 746]

Young people today tend to attach little importance to the idealization implicit in the heroic conception and feel closer to the youths who are among their presumed enemies than to their parent-leaders. They begin to understand that in war those who die are both the youths of their own group, their companions, and the youths of the enemy group. The old generation will later make peace and keep the war booty, that is, they will preserve their lives after eliminating a great part of the generational rival who is constantly disputing important functions of all kinds. However, the heroic model, as an expression of the persistence of masochistic submission to the persecutory parents, is often seen

---

[3]In Greek mythology, violence is symbolized by Bia, sister of Nike (victory), of Cratus (strength), and of Zelus (zeal), all of them children of the Titan Pallas and the nymph Styx. She is depicted as a woman in armor who is clubbing a child to death. She was considered a faithful companion of Zeus.

in the idealization of guerrillas and in the identification with their leaders in the search for heroic sacrificial death.

War is the institutionalization of the primitive murder and denigration of children with the consequent denial of their persecutors through idealization. It is social action that executes the compulsion to eliminate children. This expression of parental aggression, though its formal aspects have diminished in the process of civilization, persists and preserves the dependent condition of children imposed by universal cultural models.

ABANDONMENT

We have already said that one of the most damaging and covert forms of filial sacrifice is abandonment. We must first remind the reader of a few basic facts.

Throughout childhood, the parents form an important part of the child's own ego; they are the child's auxiliary ego. The need for the parents gradually decreases as they are internalized into the child's personality through the process of identification. Thus, after a period of dependency, the individual is able to become independent, that is, to incorporate the parents, who were at first only external, into him- or herself. For this reason, any major or minor abandonment by the parents implies that something is cut away from the child. Further, the parents are depositories of the child's innate aggression and their function is to accept it and work it through, because if it is not projected onto the parents and received by them, this aggression is blocked up and becomes self-destructive in the child. We can see how children's self-integration comes about thanks to the qualitative and quantitative presence of their parents and substitutes, including a basic quantum of constancy. The primitives understood that abandonment equals filicide, since one of the ways they killed their children was simply to leave them out in the open.

The works of Bowlby have contributed greatly to clarifying modern concepts on maternal deprivation. In his report to the World Health Organization, he stated the following principle (Bowlby 1969): "What seems essential for mental health is that the infant and child must hold a warm, intimate and continuous relationship with their mother (or with the permanent substitute mother), in which both find satisfaction and enjoyment." Later, together with the observations filmed by his colleagues, Mr. and Mrs. James Robertson, Bowlby (1956) pointed out the intense suffering and heart-rending process provoked in children when they are separated from their mothers in nurseries and hospitals.

> At that time (1956), there was no consensus on the significance and importance of these observations. Some questioned their value; others recognized the facts but attributed them to anything except the loss of the mother; others, finally, recognized that the loss was a relevant variable, but affirmed that it was not difficult to mitigate its effects and that, therefore, the loss was not as important for pathology as had been thought. [p. xiii]

Bowlby and his colleagues concluded by saying that the characteristic picture of protest and desperation, which appears specifically when a child over six months old is separated from his or her mother and placed in the care of strangers, is especially due to "the loss of the mother's care in this period of development when the child is very dependent and vulnerable" (p. xiii). Further, "the need felt by the child for his mother's love and presence is as great as his need for food" and, consequently, the absence inevitably generates "a powerful feeling of loss and rage" (p. xiii).

And Bowlby (1969) adds:

> . . . the loss of the maternal figure, in itself or in combination
> with other variables not yet clearly defined, may provoke re-
> sponses and processes of great interest for psychopathology. And
> not only that, since we can affirm that such processes and
> responses are the same ones that are recognized as being active in
> adults who continue to be disturbed by the separations they
> suffered during early childhood. In these responses and processes
> and in the disturbances we observe, on the one hand, the
> tendency to make excessive demands on others and anxiety and
> anger when such demands are not satisfied, as can be seen in
> dependent and hysterical personalities, and, on the other hand, a
> blockage of the capacity for establishing deep relationships, as
> can be seen in disaffective and psychopathic personalities. In
> other words, we believe that when we observe children during
> and after the periods in which they have been separated from
> their mother and taken to a strange establishment, we are
> registering responses and also the effects of defensive processes
> which allow us precisely to fill in the blanks between an experi-
> ence of this type and any disturbances in the development of the
> ulterior personality. [p. xiii]

Bowlby's work has led to both corroborations and new
contributions by many researchers today in experimental observation not only of children but also other primates.

Deprivation of maternal affection generates multiple
mental and physical disturbances. Only after seven months of
intrauterine life is the child able to live without total and
permanent contact in the mother's womb. After this point, the
baby can barely do without the maternal organism and although
the moments in which it can do without her increase gradually,
only in adulthood will the person be totally able to do without

the mother. This concept acquires momentous significance in parent–child relationships, since abandonment does not mean drastic removal from the mother's or father's home. More important, because of its frequency and far-reaching consequences, is the constant abandonment of all kinds that children suffer in daily life, be it due to the parents' lack of capacity for understanding and giving love to their child, or to the social conditions that oblige the parents to work excessively in order to support home and family, or to the ethics of the community, unconsciously influenced by strongly filicidal tendencies, which demand educational norms that impose lack of attention or abandonment.

In the human species, the maternal function alone is insufficient to satisfy children's needs. The father's active cooperation is required at the same time. The lack of this cooperation or its limitation is frequent and, to a certain extent, constant, and is a pathogenic factor that acts in diverse ways to the child's detriment, first and foremost because it impedes, in both sexes, the indispensable identifications with the father. In the second place, it hinders the exercise of the mother's function, since she cannot devote herself entirely to the child in its first moments of life when the father's support is lacking. In the third place, the unaccompanied mother may place an excessive burden of genital love on the child, overwhelming the child early on and creating a tie that will be difficult to dissolve exogamically in the future. It is also useful to understand the opposing and cushioning function that the two parents put into practice reciprocally in order to balance the situation of their child or children.

The effects of parental deprivation with its multiple components can be seen in the deficits the child experiences. These require thorough investigation in the future, since their study has barely begun.

There is no doubt of the detriment to physical and mental

development that children in orphanages and other institutions suffer; increased awareness of the noxious effect of certain forms of negligence toward children that are at present considered insignificant will help us to understand aspects of mental and physical illness that remain obscure at this time.

Abandonment and negligence can be seen both in daily life and in the institutionalized systems that tend to abuse the child. The most common of these is undoubtedly the nursery, the place where newborn children are taken in public and private maternity facilities. This means that when the baby leaves its uterine refuge, at the moment of greatest need for immediate and close contact with the mother, he or she is drastically separated from her for several days. Among the diverse noxious effects of this unfortunate practice is the interruption of the stimulatory and reciprocal bonding between mother and baby that assures good secretion of milk. Further, birth is the high point of the baby's paranoic increment, and this separation annuls the valuable tranquilizing action that only continuous contact with the mother can provide.

It would be impossible at this time to allot sufficient place and importance to child abandonment in all its aspects. We transcribe below the chronicle of a situation so notorious that it led to the creation of the *Casa Cuna* (Crib House) in Buenos Aires in the colonial period, during the administration of Viceroy Vertiz (Cordero 1971):

> At the end of the 18th century in Buenos Aires, babies were abandoned shortly after birth or afterwards, as if they were merely little beasts. The fact is that the frequency of those acts was such that the authorities became concerned about it . . . The *Junta Superior de Temporalidades* (High Board of Temporalities) became interested in establishing an orphanage to take in the abandoned children. They prepared and presented a document

and it was approved by Juan Jose Vertiz on July 14th, 1779. . . .
One month before the above data, the representative attorney
general wrote to the viceroy saying that one of the city's most
urgent needs was the foundation of "a home where the many
abandoned children can be taken in." And that those "many
children" abandoned "have perished before the doors and windows of the neighbors from the rigors of the night." And he
adds . . . "how many of them because they have been left on the
road have been run over; how many of them eaten by dogs and
pigs, and how many thrown out into the public streets, no one
being able to remedy their tragic fate. And being most common to
expose them without baptism; this very grave circumstance makes
their unhappy death even more painful." The representative
wanted to strengthen his request with declarations of the inhab-
itants . . . and went throughout the city to find out about the
matter directly. . . . The witnesses tell what they know. Juan Francisco de Suero says that: "it is true that he knows and has heard
that many newborn babies have been left and are left, in doors and
windows and even in other more exposed places, to their perdition . . . as happened about seven years ago when the witness
learned that a newborn infant had been moved from place to place
four or five doors, those who found it in theirs moving it to another. . ." And he confirms what other witnesses have said, that
not only have many babies died of the cold but have been devoured by animals. "As happened in the neighborhood of San
Miguel, where two babies were found eaten, of one of them all that
remained was a piece that a dog had and it was said to be this
animal that had eaten the child because of this evidence, and the
other was gnawed up to the thighs, for which accident and others
like it, this government ordered the dogs and pigs loose on the
streets killed. . . ." The following witness is Don Francisco Antonio Escalada who declares, confirming all that has been said and
then Don Francisco Cabrera. . . . He remembers that "when he
was magistrate in this district and was making the rounds one
night in the ditch they call Viera's" he found "in a herd of pigs a

newborn baby that was half-eaten by these animals and was very painful to see." Jose Antonio Ibanez, for his part, says that "over a period of 16 years, seven have been left in front of his house, of which he took in five because he was at home at the time and two are alive, one girl 14 or 15 years old and the other who is not yet six months old, that the other three deceased died when small and he attributes it to the bad weather and poor condition in which they arrived at his door, since they are usually passed from one house to another and left on the porches, at the gates, on the windowsills and in the streets until someone takes pity on them and takes them in." [*La Prensa*, Buenos Aires, 29 March 1970]

Although we have transcribed these clear testimonies from other times, we must emphasize that equally sinister facts exist today. The circumstances are not the same as those quoted in the chronicle above, but represent other forms of abandonment, cruelty, and mutilation.

Even today, markets of castrated children still exist in Baguirmi, in Chad, North Central Africa. These are legally run markets, but in our America, in Port-au-Prince, the capitol of Haiti, there is a semi-clandestine market of children. When the tourist arrives in this city by ship, a limitless number of small native boats offer the most diverse merchandise to the visitors. Among these are children between ages five and seven, who have been taught to smile and look nice and are sold for a few dollars (Otonello 1970). Further, the amputation and deliberate deformation of very small children in order to convert them into beggars is practiced on a large scale in many Asian, African, and American countries. In our own American cities, women can be seen begging with drugged children in their arms to exploit the compassion that their sad and usually false maternity elicits. In some Latin American countries there is a cruel and fairly widespread institution, "the idiot of the house" (*el bobo de la casa*), which I have been able to observe personally. This refers to one of the children of the family sometimes born with some kind of deficiency, a Down syndrome, some congenital defect, or a hypothyroid cretinism. But often, this child has fallen into that condition as a result of contemptuous and denigrating treatment, having been made the depository of all the family's pathology and hate from a very early age. Thus, he or she has suffered a slow regression or else development has been arrested tremendously. The child is then condemned to live in chains, to walk on all fours, to eat from the floor, and to endure all kinds of abuse and ill-treatment. He or she is treated with no consideration, as if the child were a despicable animal kept in the home. A lack of adequate social institutions could be a reason as well as a pretext for the family to go on depositing its hate in the "idiot of the house."

In spite of public knowledge and full awareness of its uselessness in education, it has not yet been possible to eradicate corporal punishment in highly cultured countries. The systematic punishment of children continues to be practiced in all educational systems, where it is exercised with differing degrees of harshness.[4]

Mutilation on the pretext of religious, hygienic, or surgical reasons is practiced universally in a wide variety of ways. Circumcision is the most widespread. Until only a few years ago, the tonsillectomy was a rule that few children, especially in the cities, escaped.

The effects of subtle and attenuated forms of abuse, denigration, and negligence are, in our opinion, the most promising field of investigation for the future. We have said on other

---

[4]In one period, in the majority of Christian countries, children were whipped on the Day of the Innocents (December 28th) in commemoration of Herod's murder of the innocents (Radbill 1968, p. 13).

occasions that our situation today resembles that moment in the middle of the last century when the concepts of Pasteur were discovered. The scourges that devastated the world then were the infectious diseases: bubonic plague, yellow fever, diphtheria, tuberculosis, syphilis, blenorrhagia, and so on. But the etiology of these diseases was discovered; and once their causes had been determined, the great pathology of the turn of the century was universally eradicated.

Infectious illness was interpreted and overcome in this way, and the enormous morbidity it caused diminished progressively. But human discontent was displaced. Initial attempts to understand mental illness in bacteriological terms failed, and as the effects of tuberculosis and syphilis, malaria and diphtheria, yellow fever and the bubonic plague were mitigated, today's great pathology began to increase: neurosis, manic-depressive psychosis, schizophrenia, the other diverse psychoses, suicide, perversions, drug addictions (including tobacco addiction), juvenile and adult delinquency, irrational violence, psychosomatic disturbances, and so on. It is likely that the contemporary factor that we can regard as an equivalent of the undiscovered microbe of another age is the fracture of the parent–child relationship, beginning with the disturbances and deficiencies produced by a deficit of the maternal function and by the failure, due to lack of love, of the most primary social form: the initial relationship with the parents.

Our greatest hope for prevention and therapy resides in the total modification of the factors organizing both the individual and the group so as to create a society in which today's antagonistic struggle between the generations is converted into a transcendent succession of generations.

References

Ainsworth, M., Andry, R. G., Harlow, R. G., et al. (1962). *Deprivation of Maternal Care: A Reassessment of Its Effects.* Geneva: World Health Organization.

Alighieri, D. (1977). *The Divine Comedy.* Trans. J. Ciardi. New York: W. W. Norton.

Atkins, N. (1968). El mito de Edipo y la adolescencia. *Revista de Psicoanalisis* 25:735–748.

Bakan, D. (1971). *Slaughter of the Innocents.* San Francisco: Jossey-Bass.

Berliner, B. (1966). Psychodynamics of the depressive character. *The Psychoanalytic Forum* 1:244–264.

Blin, P. C., and Favreau, J. M. (1968). Infanticidio y canibalismo puerperal. Matadoras y comedoras de pequeños. In *Psiquiatría Animal*, ed. A. Brion and H. Ey. Mexico City, Mexico: Siglo XXI.

Boas, F. (1938). Mythology and folklore. In *General Anthropology.* New York.

Bouthoul, G. (1951). *Les Guerres, Traite de Sociologie.* Paris: Payot.

Bowlby, J. (1951). Maternal care and mental health. In *Monografía # 2.* Geneva: World Health Organization.

—— (1958). The nature of the child's tie to his mother. *International Journal of Psycho-Analysis* 39:350–373.

—— (1969). *Attachment and Loss.* London: Hogarth.

Bowlby, J., Ainsworth, M., Boston, M., and Rosenbluth, D. (1956). The effects of mother–child separation: a follow-up study. *The British Journal of Medical Psychology* 29:211–220.

Bunker, H. A. (1952). "The feast of Tantalus," taken from the First Olympic Ode of Pindar. *Psychoanalytic Quarterly* 21:356–372.

Burlingham, D., and Freud, A. (1943). *Infants without Families.* London: Allen and Unwin.

Caffey, J. (1946). Multiple fractures in the long bones of infants suffering from chronic subdural hematoma. *The American Journal of Roentgenology, Radium Therapy and Nuclear Medicine* 56:163–173.

Cordero, H. A. (1971). El niño desde la época de los virreyes. In *La Prensa* [Buenos Aires], July 18, p. 4.

Culican, W. (1966). Carthage. In *The Encyclopaedia Britannica* 4:977–979. Chicago: Benton.

Darwin, C. (1906). *The Origin of the Species and the Descent of Man.* New York: Modern Library.

Dentan, R. C. (1966). Moloch. In *The Encyclopaedia Britannica* 5:676. Chicago: Benton.

Devereux, G. (1953). Why Oedipus killed Laius. *International Journal of Psycho-Analysis* 34:132–141.

——— (1966). The cannibalistic impulses of parents. *The Psychoanalytic Forum* 1:114–130.

Dostoyevsky, F. (1966). *The Brothers Karamazov.* New York: Airmont.

Eggan, F. R. (1966). Infanticide. In *The Encyclopaedia Britannica* 12:217. Chicago: Benton.

Emilianov, V. (1972). *La Nación* [Buenos Aires], October 3, p. 15.

Fornari, F. (1966). Psychanalyse de la guerre. *Revue Française de Psychanalyse* 30:135–260.

Frazer, J. G. (1910). *Totemism and Exogamy.* London: Macmillan.

——— (1913). The belief in immortality. In *The Golden Bough.* London: Macmillan.

——— (1913). Balder the beautiful. In *The Golden Bough.* London: Macmillan.

——— (1922). *The Golden Bough: A Study in Magic and Religion. Abridged*

Edition. New York: Macmillan.

———— (1944). *La Rama Dorada*. Mexico City, Mexico: Fondo de Cultura Económica.

Freud, S. (1901). The psychopathology of everyday life. *Standard Edition* 6:1-290.

———— (1913). Totem and taboo. *Standard Edition* 13:1-161.

———— (1919). The uncanny. *Standard Edition* 17:217-252.

———— (1928). Dostoyevsky and parricide. *Standard Edition* 21:173-196.

———— (1930). Civilization and its discontents. *Standard Edition* 21:57-146.

———— (1939). Moses and monotheism: three essays. *Standard Edition* 23:1-138.

Grene, D., and Lattimore, R., eds. (1954). *Oedipus at Colonus*. In *Sophocles I*. Chicago: University of Chicago Press.

Grimal, P. (1966). *Mitologías del Mediterraneo al Ganges*. Buenos Aires: Larousse.

Grinberg, L. (1963). La culpa persecutoria, pp. 95-102. In *Culpa y Depresión*. Buenos Aires: Paidos.

———— (1964). Two kinds of guilt: the relations with normal and pathological aspects of mourning. *International Journal of Psycho-Analysis* 45:366-371.

Harder, T. (1967). The psychopathology of infanticide. *Acta Psychiatrica Scandinavica* 19:196-245.

Helfer, R. E., and Kempe, C. (1968). *The Battered Child*. Chicago: University of Chicago Press.

Herodotus. (1947). *The Persian Wars*. New York: Random House.

———— (1968). *Los Nueve Libros de la Historia*. Barcelona: Iberia.

Holy Bible with Ideal Helps. (1919). United States: National Bible Press.

Hoover, J. E. (1966). *Uniform Crime Reports*. Washington, DC: U.S. Government Printing Office.

Invernizzi, G. (1971). *L'Espresso*. March 14, p. 8.

Jacobs, W. W. (1991). The monkey's paw. In *The Dracula Book of Great Horror Stories*. New York: Carol Publishing Group.

Jones, E. (1962). *Vida y Obra de Sigmund Freud 3*. Buenos Aires: Editorial Nova.

Josefo, F. (1948). *Guerra de los Judíos*. Barcelona: Iberia.

Kempe, C., Silverman, F. N., Steele, B. F., et al. (1962). The battered child syndrome. *Journal of the American Medical Association* 181:17. Also cited in Bakan, 1971, pp. 10, 55.

Kroeber, A. L. (1920a). *Totem and Taboo* in retrospect. *American Journal of Sociology* 55:446–451.

_____ (1920b). *Totem and Taboo*: an ethnologic psychoanalysis. *American Anthropologist* 22:48–55.

Lee, R. W. (1956). *The Elements of Roman Law*. London: Sweet & Maxwell.

Lévi-Strauss, C. (1969). *Antropología Estructural*. Buenos Aires: Eudeba.

_____ (1983). *Las Estructuras Elementales del Parentesco*. Buenos Aires: Paidos.

Lorenz, K. (1966). Discussion of Devereux: the cannibalistic impulses of parents. *The Psychoanalytic Forum* 1:128–129.

Malinowski, B. (1954). *Magic, Science and Religion*. New York: Meridian.

Montagu, F. A. (1966). Circumcision. In *The Encyclopaedia Britannica* 5:799–800. Chicago: Benton.

New Larousse Encyclopedia of Mythology. (1959). New York: Paul Hamlyn.

Otonello, N. (1970). Letter to the editor. *La Prensa*, March 29. Buenos Aires.

Parker, T., and Allerton, R. (1962). *The Courage of His Convictions*. London: Hutchinson.

Radbill, S. X. (1968). A history of child abuse and infanticide. In *The Battered Child*, ed. R. E. Helfer and C. Kempe. Chicago: University of Chicago Press.

Rank, O. (1981). *El Mito del Nacimiento del Héroe*. Barcelona: Paidos.

Rappoport, A. S. (1966). *Myth and Legend of Ancient Israel*. New York: K'tav.

Rascovsky, A. (1970). *La Matanza de los Hijos y Otros Ensayos*. Buenos Aires: Kargieman.

_____ (1970). Filicide and its transcendence in the unconscious motivation of war. Speech delivered at the United Nations, January 10.

―――― (1970). Spanish version of the same. Filicidio y su transcendencia en la motivación inconsciente de la guerra. In *El Psychoanálisis Frente a la Guerra.* Buenos Aires: Alonso.

Rascovsky, A., and Rascovsky, M. (1967). Acontecimientos de la sexta semana de vida y el comienzo de la posición depresiva. In *Revista de Psicoanálisis* 24:717–734.

―――― (1967). Sobre el filicidio y su significación en la génesis del acting out y la conducta psicopática en Edipo. In *Revista de Psicoanálisis* 24:7–22. (1971). Also in *Niveles Profundos del Psiquismo,* pp. 193–221. Buenos Aires: Editorial Sudamericana.

―――― (1968). On the genesis of acting out and psychopathic behaviour in Sophocles' *Oedipus. International Journal of Psycho-Analysis* 49:390–394.

Reik, T. (1945). Estudio sobre Dostoyevsky. In *Treinta Años con Freud.* Buenos Aires: Iman.

―――― (1958a). Couvade and the psychogenesis of the fear of retaliation, pp. 14–89. In *Ritual: Psychoanalytic Studies.* New York: International Universities Press.

―――― (1958b). The puberty rites of savages, pp. 91–166. In *Ritual: Psychoanalytic Studies.* New York: International Universities Press.

Rheingold, J. C. (1964). *The Fear of Being a Woman: A Theory of Maternal Destructiveness.* New York: Grune & Stratton.

Robertson Smith, W. (1956). *The Religion of the Semites.* New York: Meridian.

Roheim, G. (1952). Oedipus Rex. In *The Gates of the Dream.* New York: International Universities Press.

Rowe, H. T. (1971). *Quick Deutchlands Grosse Illustrierte,* pp. 22–32. Munich.

Seaman, J. (1971). *La Prensa,* November 27. Buenos Aires.

Silverman, F. N. (1953). The Roentgen manifestation on unrecognized skeletal trauma. In *American Journal of Roentgenology* 69:413–427.

Spiegel, S. (1969). *The Last Trial.* New York: Schocken.

Spitz, R. (1951). The psychogenic diseases in infancy: an attempt at their etiologic classification. *Psychoanalytic Study of the Child* 6:255–275. New York: International Universities Press.

_____ (1946). Anaclitic depression. *Psychoanalytic Study of the Child* 2:313–342. New York: International Universities Press.

Sturtevant, W. C. (1966). Mutilations and deformations. In *The Encyclopaedia Britannica* 15:1107. Chicago, Benton.

Sumner, W. G. (1906). *Folkways*. Boston: Ginn. Also cited in Bakan, 1971, p. 31.

Thordarson, T. K. (1966). Abraham. In *The Encyclopaedia Britannica* 1:44–45. Chicago: Benton.

Troyat, H. (1960). *Dostoievsky*. Paris: Fayard.

Werner, O. H. (1917). *The Unmarried Mother in German Literature*. New York: Columbia University Press.

Wertham, F. (1971). *La señal de Caín*. Mexico City, Mexico: Siglo XXI.

Credits

The author gratefully acknowledges permission to quote from the following sources:

Complete Greek Tragedies, Sophocles I, edited by D. Grene and R. Lattimore. Copyright © 1954 by the University of Chicago Press.

"The Feast of Tantalus," by Henry Alden Bunker, in *The Psychoanalytic Quarterly,* vol. 21, pp. 355–372. Copyright © 1952 by *The Psychoanalytic Quarterly.*

The Divine Comedy, by Dante Alighieri, trans. John Ciardi. Copyright © 1977 by W. W. Norton & Company.

"El niño desde la época de los virreyes," by Hector Adolfo Cordero, in *La Prensa,* July 18, 1971. Copyright © 1971 by *La Prensa.*

Index

About the Author

The late Arnaldo Rascovsky, M.D., was in the private practice of psychoanalysis in Buenos Aires, Argentina and was permanent honorary president of FEPAL, the Psychoanalytic Federation of Latin America. He was a founding member of the Argentine Psychoanalytic Association and was twice its president. Dr. Rascovsky was a founder of the *Revista de Psicoanalisis* (*Journal of Psychoanalysis*), which he directed for many years. He taught courses on medical psychology at the University of Buenos Aires Medical School, courses on psychology in the post-graduate program of the Department of Psychology at the University of Belgrano, and numerous seminars at the Argentine Psychoanalytic Association. Dr. Rascovsky earned his M.D. from the University of Buenos Aires.

"Humanity needs a central revolution with respect to the treatment of children. The country that wants good children must preserve the mother's assistance so that she can be with her child during the first years of life. This is not respected in the contemporary world."

                                                            —Arnaldo Rascovsky